S0-BVE-161

EXPOSITION OF HEBREWS

Notes Intended For

An Exposition
Of The
Epistle To The

Hebrews

Printed From The
Unpublished Manuscripts Of

James A. Haldane

The Newport Commentary Series

The Publication of this book is made
possible through the shared vision of the

**Grace Baptist Church,
Lebanon, Missouri**

This facsimile reprint is from an original 1860 edition
owned by C. H. Spurgeon provided courtesy of
The Curry Library
William Jewell College, Liberty, Missouri

Particular Baptist Press
2766 W. Farm Road 178
Springfield, Missouri 65810

Second Edition, 2002

Cataloging data:

Haldane, James Alexander 1768-1851
First Edition published in 1860

1. Bible Commentaries
2. Baptist Doctrinal Works

ISBN 1-888514-16-7   acid free paper

Printed in the United States of America

CONTENTS

ILLUSTRATIONS

The publishers wish to thank Mr. John Young of the Curry Library of William Jewell College for kindly loaning us this rare volume to reprint in our series.

PREFACE

The Grace Baptist Church of Lebanon, Missouri is very thankful for the Lord's provision in enabling us to assist in the reprinting of these rare works by the Particular Baptist Press.

We share the vision with brothers Gary W. Long and Terry Wolever of the Press in making available to our generation these writings of Particular Baptists of the past.

Some of these works are difficult to find and seem destined for extinction if not put back in print. The wisdom and understanding in these works must not be lost. It is important in our day and those to follow, to have these available for consideration.

It is with particular enthusiasm that we anticipate the printing of the Newport Commentary Series and trust it will be both accepted and beneficial.

Sir Francis Bacon said, "Old wood is best to burn, Old friends are best to trust, and Old books are best to read." Seasoning establishes value. These old writings have stood the tests of time and criticism and are worthy of our attention. We joyfully anticipate their use today.

Don Preusch, pastor
Grace Baptist Church
Lebanon, Missouri

J A Haldane

Æt 77

Portrait of James Haldane at the age of 77.

FOREWORD

In considering the impress of Evangelical Christianity upon the character of a nation, one is sure to conclude that it is in direct proportion to the number of devoted adherents of the faith to be found among the general population. What Dr. Henderson expressed as that "vital connection between religion and national character"[1] has certainly evidenced itself among the Scottish people. "Nor have the religious history and institutions of Scotland been the least powerful factors in inflaming Scotsmen with an ardent love of their land. Scotland is a country rich in religious landmarks," he tells us, "Wherever we turn there can be pointed out spots where great things were done for Christ and His Kingdom; here the home of early saints whose great work in spreading Christianity among the rude inhabitants is borne witness to in the nomenclature of the land; there the regions where Reformation heroes did their work and Scottish Covenanters made their great confessions, churches where holy men have exercised their ministry and great spiritual awakenings have taken place."[2]

Principally engaged in this "great work in spreading Christianity," not only in their native Scotland but to other lands as well, were two brothers, Robert (1764-1842) and James Alexander (1768-1851) Haldane. And though Robert is perhaps the better known of the two, most notably for championing evangelical Calvinism against the continental rationalism of the time during a visit to Geneva and Montauban in

---

[1] Henry F. Henderson. *Religion in Scotland: Its Influence on National Life and Character* (Paisley: Alexander Gardner, 1920), p. 40.

[2] Ibid

1816-1819 and for his resulting *Exposition of the Epistle to the Romans* (1836-1839), both brothers played a significant role in the revival of Calvinistic theology in Scotland in the nineteenth century.[3]

James Alexander Haldane, the author of this *Exposition of Hebrews*, was born in Dundee on July 14, 1768. After a few years of study at Edinburgh University, James thought he would follow in the steps of his late father and commenced the pursuit of a maritime career in the service of the East India Company in 1785. Ten years later he and his wife decided to settle in Edinburgh where he was converted to faith in Christ through the instrumentality of an Independent minister, David Bogue. In 1797 he began his first preaching tour through the north of Scotland. Though at the time still a member of the Church of Scotland, Haldane began to question and challenge the established Church, disregarding parish lines and encouraging itinerant evangelism. By 1799 he had moved away from Presbyterianism and received ordination as pastor of an Independent congregation meeting at the former Circus building in Edinburgh known as the "Tabernacle." In reviewing both doctrine and polity in the light of the Bible, and through the influence of the writings of the Scottish Baptist Archibald MacLean, and Lachlan Macintosh, James Haldane came to embrace Baptist views, and was scripturally baptized in the spring of 1808. His brother Robert, who had also become a Baptist, was baptized later that same year. For over 50 years James Haldane faithfully ministered to his beloved congre-

---

[3] It is no coincidence that when the Banner of Truth Trust began publishing in Edinburgh, Scotland in the late 1950's to promote a revival of evangelical Calvinism that Robert Haldane's *Exposition of Romans*, which had such an impact in its own time in accomplishing the same goal, would be among its first reprints (1959).

gation at the new Tabernacle, their association being terminated only by the death of pastor Haldane which occurred on Saturday February 8, 1851.

> While James Haldane was pastor of the Tabernacle he took itinerating tours throughout Scotland, the Orkneys and Shetland. He also preached at important centres in England and Ireland. Much of his work was done in the open air during the summer months. He met with much opposition, but was never discouraged. He was always the Christian gentleman as well as the fervent Gospel Preacher. How far-reaching such evangelical preaching was instrumental in awakening the religious life of Scotland, no historian can put on record.[4]

To this reprint of Haldane's valuable work we have appended what was deemed by his biographer "on the subject of faith one of the most useful and valuable of Mr. J. A. Haldane's practical works," his treatise on the *Doctrine and Duty of Self-Examination* (1806).[5]

With the recommendation of C. H. Spurgeon and fittingly reprinted from Spurgeon's own personal copy, the publishers gratefully send forth this work, "for the perfecting of the saints, for the work of the ministry, for the edifying of the body of Christ." (Ephesians 4:12).

Terry Wolever

---

[4] George Yuille. *History of the Baptists in Scotland* (Glascow: Baptist Union Publications Committee, 1926), p. 125.

[5] Alexander Haldane. *The Lives of Robert Haldane and of His Brother James Alexander Haldane* (Edinburgh: Banner of Truth Trust, 1990 reprint of the 1852 edition), p. 381.

A posthumous work stands out as a finished Exposition, but as "notes" of an intended Exposition."

Very valuable for all that.

Facsimile of Spurgeon's signature and comments from the front endpapers of his personal copy of James Haldane's *Exposition of Hebrews* now a part of the collection of the C. H. Spurgeon Library housed in the Curry Library at William Jewell College, Liberty, Missouri. Spurgeon would often pen comments in his books which he then later incorporated in his *Commenting and Commentaries* (1885), a book he compiled as a guide to his pastoral students in buying the best Bible Commentaries. The comments shown here (*left*) were printed verbatim in *Commenting and Commentaries*, and read:

"A posthumous work, and issued, not as a finished exposition, but as 'notes of an intended exposition.' Very valuable for all that."

Courtesy William Jewell College

xi

The Tabernacle in Edinburgh, Scotland, where James A. Haldane was pastor for nearly half a century. Built for him by his brother Robert, this meeting-house was opened in May of 1801. James Haldane's first sermon there was from the text, "Ye are the temple of God." As Alexander Haldane wrote, the building "was larger than any of the city churches, and calculated to accommodate a greater congregation even than St. Cuthbert's. The entrance was by a descent of some steps, which conducted to three doorways, leading into the vestibule of a spacious area, rising like an amphitheatre, at a little distance from the pulpit. Above, there were two galleries, each capable of seating about eight hundred people. It was estimated that the whole place furnished sittings for three thousand two hundred persons, whilst, on special occasions, four thousand might be crowded within its walls.

The cost was entirely borne by Mr. Robert Haldane, and when the building was furnished, he offered to make it over in perpetuity to his brother. This Mr. James Haldane declined, alleging that, so long as it was devoted to religious purposes, it was as well in his brother's hands, who could, at his death, make what arrangements he pleased. But it was never contemplated by either of them that the property should become vested in trustees, so as to remove it beyond their own control, or expose it to the risks which have befallen so many orthodox Dissenting endowments." Alexander Haldane. *The Lives of Robert and James Haldane* (Edinburgh: Banner of Truth, 1990), p. 302.

NOTES

INTENDED FOR

AN EXPOSITION

OF

THE EPISTLE TO THE HEBREWS.

PRINTED FROM

THE UNPUBLISHED MANUSCRIPTS OF

THE LATE

JAMES A. HALDANE.

LONDON:

JAMES NISBET AND CO., BERNERS-STREET.

HAMILTON, ADAMS, AND CO., PATERNOSTER-ROW.

1860.

ALEX. MACINTOSH,

PRINTER,

GREAT NEW-STREET, LONDON.

PREFACE.

In the lives of Robert and James A. Haldane it is mentioned (p. 636 of Sixth Edition) that shortly before the death of the latter, in Feb., 1851, he had in his public ministrations completed an " Exposition of the Hebrews," which had long occupied his attention. It is added, that his correspondence shows how much his mind was interested in the work, and how clear and acute were his perceptions of its difficulties. Every posthumous work must appear at a disadvantage, and more especially when not finally completed, although obviously intended for the press. It was for some years doubted whether it would be desirable to publish it under these circumstances. But, on the whole, it is felt that it would be wrong to throw away what in his last years had cost so much thought and pleasant labour.

It is, therefore, printed, not as a finished Exposition, but as " Notes intended for an Exposition;" and it is humbly committed to the blessing of Him whom it was the author's privilege for so many years to serve in the Gospel of His Beloved Son Jesus Christ.

EXPOSITION.

HEBREWS, CHAP. I.

MAN was created in the image of God, and in the glorious works of creation was surrounded with ample proofs of his Maker's eternal power and Godhead. He was also reminded of his absolute dependance on God by receiving permission freely to eat of all the trees of the garden in which he was placed, excepting the tree of the knowledge of good and evil, which was to be the test of his obedience. All this, however, did not prevent Adam from starting aside from God like a deceitful bow, thus bringing himself and his posterity under condemnation. But God, who is rich in mercy, was pleased to reveal Himself as the God of salvation, and it deserves attention that He did so, not in the form of a promise to Adam, but of a curse upon the serpent. It was, indeed, impossible for God to hold friendly intercourse, or make any direct promise to sinful man. He is of purer eyes than to behold iniquity, and cannot look upon sin; but in the curse pronounced on the serpent, which is the devil and Satan, He revealed the great Mediator between God and man, in whom all the promises are yea and amen. 2 Cor. i. 20. He was described as the seed of the woman who should bruise the head of the serpent, while His own heel should be bruised in the conflict. It was at the same time intimated that salvation was not to be universal, for mankind were divided into two great families, respectively distinguished as the seed of the woman and the seed of the serpent; the seed of the woman being the children of that family, the members of which the Son of God is not ashamed to call His brethren, chap. ii. 11; the seed of the serpent being the children of the wicked one, to whom the Judge will say, " Depart from me, I never knew you."

V. 1.—God, who at sundry times and in divers manners spake in time past unto the fathers by the prophets.

God spake.—Whatever was communicated by the prophets is here said to be spoken by God. HE spoke whatsoever was uttered by His prophets. The Scriptures are very jealous on this subject; how different from the language of many who seem desirous to exclude God from being the Author of his own word!

At sundry times.—The wonderful plan of salvation was gradually unfolded. God did not fully communicate it at once, but at sundry times, or, rather, in sundry parts, here a little and there a little. The first intimation of the Saviour was made to Adam; His coming as the judge, to Enoch; the covenant, or solemn engagement was renewed to Noah, and a visible representation of the salvation of believers was given in the preservation of Noah and his family in the Ark, which, being warned of God, he had prepared for the saving of his house.

We have seen that the Saviour was first revealed as the seed of the woman;[*] He was afterwards described as the seed of Abraham, Isaac, and Jacob; His descent was next limited to the tribe of Judah, and finally to the house of David.

---

[*] Eve was the emblem of the Church of Christ, the mother of all believers. Gal. iv. 21. She was first called woman because she was taken out of man. It is remarkable that the name of Eve, or Life, was given her after she had been the means of entailing death on all her posterity; but the Prince of Life, who hath abolished death, was the seed of the woman, hence the new name given to Eve.

The gradual manner in which God communicated His purposes of mercy to man correspond with the other parts of the divine procedure. He could have completed in a moment the work of creation, but He was pleased to accomplish it in six days, and here we see His wisdom and condescension. It enables us to follow the wonderful process; it presents to us the stupendous whole in its various parts, thus preventing our being overwhelmed with its magnitude. So likewise the herb of the field does not at once arrive at maturity; there is first the blade, then the ear, and afterwards the full corn in the ear. Thus, too, man has his age of infancy, youth, and manhood, through all of which steps the Saviour passed, thus intimating that His salvation was not confined to any age.

Divers manners.—Revelation was not only communicated in different portions, but in different ways, by angels, voices, dreams, visions, and similitudes. Such were the different modes in which the prophets received their revelations.

In times past (rather, of old).—Here there appears to be a reference to the fact that the spirit of prophecy had long ceased. No prophet had arisen in Israel for the space of three hundred years from the days of Malachi.

To the fathers.—Here the term fathers includes not only the patriarchs of the Jewish nation, but all the prophets by whom God had communicated His will from the beginning.

V. 2.—Hath in these last days spoken unto us by his Son, whom he hath appointed heir of all things, by whom also he made the worlds.

These last days.—This expression may, no doubt, refer to the present time contrasted with " time past," ver. 1 ; but it appears especially to apply to the last dispensation under the reign of Messiah. The expression is parallel to chap. ix. 26, " now in the end of the world."* The same expression is used Isa. ii. 2 ; Acts ii. 17, &c.

All the prophets declared that the days should come when the Lord would communicate His will in a clearer and more glorious manner than He had hitherto done, so that " the last days " appear to indicate the period of the new dispensation, to which those who feared God in Israel looked forward. Matt. xiii. 17.

Spoken unto us by his Son.—For four thou-

* The Apostle designates the kingdom of Israel as the world. " Wherefore if ye be dead with Christ from the rudiments of the world, why, as though living in the world, are ye subject to ordinances ? " Col. ii. 20.

sand years preparation was being made for the
manifestation of the Son of God. Jesus is
termed God's *own* Son, His *only begotten*, and
when the fulness of the time had come He was
sent forth, " born of a woman, made under the
law, that he might redeem sinners from the
curse of the law, that they might receive the
adoption of sons." Gal. iv. 5. When He
appeared, the darkness of the old dispensation
fled before the beams of the Sun of Righteousness which arose with healing on His wings.
The wages of sin is death, therefore as the
head, the substitute, and representative of His
people He was delivered for their offences; He
was made sin for them, although He knew no
sin, that they might be made the righteousness
of God in Him; and in token of the efficacy of
His sacrifice He was raised from the dead, and
became the first fruits of them that slept.
No man took His life from Him, He laid it down
of Himself; He had power to lay it down and
power to take it again. Having offered Himself a sacrifice of a sweet-smelling savour
acceptable to God, He rose to die no more,
and because He lives His people shall live also.
Adam was the source of natural life to all
his children, but he forfeited it and they all
died in him, but in Christ all His people are
made alive; and when He who is their life shall

appear, they also shall appear with Him in glory.

The name of the Saviour is Immanuel, which being interpreted is, God with us. In His wonderful person the Divine and human natures are united, and thus we have a manifestation of the closeness of that union which subsists between the head and the members of Christ's mystical body.

The Word was in the beginning with God, and was God.* He was the Creator of all things visible and invisible, the fountain of life, and the only medium of communication of light to fallen man. John i. 2—4. He was made flesh and dwelt among us. When the angels sinned they were cast down to hell and reserved in everlasting chains of darkness

---

* Thus the Apostle intimates the personal distinction in the unity of the Godhead, which is to us an unfathomable mystery, of which we can know nothing beyond the simple fact. Yet it is the basis of the Gospel. Each of the adorable persons takes an important part in the work of redemption. The Father chose his people in Christ, and sent forth His Son to redeem them from death; the Son willingly undertook their cause; and the Holy Spirit, which Christ received without measure, is through Him communicated to each of them. Thus they are led into the truth as it is in Jesus. Hence they are baptized into the name, or faith, of the Father, Son, and Holy Ghost.

unto the judgment of the great day. Sin had
interposed an impenetrable vail between them
and the only source of light and joy; but by
the incarnation and sufferings of Christ God
was pleased to cause the light to shine out of
darkness upon an innumerable multitude of
our fallen race which had also come under
condemnation. And, inasmuch as the children
given to Christ were partakers of flesh and
blood, He Himself also took part of the same,
that by death He might destroy him that had
the power of death, that is the devil, and by
showing to His people the path of life, and becoming the firstborn of many brethren, might
deliver them who through fear of death were
all their lifetime subject to bondage. Thus
He magnified the law which they had broken,
and made it honourable. He spoiled principalities and powers, and made a show of them
openly, triumphing over them in His cross.
Hence it is written, " As by man came death,
by man came also the resurrection from the
dead; for as in Adam all die, even so in
Christ shall all be made alive; Christ the first
fruits, afterwards they that are Christ's at his
coming."

Whom he hath appointed heir of all things.—
As God, the Lord Jesus had an independent
right to the sovereignty of the universe; but

as God manifest in the flesh, at once the Son
of God and the Son of man, the great Mediator, He is appointed heir of all things, He is
termed the firstborn or heir of the whole creation.
Col. i. 18. This was the joy set before him,—
" Arise, O God, judge the earth, for thou
shalt inherit all nations." Ps. lxxxii. 8.*
" Jesus, being in the form of God, thought
it not robbery to be equal with God : but
made himself of no reputation, and took upon
him the form of a servant, and was made in
the likeness of men : and being found in fashion
as a man, he humbled himself, and became
obedient unto death, even the death of the
cross. Wherefore God also hath highly exalted him, and given him a name which is
above every name : that at the name of Jesus
every knee should bow, of things in heaven,
and things in earth, and things under the
earth ; and that every tongue should confess
that Jesus Christ is Lord, to the glory of God
the Father." Phil. ii. 6—11.

Thus, we are taught that as the reward of
His obedience unto death all power in heaven
and earth is committed to Him, and He employs

* Abraham is termed the heir of the world, Rom.
iv. 13, as being the father of Christ; just as it is written
in thee shall all families of the earth be blessed, because
this was to be fulfilled in his seed, which is Christ.

this power in gathering in His blood-bought sheep. The exaltation of the Son of God at His Father's right hand, surrounded by a countless multitude delivered from the power of Satan and translated into His everlasting kingdom, was the grand end of the creation of the world, which was not only made by Christ, but for Christ as a theatre on which His glory should be displayed. Col. i. 16. It was God's eternal purpose to make known to the principalities and powers in heavenly places His manifold wisdom by the Church redeemed with the Saviour's blood. Eph. iii. 10.

Christ is the head of the Church, and all of its members are members of His body, of His flesh, and of His bones. They are brought into a state of union so close and intimate that their sins are His, and His righteousness theirs. Hence, although He did no sin, nor was guile found in His lips, He says, " Mine iniquities have taken hold upon me, so that I am not able to look up; they are more than the hairs of my head, therefore my heart faileth me," Ps. xl. 12; while they who drank up iniquity as the ox drinketh up water are enabled with confidence to demand, " Who shall lay anything to the charge of God's elect?" arrayed in His unspotted righteousness, they shall all sit down on His glorious high throne and reign with Him for ever. He is their elder brother, their surety, their life. They were given to Him by His Father in the everlasting council; He undertook for them, has cancelled all their debt, and has entered into His glory to prepare for them mansions in which they shall for ever dwell. The Church of Christ, ransomed with His precious blood, shall abide an imperishable monument of the manifold wisdom of God, showing that with Him nothing shall be impossible.

By whom also he made the worlds.—That is, the universe; all things were made by Him, and without Him was not anything made that was made. John i. 3. Such is the glorious Personage by whom God hath spoken to us in these last days. The prophets were employed to unfold the revelations which God thought fit to communicate, but the Son has completed the discoveries which are necessary for our instruction, and to Him alone we are directed to look.

This was strikingly exhibited on the holy mount. Moses and Elias, the two most illustrious prophets of the old dispensation, conversed with Jesus on His decease which He was to accomplish at Jerusalem. The Apostles were desirous of detaining the heavenly visitors, but a bright

cloud overshadowed them, and behold a voice
out of the cloud which said, This is my beloved
Son: HEAR YE HIM.   They lifted up their eyes,
and Jesus alone remained, the great Prophet of
His Church.   The darkness was past and the
true light now shone.

*V. 3.—Who being the brightness of his glory, and the
express image of his person, and upholding all things by
the word of his power, when he had by himself purged
our sins, sat down on the right hand of the Majesty on
high.*

Who being the brightness of his glory.—God
has revealed Himself in the works of creation
and providence, but the brightness or effulgence
of His glory is only seen in His Son.   In Him
God has fully made known the glory of His
character.   Moses put a veil on his face when
declaring the message from God to Israel, but
we see the glory of God in the unveiled face of
Jesus.   No man hath seen God at any time;
the only begotten Son who is in the bosom
of the Father, intimately acquainted with all
His counsels, He hath declared Him.   John
i. 18.

And the express image of his person.—Christ
is the image of the invisible God, Col. i. 15;
and this image is so perfect that Christ Himself
tells us, " He that hath seen me hath seen the

Father." John xiv. 9.* By contemplating in
Him the glory of the Lord, we are changed into
the same image from glory to glory as by the
Spirit of the Lord. This is the new creation
in Christ Jesus, which is essential to our being
His disciples.

*And upholding all things by the word of his
power.*—All power is committed to Christ in
heaven and on earth. This is the reward of
His obedience to death, all things are put under
Him—all the vessels of His Father's house hang
on Him. The Father judgeth no man, but hath
committed all judgment to the Son.

When he had by himself purged our sins.—
Removing them by His atonement as far as the
east is from the west, having washed His people
from their sins in His own blood, they are whiter
than snow. The priests under the law purified
the people with the blood of bulls and goats,
but Christ obtained eternal redemption for all
believers by the shedding of His own blood.
When their sins are sought for they shall not

---

* It is unnecessary to state that this does not refer to
seeing the Saviour with our bodily eyes. It means a
right apprehension of His person, character, and offices.
Those who are thus enlightened behold the glory of
God in the face of Jesus Christ, and are changed into
His image.

be found, He will present them faultless before the presence of His glory with exceeding joy.

The resurrection and ascension of Jesus demonstrated the perfection of His sacrifice. One generation after another had gone down to the grave, which had never said, It is enough; but the Son of God, who knew no sin, having by His union with His people, so to speak, appropriated their sin, was delivered for their offences. He went down into the lower parts of the earth, but it was not possible He could remain there; not only because He was the Prince of Life, having life in Himself, but because He had cancelled the guilt of His brethren. What, then, could retain Him under the power of death? Death had lost its sting, its power was gone, and of necessity the earth cast forth its dead. Jesus rose to the power of an endless life as the head of his body the Church, as the first fruits of an abundant harvest; it was the seal of His Father's approbation of the work which He had undertaken and accomplished. As our great high priest He offered the body which had been prepared for Him. This is the will of God which He came to do, by which, says the Apostle, we are sanctified through the offering of the body of Christ once for all. Heb. x. 5—10. He is

the Captain of the salvation of a countless
multitude, who, in virtue of their union with
the Only-begotten, shall reign with Him in life
for ever.

*Sat down on the right hand of the Majesty on
high.*—When the Jewish high priest entered
the holy place, he *stood* while he performed
the service, for he was to remain but for a short
time, and only as a minister; but our great
High Priest *sat down* as a Prince on the right
hand of the Majesty on high. He occupies the
highest place. To Him everything in heaven
and on earth is subjected. He sits as a Royal
priest on His throne, consecrated for evermore,
—and His sitting on the right hand of the Majesty *on high*, implies that all things are put
under Him, excepting Him who did put all
things under Him. 1 Cor. xv. 27.

*V. 4.—Being made so much better than the angels, as
he hath by inheritance obtained a more excellent name
than they.*

Being made so much better than the angels.—
It is abundantly manifest that the title of the
Son of God, who is said to be appointed heir
of all things, to have been the brightness of
God's glory and the express image of His
person, purging our sins, and sitting down
at the right hand of the Majesty on high,
is descriptive of Immanuel, God manifest in

the flesh. God is invisible, and could not be the image of Himself; and the Son, in His Divine nature, is as invisible as the Father. Besides, where was the necessity for proving God to be superior to angels? But the Divine and human natures were united in the one person of Christ, and it is in this character that the Apostle establishes His superiority to angels.

As he hath by inheritance obtained a more excellent name than they.—Angels are, indeed, termed by courtesy the sons of God, but to Christ this name belongs by inheritance.* He is possessed of the Divine nature, as a son partakes of the nature of his father, while from His mother Christ equally partook of human nature. Hence He is indifferently described as the Son of God, implying His Divinity, and as the Son of man, implying His humanity. God does nothing in vain; He accomplishes His purposes by means exactly adapted to the end He has in view. In the first creation He spoke and it was done, He

* This is illustrated by a passage in English history. Henry II., having admitted his son to a share of the sovereignty, caused him to sit at table while he waited on him, at the same time observing that never king was more royally served. The prince pleasantly replied, that there was nothing extraordinary in the son of a Count serving the son of a king. The son's rank came to him by inheritance, the father's by conquest.

commanded and all things stood fast; but to reconcile justice with mercy, to destroy the works of the devil, the Son of God was manifested, and suffered, and died, and revived, that He might be the Lord both of the dead and the living.

V. 5.—For unto which of the angels said he· at any time, Thou art my Son, this day have I begotten thee? And again, I will be to him a Father, and he shall be to me a Son?

For unto which of the angels said he at any time, Thou art my Son, this day have I begotten thee?—Here the Apostle proceeds to prove his assertion, that Christ possesses by inheritance a more excellent name than the angels. This he demonstrates by a quotation from the second Psalm, which not only gives Jesus the title of Son, but describes Him as *begotten.* The Apostle elsewhere applies this prediction to the resurrection of Christ, Acts xiii. 33, because He was thus declared to be the Son of God with power. Rom. i. 4. In various ways had He been declared to be the Son of God, by His doctrine and miracles, the perfection of His character, and repeated testimonies by a voice from heaven; but His resurrection was the demonstration of His being the Son of God, the promised seed of the woman, the Judge of

the world. Acts xvii. 31. Hence, the sign
which He gave in token of the dignity of His
person was the sign of the prophet Jonas.
Jesus was to be three days and three nights in
the heart of the earth. The temple of His
body, in which dwelt all the fulness of the
Godhead bodily, was to be destroyed, and in
three days He would raise it up.

He appeared in our nature, that He might
lay down His life. He came in the character
of the Father's servant to accomplish the salvation of the children given to Him. He is
the seed of the woman, the Head of God's
elect; and having identified Himself with them,
that He might raise them to life and glory, He
in their nature endured the curse which they
had incurred that they might inherit a blessing,
and might all through union with Him be
acknowledged to be the sons of God. He
subjected Himself to suffering and death that
they might partake of eternal life with Him.
It was an easy service imposed on Adam to
abstain from the fruit of one tree, but the
service required of the second Adam included
not only sorrow, shame, and grief in this
world, but the pains of death. To all this
He cheerfully submitted, knowing that His
Father's commandment was life everlasting,
not only to Himself, but to a countless mul-

titude. As the Father hath life in Himself,
so hath He given to the Son to have life in Himself, and hath given Him authority to execute
judgment also, because He is the Son of man.
John v. 26, 27.   The reason of all judgment
being committed to the Son is very remarkable,
"that all men should honour the Son even
as they honour the Father."

The Apostle adds another testimony to the
Sonship of Christ.

*And again, I will be to him a Father, and he
shall be to me a Son.*—It is evident that this
passage refers primarily to Solomon, 2 Sam.
vii. 14 ; 1 Chron. xvii. 12, who was a remarkable type of Christ, but we learn from the
Apostle that a greater than Solomon is here.
Indeed, this is evident from the passage quoted,
for God promises to establish His kingdom *for
ever*.   The Lord Jesus is frequently described
both as David and the Son of David.   David
was a man after God's own heart, which denotes his zeal for the worship of God; but it
has its full accomplishment in Christ, who is
in all respects a man after God's own heart, for
He always did those things which pleased His
Father.   He now sits on the throne of His
father David, and is indeed the King of Israel.
John i. 49.

We repeatedly find a double type in consequence of the different aspects in which Christ is presented to our view. He was in the form of a servant, engaged in a work committed to Him by His Father, which required Him to be a man of sorrows and acquainted with griefs, a stranger and pilgrim, a houseless wanderer in this world, and finally to be made a curse by hanging on a tree, thus becoming obedient to the death of the cross. Again, we behold Him a resistless conqueror triumphing over death, His foot on the neck of Satan, and invested with all power in heaven and on earth. Hence a double type was necessary to denote His sufferings and glory. The former was typified by " David and all his afflictions," the latter, by Solomon, who enjoyed a long, glorious, and peaceful reign; a remarkable type of Him of the increase of whose government and peace there shall be no end, upon the throne of David and of his kingdom, to order it and establish it with judgment and justice, from henceforth and for ever. Hence the Apostle applies to Jesus what was primarily said of Solomon,—I will be to him a Father, and he shall be to me a Son.

Besides David and Solomon prefiguring Christ in His humiliation and exaltation, we find other instances of a double type. Thus, on the great day of atonement there were two goats, one of which, when the sins of Israel were laid upon it, was slain, while the other was set free, denoting Christ dying for the sins of His people and raised for their justification.

Again, in cleansing the leper, there were two birds, the one of which was slain, the other, after being dipped in its blood, was set free. This represented the great Shepherd of the sheep brought again from the dead through the blood of the everlasting covenant. Heb. xiii. 10.

Moses, the Mediator of the old covenant, was a remarkable type of our great Mediator, and in correspondence with the antitype, Israel could not enter Canaan till after his death. When the people sinned in the matter of the golden calf, and Moses had broken the tables in token of the covenant being broken, he said to the people, " Ye have sinned a great sin, and now I will go up unto the Lord, peradventure I shall make an atonement for your sin." Exod. xxxii. 30. He accordingly returned to the Lord, and said, " Oh, this people have sinned a great sin, and have made them gods of gold. Yet now, if thou wilt forgive their sin—; and if not, blot me, I pray thee, out of the book which thou hast written." Exod. xxxii. 31, 32. Thus he offered his life

to atone for the sin of Israel. We know that
God spoke to Moses mouth to mouth, even
apparently, and not in dark speeches. Num.
xii. 8. There is therefore reason to suppose
that Moses communicated to Israel in parables
what he had heard plainly in the mount. Israel
was a carnal, stiffnecked people, and could not
have borne the truth of the Son of God dying,
and reviving, and rising. The doctrine of
Christ was a stumblingblock to their children, after they had received all the additional
instructions contained in the Scriptures of the
prophets, had seen His own mighty works, and
heard Him declared to be the Son of God by a
voice from heaven,—notwithstanding all this,
they crucified Him as a blasphemer. Hence,
it is not improbable that Moses concealed in
parables what he had been taught in the
mount, and that this was intimated by the
veil which he put upon his face while speaking
to the people, and which he took off when he
went in before the Lord. Exod. xxxiv. 33, 34.
If this were the case, Moses knew that Christ
was to die for His people, and as the mediator
of the old covenant he offered to expiate by
death the sin of which Israel had been guilty.
But Moses, however eminent, was but a sinful
man, and a sin-offering must be perfect to be
accepted—"There shall be no blemish therein."

Lev. xxii. 21. But, although the death of Moses could not be accepted as an expiation for the sin of Israel, it was necessary for the correspondence of the type and the antitype, that the mediator should die before Israel could enter Canaan. Hence it is written, " Moses, my servant, is dead; now, therefore, arise, go over this Jordan, thou and all this people, unto the land which I do give to them, even to the children of Israel." Joshua i. 2. Thus Moses and Joshua were each a type of Christ, who, having by His death expiated the sins of His people, rose from the dead as the Captain of their salvation, and puts them in possession of the eternal inheritance.

V. 6.—And again, when he bringeth in the first-begotten into the world, he saith, And let all the angels of God worship him.

And again, &c.—There is a great difference of opinion with respect to the construction of the word rendered " again." It may be understood either as an additional proof of what had been asserted in verse 5, or it may refer to Christ being brought again into the world by His resurrection. The quotation is taken from Ps. xcvii., which is descriptive of the reign of Christ. During His humiliation he was made for a little while lower than the angels, being exposed to suffering and death; but when at His resurrection He was brought again into the world, all power in heaven and in earth was committed to Him, and all the angels of God were commanded to worship Him. The passage, therefore, appears to refer to His resurrection. In our version Ps. xcvii. 7 is rendered " Worship him all ye gods ; " but the expression is elliptical, and may be rendered " All ye angels of God."

Jesus is here termed the firstborn, or first-begotten, while personally distinct He is one with the Father. The firstborn had various privileges,—he had authority over his brethren. Hence the Lord said to Cain, after testifying his approbation of his brother's sacrifice, " Unto thee shall be his desire, and thou shalt rule over him." Gen. iv. 7. God's accepting Abel's offering was not to interfere with Cain's superiority as the firstborn. Again, Jacob describes Reuben, his firstborn, as the excellency of dignity and the excellency of power. Gen. xlix. 3. This privilege was forfeited and transferred to Judah, of whom came the " chief ruler." 1 Chron. v. 2. Another privilege of the firstborn was a double portion. This, also, Reuben forfeited, and the privilege was transferred to Joseph, who was the father of two of the twelve tribes ; while from each of Jacob's other sons sprang only

one tribe. Another privilege was the priesthood, which was also forfeited by Reuben
and bestowed on Levi.

Christ, as the firstborn in all things, had the
pre-eminence; to Him every knee shall bow, of
things in heaven and things on earth, and every
tongue shall confess that He is Lord, to the glory
of God the Father. The angels are all commanded to worship Him.; He is exalted "far
above all principality, and power, and might,
and dominion, and every name that is named,
not only in this world, but also in that which
is to come." Eph. i. 21.

*V. 7.—And of the angels he saith, Who maketh his
angels spirits, and his ministers a flame of fire.*

And of the angels, &c.—The angels are
here described as spirits, and as a flame
of fire. The word "spirits" also signifies
" winds," and some, therefore, understand
the passage as teaching us that the Lord
makes winds His messengers and flaming fire
His ministers; but the Apostle does not here
teach us the nature of winds and of lightnings,
but the nature of angels. The best interpretation seems to be, that the angels when sent
by the Lord to perform His will, do so in the
form of winds and fire. When Elijah was
taken up into heaven, "there appeared a

chariot of fire and horses of fire." "Elijah went up by a whirlwind into heaven." This seems to be a work performed by the ministry of angels, the chariot and the horses of fire appear to have been angels. We also read, that when Elisha was surrounded by the Syrian army, the mountain was full of horses of fire round about the prophet. That these were *persons* is evident from what Elisha said to his servant, " Fear not, for there be more with us than with them." This interpretation both suits the phraseology and presents the angels in a very humble situation. Or, perhaps the meaning may be that the angels serve their Maker with the rapidity of the winds and the resistless power of the lightnings.

V. 8.—But unto the Son he saith, Thy throne, O God, is for ever and ever : a sceptre of righteousness is the sceptre of thy kingdom.

Christ is described, Ps. xlv. 6, from which this is a quotation, as God sitting on His eternal throne, holding a sceptre of righteousness. This is eminently the characteristic of the Mediator's government, which is conducted on principles of the most perfect justice. While He has taken his redeemed from the fearful pit and the miry clay, He has magnified and made honourable the law which they had broken, they are clothed with a robe of unsullied righteousness. His Gospel, which proclaims God to be just while He justifies the ungodly, is the revelation of this righteousness, Rom. i. 17; and when He has reduced the creation to order and harmony, He will deliver up the kingdom to His Father, and for ever remain the glorious Head of that Church which He hath purchased with His own blood, as well as of all principality and power. The kingdom here spoken of is that kingdom upon the throne of which the King sits who reigns in righteousness, Isa. xxxii. 1, and on which He sat down after having finished transgression, made an end of sin, made reconciliation for iniquities, and brought in everlasting righteousness. Dan. ix. 24.

That the forty-fifth Psalm refers to Christ is evident, not only from the authority of the Apostle in this passage, but from the whole tenour of the Psalm. God promised David respecting him, "I will establish the throne of his kingdom for ever;" and when Gabriel announced his birth to Mary, he said, "And, behold, thou shalt conceive in thy womb, and bring forth a son, and shalt call his name Jesus. He shall be great, and shall be called the Son of the Highest: and the Lord God shall give unto him the throne of his father

David : and he shall reign over the house of
Jacob for ever; and of his kingdom there
shall be no end." Luke i. 31—33. In the
Psalm He is described as riding forth in
majesty, vanquishing His enemies, and placing
on his right hand the " Queen," the mother
of a numerous offspring.

It is evident that the Apostle here speaks
of Jesus in the character of Mediator, the
Son of man. In this character alone could
any comparison be instituted between Him and
the highest of created beings.

*V. 9.—Thou hast loved righteousness, and hated ini-
quity; therefore God, even thy God, hath anointed thee
with the oil of gladness above thy fellows.*

*Thou hast loved righteousness and hated
iniquity.*—This refers to the character of Jesus
while in this world, not, as some have supposed, after His government is over. It was
the perfection of the character of Jesus that
He loved righteousness and hated iniquity.
In the days of His flesh He always did the
things which pleased His Father; the law was
within His heart. His language was, " O how
love I thy law! it is my meditation all the
day." He challenges His enemies to convict
Him of sin. Indeed one flaw in His character
would prove the Gospel a fable, for He is
God manifest in the flesh, and therefore must

have been absolutely perfect. Again, He received the Holy Spirit without measure, which was inconsistent with the slightest deviation from the path of righteousness. The character of Jesus is in itself a demonstration of the truth of the Gospel. Man could not have imagined such a character; and, we may say with the infidel Rousseau, that to suppose the four Gospels a forgery is more incredible than the admission of its truth.*

Such was the Lord's love of righteousness, that He gave Himself for His people to deliver them from all iniquity, that He might purify unto Himself a peculiar people, zealous of good works. He walked in the perfect law of liberty. His undertaking was entirely voluntary; hence He said, "Lo I come, to do thy will, O my God!" Amidst all the discouragements He met with, He never swerved by a hair's breadth from the path of rectitude. Amidst all the shame and reproach which He encountered He set his face as a flint, nor did

---

* Why then did Rousseau remain an infidel? Because, as he tells us, the Gospel contains many things to which his reason could not assent. What a comment on 1 Cor. ii. 14, "But the natural man receiveth not the things of the Spirit of God: for they are foolishness unto him: neither can he know them, because they are spiritually discerned."

He fail or become discouraged till He set judgment on the earth. He had only to will it, and
legions of angels were ready to vindicate His
glory; but He endured the cross, despising the
shame, and thus was His mediatorial throne
established in righteousness. All His subjects
are righteous, without spot and blemish.

Therefore—on this account.—The anointing
was the reward of Christ's love of righteousness
and hatred of iniquity while on earth. Some
suppose that the anointing takes place subse-
quently to His government, but it is not connected with His government, which is spoken
of before. The eighth verse speaks of Him as
a king, and the ninth verse shows why the
kingdom was given Him, consequently it was
not the reward of His administration of the
kingdom. This would imply that Christ has
not yet received the anointing, for the mediatorial kingdom will not cease till He hath put
all enemies under His feet.

God, even thy God.—Some render this
" therefore, O God thy God." The difference
is not material. Owen observes, that the
phrase is generally translated as in our version.

Hath anointed thee.—What is the anointing
here meant? Is it that by which He was consecrated to the kingly office? or, has it reference
to the anointing which was usual in cases of

festivity and joy? The latter appears to be
the meaning. Christ was anointed to all His
offices after His baptism, when He received the
Holy Ghost without measure. The anointing
here spoken of took place after the manifestation of His love of righteousness and hatred
of iniquity while in this world. It was that
happiness and glory which He received as
Mediator after his ascension.

Above thy fellows.—Some suppose that "by
his fellows" is meant the angels, because the
Apostle is here proving His superiority to
angels, but He never assumed the nature of
angels. In this respect He never had fellowship with them. Others think that "by his
fellows" we are to understand the prophets,
priests, and kings who were anointed with oil
to their respective offices, which were all con-
centrated in Him while He was anointed with
the Holy Ghost. It appears, however, rather
to mean His people, whom He is not ashamed
to call brethren. He took part with them in
flesh and blood. He is the connecting link by
which the whole family in heaven and in earth
is united to God. The closeness and perpetuity
of this union is exhibited in His person as God-
man. Hence he says, " I ascend to my Father
and to your Father, to my God and your God."
His fellows, then, are those with whom, by His

incarnation, He has fellowship; and so close is this fellowship, that both He that sanctifieth and they that are sanctified are all of one—children of one family. But in all things He hath the pre-eminence; all their well-springs are in Him. He is anointed with the oil of gladness above His fellows, He received the Holy Spirit without measure, of which no creature was capable, which is therefore a conclusive proof of His Divinity. The Jewish prophets, priests, and kings were anointed with oil, which was the emblem of the Spirit; they were types of Him who is the Christ, or Anointed One, and His people are called Christians because they have all an unction from the Holy One. As the precious oil, poured on the head of Aaron, ran down to the skirts of his garments, so the Spirit, poured on the great Head of the Church, is conveyed from Him to all His people, and thus they are one spirit with Him, 1 Cor. vi. 17; they are all baptized by one Spirit into one body, 1 Cor. xii. 13; and we are taught, that if any man have not the Spirit, he is none of His.

V. 10.—*And, Thou, Lord, in the beginning hast laid the foundation of the earth; and the heavens are the works of thine hands.*

And, thou, Lord.—The 102d Psalm, from which this quotation is taken describes, in an

address to His Father, the sufferings of Christ
and the depth of His humiliation. Ver. 1—11.
The sweet Psalmist of Israel then contemplates
Jehovah arising in His might to favour Sion, and
anticipates the universal spread of the Gospel.
Ver.16—22. He then adverts to His own suffering
and death, ver. 23, and describes the supplications which He offered to Him who was able to
save Him from death. Ver. 24. The concluding
verses contain the answer to the prayer. Had
the Psalm not been quoted by the Apostle, we
should, probably, have understood the conclusion of the Psalm as the continuance of the
prayer, but we learn from the Apostle that it
is the answer which Christ received. In the
depth of His humiliation He is acknowledged
as the Creator of heaven and earth. John i. 3.
The Apostle had previously stated that God
had made the worlds by His Son, ver. 2; and
here, in reply to the expression of Christ's
deep and overwhelming affliction, He is reminded that His years are throughout all
generations:—"Of old hast thou laid the
foundations of the earth: and the heavens are
the work of thy hands. They shall perish,
but thou shalt endure: yea, all of them shall
wax old like a garment; as a vesture shalt
thou change them, and they shall be changed;
but thou art the same, and thy years shall have

no end." Ps. cii. 25—27. It had been given
to the Son to have life in Himself, although in
connexion with his humanity He had received
a commandment to lay it down, that He might
take it again; and not only so, but the children
of His servants should continue, and their seed
should be established before Him, which exactly
corresponds with our Lord's words—"Because
I live, ye shall live also." John xiv. 19.

*V. 11.—They shall perish: but thou remainest: and
they all shall wax old as doth a garment.*

They shall perish.—However glorious the
work of creation, the heavens and earth shall
perish. They are, so to speak, the scaffolding
for the erection of a more glorious fabric.
2 Pet. iii. 10—13. Here we may apply the
Apostle's reasoning,—"Howbeit that was not
first which is spiritual, but that which is natural; and afterward that which is spiritual."
1 Cor. xv. 46. So the visible heavens and
earth are intended to introduce the new
creation,—"And I saw a new heaven and a
new earth: for the first heaven and the first
earth were passed away; and there was no
more sea. And I John saw the holy city, new
Jerusalem, coming down from God out of
heaven, prepared as a bride adorned for her
husband. And I heard a great voice out of

heaven saying, Behold, the tabernacle of God
is with men, and he will dwell with them,
and they shall be his people, and God himself
shall be with them, and be their God. And God
shall wipe away all tears from their eyes; and
there shall be no more death, neither sorrow,
nor crying, neither shall there be any more
pain: for the former things are passed away.
And he that sat upon the throne said, Behold,
I make all things new. And he said unto me,
Write: for these words are true and faithful."
Rev. xxi. 1—5. The heavens and the earth shall
be changed; but He, the Messiah, remains; He
is the same, yesterday, to-day, and for ever.

They all shall wax old as doth a garment.—
As a garment becomes unfit for being worn, so
shall they wax old.

*V. 12.—And as a vesture shalt thou fold them up, and
they shall be changed: but thou art the same, and thy
years shall not fail.*

*And as a vesture shalt thou fold them up, and
they shall be changed.*—The first creation shall,
like a vesture, be folded up and laid aside.

*But thou art the same, and thy years shall not
fail.*—This is a most decided testimony to the
supreme Divinity of the Lord Jesus. He is
the same. The word is used, chap. xiii. 8.
He is the unchangeable Jehovah. The years

of the heavens and the earth are numbered, and shall fail, not so the years of the Son of God, the Ancient of days.

The expression "*changed*" merits attention. We know nothing of annihilation; probably there is no such thing in the universe. God created nothing in vain; annihilation means any substance being reduced to nothing. We have no experience of this; the body is changed to dust, fuel into smoke, water into steam, and here we read that the heavens and the earth shall be changed.

Even had the Apostle not applied Ps. cii. 24—27 to Christ, we might have been led to it by the last verse: "The children of thy servants shall continue, and their seed shall be established before thee." Applying the Psalm from verse 24 to Christ, all is plain and easy. In the depth of His humiliation He is acknowledged as the great Creator, and assured that the children of His servants should continue, and their seed be established before Him. This is very beautiful and consoling as applied to Christ, and exactly corresponds with many promises made to the Lord Jesus. Ps. xxii. 30, 31; xlv. 16; lxix. 36. Isa. liii. 10 and lix. 21.

In this quotation we have another most explicit testimony to the supreme Divinity of

Christ.   He is not only declared to be superior
to angels, but to be "over all, God blessed
for ever."   Rom. ix. 5.   This is shown by His
being represented as seated on His eternal
throne, Heb. i. 8; and not only having in His
character of mediator the pre-eminence over all
those with whom he had condescended to unite
himself, but as the Creator of all things.   Amidst
all the changes which he would effect on the
works of His hands, in order to adapt them to
His infinitely wise purposes, HE remains for ever
the same, and with Him there is no variableness
or shadow of turning.   James i. 17.

*V. 13.—But to which of the angels said he at any time,
Sit on my right hand, until I make thine enemies thy
footstool?*

The Apostle here returns to his argument to
prove the superiority of the Lord Jesus to
angels, of which, indeed, he had never lost
sight; but had soared so high in describing the
Divinity of the Son of God, as to leave every
created being far beneath Him.   The honour
of sitting at the right hand of God is such,
that it never was given to any of the angels.
They are described as *round about* the throne;
but Christ, in the character of mediator, sits
upon the throne at the Father's right hand.
Thus Christ is distinguished from all angels
of every order, from the highest to the lowest.

Sit on my right hand, is a quotation from
Ps. cx. 1 and 5; it was quoted by our Lord
in the days of His flesh, as having been written
by David under the inspiration of the Holy
Spirit in reference to Christ. The great mystery of godliness, God manifest in the flesh,
was hid from the scribes and pharisees, although
plainly declared in the Scriptures; but, like
many other predictions, was not understood
till its fulfilment.

The reference to Ps. cx. was exactly to the
Apostle's purpose in proof of Messiah's superiority to angels. It also contained a powerful
argument to induce the believing Hebrews to
hold fast their allegiance to Christ, because all
His enemies must be made His footstool. Isa.
lx. 12. Ps. lxxii. 9.

Enemies.—The devil and his angels are in
a state of rebellion against God; and it would
appear that their rebellion arose from the intimation of the exaltation of Christ, and that
our Lord refers to this when He said, " He
was a murderer from the beginning, *and abode
not in the truth.*" John viii. 44. It was God's
eternal purpose to make known by the Church
to the principalities and powers in heavenly
places His manifold wisdom. Eph. iii. 10. In
furtherance of this design He seems to have
revealed to the heavenly hosts His determina-

tion to put all things under the Son of man. Satan, then an angel of light, and, it may be, superior to all other angels, scorned the thought of being subject to a creature formed of the dust. He therefore set himself to defeat his Maker's purpose. He knew His justice and His truth; he heard the intimation, "in the day that thou eatest thereof thou shalt surely die." If, then, he could lead man to transgress, the exaltation of Adam, or any of his posterity, appeared absolutely impossible. He succeeded, he brought mankind under the curse; but there is no counsel or divination against the Lord. His purpose was accomplished by the very means employed to defeat it; for, in the fulness of time, the Son of God was manifested to destroy the works of the devil, and now in human nature is seated at God's right hand to gather in his redeemed, and to take vengeance on all his enemies. Satan has thus become the dupe of his own subtlety, and has been made the unwilling instrument of accomplishing the Divine purpose.

Not only are the devil and his angels the enemies of Christ, but all the children of men who have not been chosen in Him—called by His grace, are among the number of His enemies. But all His enemies shall be made His footstool. They shall not only fail in their attempts to injure those who are called into the fellowship of God's dear Son, but their enmity shall be overruled to promote the benefit of Christ's people. As *a footstool* is a convenience to one seated on a chair of state, so all the machinations of Satan and his adherents shall advance the glory of the Son of God.

V. 14.—Are they not all ministering spirits, sent forth to minister for them who shall be heirs of salvation?

Are they not all ministering spirits, &c.—This form of expression may imply that the thing asserted was known and admitted by the Hebrews; yet our belief of it does not rest on this foundation, but on the authority of the Apostle. The question implies no doubt, on the subject of inquiry; it is a strong mode of asserting a proposition. The existence of angels was believed by the Jews, with the exception of the Sadducees. We have many instances in the Old Testament of angels being employed to convey messages to men, and in defending the people of God. Such is not now visibly the case: we have no reason to expect an extraordinary message to be conveyed to us by angels, or that they shall visibly come to our aid; but it is well that we should know that all the angels are employed by our

Lord to minister to the heirs of salvation. It may be asked, of what use is this ministry? Had the Lord any need of such agents as instruments in taking care of his people? Certainly not; but can anything more clearly prove the dignity of the saints? They are despised among men, yet all the angels in heaven wait on them. Many of God's people may be engaged in the meanest offices among men, yet they have a retinue of angels to watch over them.

Heirs of salvation.—The saints have their privileges, not by works of righteousness, but by inheritance. They are joint-heirs with Christ. Adam was the heir of the world, Gen. i. 28, 29, but he lost his inheritance. The second Adam is appointed heir of all things, and the inheritance is secured by his love and power to all the children of promise. Those who are saved inherit glory, therefore salvation includes, not only deliverance from misery, but also the possession of glory. Here it signifies whatever the people of God shall enjoy throughout eternity.

Shall be.—Hence it appears that the ministering of the angels belongs to the heirs of salvation from the earliest period of their existence. It is said of Jeremiah,—"Before I formed thee in the belly I knew thee; and before thou camest forth out of the womb I sanctified thee, and I ordained thee a prophet unto the nations." Jer. i. 5. The Lord separated Paul from his mother's womb, and no doubt the angels were employed in ministering to him while breathing out slaughter and threatening against the disciples of Christ.

Such is the introduction of this most instructive epistle. The Apostle begins by referring to the revelations which God had given by that succession of prophets who were raised up from the beginning. He had now spoken by His Son, whom He had constituted heir of all things. By Him and for Him all the worlds were made. He is the image of the invisible God, and has revealed Him to us, clearly exhibiting his glorious perfections. Having, by offering the body which had been prepared for Him, cast the sins of His people into the depths of the sea, so that they should be no more remembered, He sat down on the right hand of the Majesty on high, denoting His absolute and universal dominion. He is the Judge of the quick and the dead, to whom every knee shall bow and every tongue confess. The name which He inherited, and which in its proper sense exclusively belongs to Him, was far more glorious than the name given to the angels. To none of them had God said,

Thou art my Son, this day have I begotten thee. He had described none of them as standing to Him in the relation of a Son. On the contrary, when He foretold the appearance of the first-begotten, the Lord and heir of all, He commanded all the angels of God to worship Him.

The angels are described as executing His will with the rapidity of winds and the resistless power of the lightnings; but the Son is addressed as God sitting on his eternal throne, and as a King reigning in righteousness. He humbled himself, so that, although he was truly God, the Father stood to Him in the relation of His God; and, lest this should derogate from His innate dignity, He is described as the Creator of all things, who, amidst all their mutations, abideth ever the same. Once more, which of the angels was ever invited to sit at God's right hand until their enemies were made their footstool? So far from their being thus honoured, they are all only ministering spirits, sent forth by their glorious Head to minister to the heirs of salvation.

CHAPTER II.

V. 1.—Therefore we ought to give the more earnest heed to the things which we have heard, lest at any time we should let them slip.

Therefore, or, on this account, viz., the consideration of the surpassing dignity of the Son of God, by whom God had spoken in these last days.

We ought to give the more earnest heed.— Here we are taught that our regard to what is spoken, ought to be in proportion to the dignity and authority of the speaker. Now, if attention is to be given to the Gospel in proportion to the dignity of its author, who is no less a personage than the Son of God, with what solemn reverence ought we to listen to His words! They are not only to be at first received, but to be kept in memory. The persons addressed had already received the Gospel, but they were to continue in faith and obedience to the end of their lives. Matt. xxiv. 13.

To the things which we have heard.—Be-

lievers ought diligently to attend to whatever
the Lord Jesus has said in His Word. The
Gospel itself is the great truth, the belief of
which is salvation, however great men's ignorance in other respects may be; yet nothing
which God has said is to be overlooked, but
everything is to be attended to as far as it is
understood. All things said by Jesus are not
of equal importance, but all things are important, and to be received and obeyed at
every hazard and every loss. The consideration
that the Lord forgives the ignorance of his
people ought never to be alleged in justification of inattention to whatever he hath spoken,
or of the neglect of the least of his commandments. It may also be observed that we are
to give heed to the things *that we have heard*,
that is, the things recorded in the Scriptures.
Christians have nothing to learn from other
sources. They are not to employ speculations
of their own to eke out their information with
respect to Divine things, far less are they to
receive the doctrines and commandments of
men. The word which I have spoken, says
the Lord, it shall judge you. The word
rendered " let slip," literally signifies " to run
out," as a leaky vessel, which strikingly corresponds with our proneness gradually and
insensibly to lose sight of one or another

part of the doctrine of Christ.   It is evidently
a warning not to depart from the faith.

*V. 2.—For if the word spoken by angels was stedfast,
and every transgression and disobedience received a just
recompence of reward.*

The word spoken by angels.—The law spoken
by angels, is the law delivered at Mount Sinai.
Stephen speaks of the Jews having received
the law by the disposition of angels, Acts vii.
53, and the Apostle describes the law as being
ordained of angels. Gal. iii. 19.   We are,
however, expressly taught that God spake the
Ten Commandments. Exod. xx. 1.   This may
be explained by the 11th verse of Psalm lxviii.,
" The Lord gave the word : great was the
company of those that published it."   Angels
were employed in publishing the law given by
God.
    But, perhaps, the difficulty may be solved
by the consideration that He who was afterwards manifested in the flesh ruled over the
Mosaic dispensation in the character of an
angel. He is called the Messenger of the
Covenant,—the Lord whom they sought, who
was to come suddenly to his temple. Mal.
iii. 1. This is evidently descriptive of Christ.
Again, it is said my name is in Him, Exod.
xxiii. 21, and under the guidance of this

angel Moses had no scruple to proceed. But
when the Lord said he would send an angel
to drive out the nations, and to give them the
land, but that HE would not go in the midst
of them, Moses objected. He was not satisfied with being under the protection of a
created angel, and requested, that if God's
presence went not with them, he would not
command them to pursue their journey. Exod.
xxxiii. 15. The angel who had hitherto conducted Israel is frequently called Jehovah; He
is the angel of God's presence. Isa. lxiii. 9.
Thus, He who was afterwards manifest in the
flesh ruled that dispensation in the character
of an angel; but this was only for a season,
and to this the prophet refers,—" O the hope
of Israel, the Saviour thereof in time of
trouble, why shouldest thou be as a stranger
in the land, and as a wayfaring man that
turneth aside to tarry for a night?" Jer.
xiv. 8.

The Apostle had previously established the
infinite superiority of the Son of God to
angels, and hence he argues the inferiority
of the Law to the Gospel,—the Law having
been promulgated by God in the temporary
character of an angel, implying the temporary
nature of the dispensation; the Gospel by the
Son of God who abideth for ever, and who

has said, "Heaven and earth shall pass away, but my Word shall not pass away." Matt. xxiv. 35.

Was stedfast.—Many prophets were raised up in Israel, but no alteration of the law was permitted. Malachi, the last of the prophets, concludes his testimony by enjoining upon Israel to remember the Law of Moses, with the statutes and judgments. Mal. iv. 4.

Every transgression and disobedience.—The words are nearly synonymous; when used together, transgression implies the doing of what is forbidden, and disobedience the omission of what is required. This exactly corresponds with the injunction neither to add to, nor diminish, what Moses had commanded. Deut. xii. 32.

Just recompence of reward.—The punishment justly awarded according to the offence. It would be unjust not to visit transgression with merited punishment.

V. 3.—How shall we escape, if we neglect so great salvation; which at the first began to be spoken by the Lord, and was confirmed unto us by them that heard him?

How shall we escape.—This implies that there is no possibility of escaping the wrath of God revealed from heaven against sin. Men may deceive themselves by hopes founded on false views of the mercy of God; but the door of mercy is for ever shut against all transgressors who do not avail themselves of the only remedy provided by God through the death of His Son.

If we neglect so great salvation.—The Apostle includes himself and his fellow-believers, because it was as true of them as of others. Had they neglected the great salvation there would not have been any way of escape for them. Believers are secured by having been chosen in, and given to Christ, and, consequently, they are secured from neglecting the great salvation; for He who has begun a good work in them, has engaged to perform it until the day of Jesus Christ. Phil. i. 6.

It is a wonderful proof of the wisdom of God that, in the salvation of sinners, He has given a more awful manifestation of the exceeding sinfulness of sin than in the destruction of the rebel angels. So far from sin appearing less pernicious by an unlimited pardon being proclaimed to the chief of sinners by faith in Christ, its malignity is more fully displayed. It was God's eternal purpose to pluck a multitude of our fallen race, which no man should be able to number, as brands from the burning, and His purpose could only be effected by the incarnation, sufferings, and death of His only-begotten and well-beloved Son. If there was no other channel through which mercy could

E

flow to sinners of mankind, how could any
who neglected so great salvation possibly
escape ?

The salvation here spoken of is deliverance
from the love and power of sin, hence the Son
of God was named Jesus. Matt. i. 21. It is
great in every point of view, whether we consider the ruin and misery from which it delivers
us, the means by which the deliverance was
accomplished, or the glory into which those
who receive it are introduced. On the other
hand, he that believeth not the record that God
gave of His Son, hath made Him a liar.
1 John v. 10.

Some openly reject the Gospel, accounting
it a cunningly-devised fable ; others, although
they do not openly reject it, are so much
occupied with the things of time and sense as
altogether to neglect it. All men neglect the
great salvation who do not consider it as the
one thing needful. All men neglect it who
do not receive it. All men neglect it who are
not influenced by it, for it *effectually works* in
them that believe.

Perhaps, in speaking of the great salvation,
the Apostle refers to the deliverance of Israel
from the iron furnace. In bringing them out
of Egypt, God gave a glorious display of his
power and goodness. This, however, was only

a temporal salvation, but the salvation announced in the Gospel is eternal. It is
deliverance from the bondage of Satan, and,
consequently, from the wrath to come—from
that lake of fire, where there is weeping, and
wailing, and gnashing of teeth. It translates
the lost and ruined sinner into the kingdom
of God's dear Son. It restores him to the
image of God in which he was created. So
long as God's Word abode in the heart of
Adam, he stood firm in that estate of holiness
and happiness in which he was created; but
Satan gained admission into his heart in the
form of a lie, and thus was man changed into
the image of him who was a liar from the
beginning. But the believer is created anew
in Christ; by receiving the love of the truth
he is saved; Christ, who is the truth, takes
possession of his heart, and he is thus delivered
from the power of darkness and translated into
the kingdom of God's dear Son; and, after
having fellowship with Christ in His death and
resurrection, shall sit with Him for ever on
His throne. Such is the great salvation, and
how shall the sinner who neglects it escape?

Began to be spoken by the Lord.—The great
salvation began to be spoken by the Lord.
The title, " The Lord," belongs to Jesus as
fully as to the Father. He is Lord of heaven

and earth, the Lord of life and glory. The great salvation had been announced to our first parents, and intimated by all the prophets by types, and figures, and shadows ; but the full and clear declaration of it was made by the Lord during his personal ministry.

Confirmed unto us by them that heard him.— That is, by the Apostles, who were the Lord's chosen witnesses. John xv. 27. They had attended Him during His public ministry, they went about with Him and heard all His discourses.   When he spoke in parables, He explained them in private to the Apostles. But after all, their' views were dark, they still expected a worldly kingdom,—that He would restore the kingdom to Israel, and raise it to additional splendour, and that He should sit on the throne of His Father David.   Even after His resurrection they still fondly adhered to this notion.   They were therefore, after all the advantages they had enjoyed, not qualified to preach the Gospel.   He, therefore, commanded them to tarry at Jerusalem till they were endued with power from on high, and on the day of Pentecost they were baptized with the Holy Ghost, and not only qualified to preach the Gospel with unerring certainty, but to do so in all the various languages of the assembled multitudes.   A new proof was also

given of the truth of their doctrine by multitudes receiving the love of the truth. The
Gospel came to them not in word only, but
in power and in much assurance. Those who
believed, according to the Lord's commandment, were baptized, thus putting on Christ,
professing their faith in Him who died for
their sins and was raised for their justification,
and that by His resurrection they were begotten
again to a lively hope of an inheritance incorruptible, undefiled, and that fadeth not
away. The Apostle, as was customary with
him, classes himself with his brethren whom
he was addressing; he says, confirmed *to us.*
It was, indeed, confirmed to believers in every
age and country. This does not imply that
the previous evidence from the discourses and
miracles of the Lord was not satisfactory, but
it proves that the believer's faith is capable of
increase. It is like the path of the just, which
shineth more and more to the perfect day.
The same Apostle gives thanks for the Thessalonians, because their "faith groweth exceedingly."

*V. 4.— God also bearing them witness, both with signs
and wonders, and with divers miracles, and gifts of the
Holy Ghost, according to his own will?*

God also bearing them witness.—Not only

did the descent of the Holy Ghost upon the
Apostles on the day of Pentecost establish the
truth of the Gospel, but they were enabled to
confirm their doctrine by the most astonishing
miracles, giving feet to the lame and life to the
dead. The Lord had promised that the Spirit
of Truth, whom He would send from the
Father, should testify of Him, and that the
Apostles also should bear witness. John xv.
26, 27. In this and the preceding verse we
see his promise fulfilled, in verse 3 we have
the testimony of the Apostles, and here we
have the testimony of the Spirit.

Signs—are evidences of Divine interposition,
and may, or may not, be beyond the course of
nature; *wonders*—things that excite wonder,
prodigies; *divers miracles*—a variety of miraculous attestations to the truth of the Gospel.

Gifts of the Holy Ghost.—Rather distribu-
tions or divisions. The word employed here
does not signify gifts, but that the powers
conferred by the Holy Spirit were variously
divided,—to some, one power; to others, another. 1 Cor. xii. 28—30.

According to his own will.—In the distribu-
tion of these powers, or gifts, God acted as a
sovereign. Miraculous gifts, are termed the
manifestation of the Spirit. 1 Cor. xii. 7.
The Spirit dwells in every believer, but they

do not all possess what is termed the manifestation of the Spirit. " But the manifestation of the Spirit is given to every man to profit withal. For to one is given by the Spirit the word of wisdom; to another the word of knowledge by the same Spirit; to another faith by the same Spirit; to another the gifts of healing by the same Spirit; to another the working of miracles; to another prophecy; to another discerning of spirits ; to another divers kinds of tongues; to another the interpretation of tongues: but all these worketh that one and the selfsame Spirit, dividing to every man severally as he will." 1 Cor. xii. 7—11. These gifts were bestowed, not according to the will of man, but according to the sovereign will of God. The will of God is His only guide in all His works. This will is always holy, just, and wise—but it is always sovereign.

V. 5.—For unto the angels hath he not put in subjection the world to come, whereof we speak.

For unto the angels.—Here the Apostle returns to the subject of Christ's superiority to angels. The Apostles reasoned from the Scriptures, not because their own authority was insufficient, confirmed as it was by the miracles which they wrought, but to show that the Old and New Testaments are in perfect harmony,

and that the latter is the fulfilling of the
former. Believers are, also, thus taught to
prove everything by the Word of God. If
the ambassadors of Christ proved their doctrine
by the Scriptures of the Old Testament, much
more should uninspired men prove what they
teach by the Word of God. What is not
contained in Scripture is no part of Divine
truth.

World to come.—This is evidently the new,
or Gospel dispensation ; and, perhaps, in contrast with this the Apostle speaks of " this
present evil world," Gal. i. 4, from which
Christ came to deliver His people. The first,
the earthly or natural Adam, was at the head
of the first world. The second, the heavenly
and spiritual Adam, is at the head of the new
world, which God foretells by the prophet as
a new creation. " For, behold, I create new
heavens and a new earth : and the former shall
not be remembered, nor come into mind." Isa.
lxv. 17. God made the worlds, both the present and that which is to come, by His Son.
Heb. i. 2. We have seen that the old dispensation was subjected to the angel of the
covenant; but He rules the new dispensation,
in the character of the Son of God, God
manifest in the flesh. The great object of
the epistle is the development of the glory

of the new dispensation, and he begins by
giving the most conclusive proof of the superiority of its Author to the angels of God.
We enter the first world by birth; we are
introduced to the second by being born again.
Adam, the head of the old creation, was of
the earth earthy; Christ, the head of the new,
is the LORD from heaven.

Whereof we speak.—The Apostle's object
was to speak of the things belonging to the
world to come, the new creation.

*V. 6.—But one in a certain place testified, saying,
What is man, that thou art mindful of him? or the son
of man, that thou visitest him?*

But one in a certain place testified.—Here
the Apostle proves his assertion by quoting
the eighth Psalm, and establishes the universal
dominion of the Son of man, the title which
Jesus commonly assumed while on earth. The
culminating evidence of his being the Son of
God was not given till his resurrection.

It is to be observed that the Apostle does
not name the Psalm, although this is not
always the case, Acts xiii. 33—35; but all
Scripture is given by inspiration of God, and
the Lord establishes its authority by so frequently referring to it during His personal
ministry. He divides it into three parts—the

Law, the Prophets, and the Psalms. To the Jews were committed the lively oracles; and, amidst all their wickedness, they have been faithful to this trust, and have preserved the Scriptures as delivered to them by the prophets. On this subject they have been very cautious; and, although they have adopted many false interpretations, they have never trifled with the purity of the sacred books.

Testified, saying, What is man, that thou art mindful of him? or the son of man, that thou visitest him?—It has been observed, that, were it not for the Apostle's authority, we should not have considered the conclusion of the 102d Psalm as an answer to the prayer of Christ, and a similar remark may be made respecting the eighth Psalm, which we should have confined to a description of the dominion over the creatures with which man is invested, Gen. i. 26; but the question is decided by the Apostle's application of it to the Lord Jesus, showing that it contains a prophetic intimation of the universal dominion of the Son of man. At the same time it holds true, in a measure, of the authority bestowed on man over the creatures as a type of the unlimited power of Jesus. One testimony from the Scriptures is amply sufficient for the establishment of any truth; but, by comparing one passage with another referring to the same subject, we have a confirmation of the interpretation just given. Now, in 1 Cor. xv. 27, Eph. i. 22, Matt. xxi. 16, where the eighth Psalm is applied to Christ, we have a confirmation of the true application of the Psalm. Compared with the magnitude and glory of creation, man appears very insignificant; but this evidently refers to man in his fallen state. Man was made in the image of God, and the world which contains all within his reach was subjected to him; but now man is altogether vanity, he is cut down as a flower. All flesh is grass; man is of few days, and full of trouble, and in this state he is viewed by the Psalmist.

That thou art mindful of him.—Considering the glorious majesty of God, how could it be expected that God should be mindful of him?

Son of man.—This is not applicable to Adam, he was a man but had no father; he was created of the dust by God.

Visitest him.—God condescended to visit man, as we read of his walking in the garden.

V. 7.—Thou madest him a little lower than the angels; thou crownedst him with glory and honour, and didst set him over the works of thy hands:

Thou madest him a little lower than the

angels.—Commentators are divided as to the
expression—*a little lower;* some refer it to the
shortness of time—*a little while* lower.

It holds true in a measure in both senses.
Man held the next place in creation to the
angels; he is now *not* a little, lower than they.
In his natural state he is like the beasts that
perish.

*V. 8.—Thou hast put all things in subjection under his
feet. For in that he put all in subjection under him, he
left nothing that is not put under him. But now we see
not yet all things put under him.*

*Thou hast put all things in subjection under
his feet.*—In a very limited sense this is true
of Adam and his posterity. The subjection
of the animals, even to a child, is very wonderful, and can only be accounted for by the fear
and dread of man being on all the creatures.
Gen. ix. 2.

*For in that he put all in subjection under
him, he left nothing that is not put under him.*—
We have seen that the words quoted by the
Apostle, in a limited and modified degree,
hold true even of fallen man; but the Apostle
takes them in their full extent, without any
modification. *But now we see not yet all
things put under him.*—Not unfrequently the
word *all* must be understood with limitation;
but the Apostle teaches us that the word *all,*

in the eighth Psalm, is to be understood in the fullest and most unlimited sense, as leaving nothing in the universe which is not put under the Son of man, whether in the heavens above, or in the earth beneath. Even in this world there are many things which man, by his utmost exertions, is unable to accomplish; and, although the animals are in a measure subjected to him, yet there are many of which he is justly afraid, and which devour him when they find opportunity.

V. 9.—But we see Jesus, who was made a little lower than the angels for the suffering of death, crowned with glory and honour: that he by the grace of God should taste death for every man.

But we see Jesus who was made a little lower than the angels.—While the language of the Psalm can only be applied to mankind in general in a very limited and confined sense, it has its full accomplishment in the Lord Jesus.

He was made for a little while lower than the angels by His incarnation—coming in the likeness of sinful flesh.

There is in our translation some confusion from the order in which the words are placed. Christ is represented as being crowned with glory and honour, that He might taste death; whereas He first tasted death, and then, as the reward of His sufferings, was crowned with glory and honour. This was the joy set before Him, for which He endured the cross, despising the shame, and is now set down at the right hand of God. He has ascended far above all heavens, such is the uniform doctrine of Scripture. "Let this mind be in you, which was also in Christ Jesus: who, being in the form of God, thought it not robbery to be equal with God: but made himself of no reputation, and took upon him the form of a servant, and was made in the likeness of men: and being found in fashion as a man, he humbled himself, and became obedient unto death, even the death of the cross. Wherefore God also hath highly exalted him, and given him a name which is above every name: that at the name of Jesus every knee should bow, of things in heaven, and things in earth, and things under the earth; and that every tongue should confess that Jesus Christ is Lord, to the glory of God the Father." Phil. ii. 5—11. Christ drank of the brook in the way, therefore He lifted up His head. He is seated at the right hand of God, till all His enemies be made His footstool. Ps. cx. i. At the same time it is true that our translators have followed the order of the words in the original; but, although the Greek may admit of this inverted order, it is

evident that Christ was made for a little while
lower than the angels by His incarnation and
that, in consequence of His voluntary humiliation, He is crowned with glory and honour.

*That he by the grace of God should taste
death for every man.*—Here we are taught the
object of the death of Christ. A multitude
whom no man shall be able to number were
chosen in, and given to Christ. They came
under the curse of the broken law, and by the
grace of God He laid down His life for them,
that He might redeem them from death, might
ransom them from the power of the grave, and
swallow up death in victory. Adam was the
source or fountain of their natural life, but
it was dried up, the streams, consequently, all
failed; but Jesus said, " Lo, I come to do thy
will, O God." Heb. x. 9. " By the which
will we are sanctified through the offering
of the body of Jesus Christ once for all."
Chap. x. 10.

Having risen from the dead to die no more,
He is to all His people the fountain of eternal
life; because I live, ye shall live also.

By the grace of God.—The gift of Christ to
die for His people was an act of pure grace; but
if so, the withholding of this boon, and the consequent condemnation of all mankind would have
been no injustice. Many seem to think, that it

would have been unjust to punish mankind without opening for them a way of escape, and putting them a second time in a state of probation. Were this correct, all mankind must have heard the Gospel, whereas the number of those to whom the glad tidings have come is comparatively small. There would be no more grace in the salvation of believers than there would have been justice in their condemnation. But if mankind were lost in their first father Adam, then their redemption in Christ is wholly of grace.

Taste death.—Death is the king of terrors. Those who know not God are described as being, through fear of death, all their lifetime subject to bondage. It is bitter and distasteful, and hence the figurative expression, " tasting death." So distasteful was it to the Lord Jesus, that in the days of His flesh He offered up supplication with strong crying and tears, to Him that was able to save Him from death, and was heard in that He feared; not that He was unwilling to drink the bitter cup, or endeavoured to avoid it, but He thus earnestly prayed for victory over this last enemy.

*For every man.**   This general expression is

* *Man* here is a supplement. Macknight says the supplement may be " υἱοῦ," *every son*, which exactly corresponds with the following verse.

frequently employed when a limitation is absolutely necessary. For instance, "*every man* shall have praise of God." 1 Cor. iv. 5. God deals to *every man* the measure of faith. Rom. xii. 3. The blind man, when the Lord opened his eyes, saw *every man* clearly. "*Every man*" is said to press "into the kingdom of God." Luke xvi. 16. In the passage before us, the context proves that the general expression must be limited to those to whom Christ stands in the relation of the Captain of their salvation. Ver. 10.

He tasted death for *every one* of the "many sons" whom He brings to glory. Here the expression imports that Christ died for each of His people; he died for them (as Israel is to be gathered) "one by one." * He tasted death for every one of the *sanctified*. Ver. 11.

---

* See the author's "Doctrine of the Atonement." Second Edition. Pp. 276, 277.

[Mr. Haldane's work on the Atonement was his last and, probably, his ablest publication. The Rev. Dr. Stanford, of Dublin, so well known as the able editor of Mr. Krause's sermons, has alluded to it in his preface to a new edition of the celebrated Elisha Coles' "Discourse on God's Sovereignty." Dr. Stanford says,—"After so " much experience as, I trust, may secure me from the " charge of presumption, in venturing an opinion of my " own, I do not hesitate to say, that if the expositor of " Divine truth would desire to be consistent in his doc-

F

For *every one* of his brethren, ver. 11, 12;
for *every one* of the *Church*, for which He

" trine,—if he would avoid being self-contradictory,—it
" can be only by the vivid and unclouded perception,
" and the unqualified adoption, of such views as are to
" be found in this [Coles'] and similar works. Rare, I
" regret to say, they are; but though few, they are
" inestimable. I shall just here mention one, which is
" happily of easy attainment, and which, I think, no
" inquirer into truth should fail to provide himself with,
" —I mean ' *The Doctrine of the Atonement*,' by J. A.
" HALDANE. The object is in a good measure parallel
" with Elisha Coles' work; of course it has the advan-
" tage of a more modern and polished style. It is a
" *singularly able and unanswerable advocacy* of those
" views which, no matter how men may recoil from them,
" it has, nevertheless, been God's will to reveal."

The first editions of Elisha Coles' work were published
with the strong recommendations of such men as Owen,
Annesley, and Goodwin. At the great revival of the
Church of England, a new edition was published by the
celebrated WILLIAM ROMAINE, who states that it is " from
these doctrines only that settled peace can rule in the
conscience, the love of God be maintained in the heart,
and a conversation kept up in our walk and warfare as
becometh the Gospel. It is from them all good works
proceed, and that all fruits of holiness abound, to the
praise of the glory of the grace of God."

It may here be remarked that the errors revived in the
present day, involving universal pardon and the denial
of eternal punishments, render the enforcement of the
old doctrines taught by the Reformers and the Puritan
divines all the more important. One of the last acts of

gave Himself. Eph. v. 23. Heb. ii. 12. For
every one of the children whom God gave unto

the judicious THOMAS SCOTT was to republish in English
the decisions of the Synod of Dort, with a preface, in which
is contained the manly concession that he had been himself prejudiced against them. It may, however, be fairly
said, that if good men, who hold the doctrines of free
grace were to compare their respective views, it would
be found that their differences on the questions of general
and particular redemption, are often reduced to a mere
logomachy, or war of words. If disobedience to God's
Holy Commandments be a sin against God of *infinite*
demerit, it could only be atoned for by a sacrifice of
infinite value. The sacrifice of Christ is admitted by
every Christian to be of *infinite* value, and such a sacrifice was necessary to atone for the sin of Adam, even
had he stood alone before his Maker, the solitary inha-
bitant of this world. But that sacrifice being *infinite* in
value, it must have been *sufficient* for the salvation not
of Adam only, but of all the countless millions of his
posterity. It is from no defect in the value of Christ's
blood, that His *sacrifice* is *efficacious* only for the salvation of the elect. But it can hardly be said, without an
abuse of words, that there is an actual *atonement*, or
reconciliation, accomplished for those who are lost. "No
man cometh unto me except the Father draw him" are
the words of Christ Himself. "But why are not all
drawn? Ask not the reason why," says Benedict Pictet.
"It is secret, but not unjust." All true Christians agree
that the value of Christ's *sacrifice* was infinite. All who
receive the doctrines of grace through the electing love
of God, believe that the *atonement* purchased by that
sacrifice is efficacious only for the elect given to Christ

Him. Ver. 13. For every one of the seed of
Abraham. " And if ye be Christ's, then are
ye Abraham's seed, and heirs according to the
promise." Gal. iii. 29. So far from dying
for all, Christ will say to many, " I *never*
knew you." He prays for the men whom His
Father had given Him out of the world, while
He expressly states He prays not for the world.
John xvii. 6—9. In point of fact, the greater
part of mankind have never heard of a Saviour,
and are not only living without God, but
without hope in the world. If Christ died
for all, no man is saved by His death. But
perhaps it is said, that they are saved by faith
in His death. Still, faith is the gift of God,
which, like every other gift, is imparted to
sinners through the atonement by which

in covenant by the Father. Is there not then in the
dispute often a confusion as to the meaning of the word
atonement? The *sacrifice* was infinite in value, but
limited in its effects; for, unless we adopt the fatal error
of universal pardon, it will be admitted that it is the
procuring cause of an *atonement* only for the saved who
are reconciled to God by the priceless blood of His beloved Son. Here there is no fetter on the free proclamation of the Gospel. Salvation is proclaimed to all who
will believe in Christ, to all who will come to Christ, to all
who will trust the promise that He is able and willing to
save. It is not for us to try to reconcile God's sovereignty
with man's undoubted responsibility, by bending the truths
of revelation either to the one side or the other.]—ED.

God's righteousness in the remission of sins is manifested.

If salvation be purely of grace, no difficulty is got rid of by holding that Christ died for all. Besides, if the atonement of Christ was not made exclusively for the elect and saved, but for all, even for those who are lost, the unity of the Godhead is denied. If Christ died for all, and the Spirit effectually reveals the truth only to some, where is the unity of operation between Christ and the Holy Spirit?

V. 10.—For it became him, for whom are all things, and by whom are all things, in bringing many sons unto glory, to make the captain of their salvation perfect through sufferings.

For it became him, for whom are all things, &c.—Here the salvation of sinners, through the sufferings and death of Christ, is ascribed as resulting from the character of God. He hath made all things for Himself. His own glory is the ultimate end of all His works. Why did He make the Captain of Salvation perfect through sufferings? Because it became Him; it was suitable to His glorious character to make the Captain of their Salvation perfect through sufferings. Hence it was not possible that the cup should pass from Jesus. Matt.

xxvi. 39. This is more fully explained in other parts of the Scriptures; but here we are simply told,—it became the great Creator, who has made all things for Himself, and for whose pleasure they are and were created.

In the works of creation and providence, and especially in the work of redemption, the glorious attributes of God are manifested.

His character is perfect, His wisdom, goodness, and compassion are infinite; but the exercise of one attribute at the expense of another would derogate from this perfection, and therefore it became Him, in bringing many sons unto glory, to make the Captain of their Salvation perfect through sufferings. Eternal life is the gift of God; but the boon could only be bestowed on sinners through the Saviour's sufferings. The justice of God must be satisfied and His truth vindicated by the surety and representative of His people enduring the penalty of their disobedience,—grace must reign through righteousness unto eternal life by the sufferings of Christ.

Many sons.—Well might the Apostle John exclaim,—" Behold what manner of love the Father hath bestowed on us, that we should be called the sons of God " (and it is not an empty title); "if children, then heirs; heirs of God and joint-heirs with Christ." " He

that overcometh shall inherit all things; and
I will be his God, and he shall be my son."
Rev. xxi. 7. Believers are so inseparably
united to the only-begotten, that they shall sit
with Him upon His throne; indeed, they are
represented as already enthroned. Ephes. ii. 6.
They shall judge angels, and reign with Christ
for ever and ever. Rev. xxii. 5.

Captain of their salvation.—When Israel
were entering upon the wars of Canaan,
Joshua, their leader, beheld a warrior with
his sword drawn in his hand, who announced
himself as the Captain of the Lord's Host.
Joshua fell on his face to the earth, loosed
his shoe from off his foot, worshipped, and
received instructions respecting the siege of
Jericho. He, who was in the Church in the
wilderness, Acts vii. 38, the Captain of the
Lord's Host, after having thus appeared to
Joshua, although afterwards unseen, conducted
Israel to their promised rest.

The word here rendered " Captain " is elsewhere rendered " Prince," Acts iii. 15; v. 31;
and " Author," chap. xii. 2. He is the leader
and commander of His people, Isaiah lv. 4;
who by Him are brought to glory, are healed
by His stripes, and live by His death.

But how is He said to be made perfect?
Was He not absolutely perfect? He did no

sin, nor was guile found in His lips. He always did the things that pleased His Father. How, then, was He made perfect through sufferings? The reference is not to moral but official perfection. In order to redeem His people from the curse of the law, it behoved Him to be made a curse for them. He could only swallow up death in victory by coming into contact with it—grappling with it—tasting it, —and thus was He made perfect through sufferings. Thus He restored what he took not away. To this He alluded in His message to Herod. Luke xiii. 32. The flaming sword, which turned every way, kept the tree of life; but He, having submitted to the deadly stroke, returned laden with its fruit, and dispenses it to the heirs of salvation. Having risen from the dead, He dieth no more; and because He lives, they shall live also. There is a passage exactly parallel. "Though he were a Son, yet learned he obedience by the things which he suffered; and being made perfect, he became the author of eternal salvation unto all them that obey him." Heb. v. 8, 9. The consecration of Aaron and his sons was completed by the offering up of a ram, Lev. viii. 22; which is therefore termed the ram of perfections. To consecrate a priest is to perfect him. Exod. xxviii. 41. Now, the Captain of Salvation was made perfect through sufferings. His consecration was thus completed, as the great High Priest of our profession. Having, according to the will of God offered the body prepared for Him, He is now fully invested with the office of our High Priest; and, having received all power in heaven and in earth, He is able to save to the uttermost all that come to God by Him, seeing He ever liveth to make intercession for them. His intercession is founded on the perfection of His one offering, to which His Father hath set His seal, by raising Him from the dead and giving Him glory, that our faith and hope might be in God.

V. 11.—*For both he that sanctifieth and they who are sanctified are all of one: for which cause he is not ashamed to call them brethren.*

For both he that sanctifieth and them that are sanctified.—Christ says: " And for their sakes I sanctify myself, that they also may be sanctified through the truth." John xvii. 19. Israel were sanctified, or set apart, as God's peculiar people, by the blood of the Sinai covenant, which could not take away sin, but only sanctified to the purifying of the flesh. Christ sanctified His people with His own blood, Heb. xiii. 12, which cleanseth them from all sin.

Of one.—Some explain this, of one Father;
others, of one nature; but it is evidently, of
one family. Christ is the seed of the woman;
and all believers, in common with the rest of
mankind, are born of a woman. It has been
already observed, that, immediately after the
fall, mankind were divided into two families,
—the seed of the woman and the seed of the
serpent. Christ was eminently the seed of the
woman, the head of the family, and all His
people are His brethren.

He is eminently the Son of the Father,
2 John 3; and, as the sanctifier and the
sanctified are all of one family, He acknowledges them as His brethren, Mark iii. 34;
Luke viii. 21; John xx. 17; and, in virtue of
their union with Him, they are called the sons
of God, 1 John iii. 1.

Sanctification means separation. Christ, that
He might sanctify the people with His own
blood, suffered without the gate. Heb. xiii. 12.

This is the blood of sprinkling of which the
Apostle speaks. Heb. xii. 24. The blood of
the old covenant was sprinkled on the bodies
of the children of Israel at Sinai, and thus
they became externally holy. The blood of
Christ is sprinkled upon the consciences of all
His people, and gives them confidence in
coming to God. The firstborn of the family

received the Spirit without measure, and through Him it is communicated to the whole family. " But when the fulness of the time was come, God sent forth his Son, made of a woman, made under the law, to redeem them that were under the law, that we might receive the adoption of sons. And because ye are sons, God hath sent forth the Spirit of his Son into your hearts, crying, Abba, Father. Wherefore thou art no more a servant, but a son ; and if a son, then an heir of God through Christ." Gal. iv. 4—7.

For which cause; that is, because they belong to the same family, Christ is not ashamed to call them brethren.

V. 12.—*Saying, I will declare thy name unto my brethren, in the midst of the church will I sing praise unto thee.*

The Apostle here confirms his assertion by a quotation from Psalm xxii., which he applies to Christ. Indeed, it is evident that this Psalm is descriptive of the sufferings of Christ and of the glory which should follow. If it has any relation to David, it is very remote. In the passage quoted by the Apostle, Christ expressly calls His people brethren. Through Him they are all adopted into God's family, and are even now the sons of God. 1 John

iii. 2. This, like other mysteries of the kingdom of God, was represented in His dealings
with Israel, concerning whom He says,—"Israel
is my son, even my firstborn," Exod. iv. 22,
in reference to which the Apostle writes,—
"To whom pertaineth the adoption." Rom.
ix. 4.

God promised to Abraham a numerous posterity, to be a God to Him and to his seed after
Him, and to give them the land of Canaan.
These promises were all limited to that branch
of the family from which Christ was to spring;
for one great object which God had in view,
was to manifest His faithfulness in the promise, that all the families of the earth should
be blessed in the seed of Abraham. It was
therefore necessary that this family should be
kept distinct; and therefore was the middle-
wall of partition set up between it and all
other families.

Isaac, as being the progenitor of Christ, was
the child of promise, Gal. iv. 23; and for the
same reason Jacob was beloved and Esau hated.
Abraham had seven sons besides Isaac, but
they had no part in the covenant. The Apostle
teaches us that the promise, "I will be a
God to thee and to thy seed," does not refer to
Abraham's posterity in general, but to *one* of
his descendants, namely, Christ. Gal. iii. 16.

Now, the Jewish dispensation was a model of
the kingdom of God; and, as only they that
are Christ's are Abraham's seed and heirs according to the promise, Gal. iii. 29, so the
first covenant was exclusively made with that
branch of the family from which Christ was
to spring. That family alone, of all the
families of the earth, was acknowledged of
God as His people. He dwelt among them.
He showed His Word unto Jacob, His statutes
and His judgments unto Israel, while He suffered all the other families of the earth to walk
in their own ways. The carnal relation of
Israel to Christ was a shadow of the spiritual
relation of the true Israel to their glorious
Head; and the carnal blessings in earthly
places, with which Israel after the flesh was
blessed, were a figure for the time then present
of the spiritual blessings bestowed on the true
Israel. When our Lord was informed that
His mother and His brethren stood without
desiring to speak with Him, He replied,—
" Who is my mother? and who are my brethren ? " He knew, or acknowledged no man
after the flesh; but " stretched forth his hand
toward his disciples, and said, Behold my
mother and my brethren ! For whosoever shall
do the will of my Father which is in heaven,
the same is my brother, and sister, and mother."

Matt. xii. 49, 50.   Hence we learn, that those
whom Christ is not ashamed to call brethren
are the members of His Church.   The children
of the new covenant, who are all taught of God,
have all heard and learned of the Father; are
delivered from the power of darkness, and
translated into the kingdom of His dear Son.
These alone are the brethren of Christ whom
He is not ashamed to acknowledge.

Thy name.—The name of God is the expression of his character. One man is distinguished
from another by his name. Jesus declared the
name of God to His brethren, John xvii. 26, by
manifesting His own character. God proclaimed
His name before Moses. Exod. xxxiii. 19. He
was alone, no man was to be seen throughout the
mount, Exod. xxxiv. 3; and when he came
down, Moses wist not that the skin of his face
shone, so that Aaron and the children of Israel
were afraid to come nigh him. Exod. xxxiv.
30.   This transaction is explained by the
Apostle, when he says,—" We all, with open
face," or, perhaps rather, in an unveiled face,
" beholding as in a glass the glory of the Lord,
are changed into the same image from glory to
glory, even as by the Spirit of the Lord."
2 Cor. iii. 18. A view of God's character has
a transforming influence. Here we see through
a glass darkly; but hereafter we shall see Him

as He is, and shall be satisfied when we awake with His likeness. Psalm xvii. 15. 1 John iii. 2.

In the midst of the Church will I sing praise unto thee.—Jesus sang praises to God in the midst of the great assembly in the temple, which was typical of the Church. He is still present in the Churches of the saints; and through His brethren, and in the midst of them, He still praises His Father.

V. 13.—And again, I will put my trust in him. And again, Behold I and the children which God hath given me.

And again, I will put my trust in Him.— There are several passages of Scripture in which this expression occurs, Psal. xviii. 2; 2 Sam. xxii. 3; and in Isa. viii. 17 the same sense, with a slight variation, is expressed; to whatever passage the reference is made, the sense in the argument is the same. We have here a decisive proof of Christ being made like unto His brethren.

In the preceding verse he had been represented as saying, " I will declare thy name unto my brethren, in the midst of the Church will I sing praise unto thee; " thus acknowledging them as His brethren, and His Church, which, we are elsewhere taught, is His body,

1 Cor. xii. 27; Eph. i. 23; like the human body it is one, although composed of many members. The next quotation is either from Psalm xviii. 2, or Isaiah viii. 17. In the Psalm the words are the same with those used by the Apostle, and in Isaiah the sense exactly corresponds. That the eighteenth Psalm is a prediction of the humiliation and exaltation of the Lord Jesus is manifest. With his dying breath the Lord Jesus cried, "Father, into thy hands I commend my spirit;" and the cry came into His ears. The earthquake which accompanied His resurrection, and His being drawn out of many waters, are then described, Ps. xviii. 7, 16, 17, together with the punishment which He inflicted on His enemies, ver. 37, and His being made the head of the heathen, ver. 43. Now the quotation, "I will put my trust in Him," ver. 2; or, "I will wait upon the Lord, and I will look for him," Isaiah viii. 17, proves the unity of Christ and his people. He has left us a perfect example of confidence in God. This is plainly exhibited in innumerable passages of the Book of Psalms, which may be viewed as our Lord's diary, describing His manifold sorrows and afflictions, and His triumph over all His enemies.

The Apostle adds another quotation, cited

from Isaiah viii. 18. In the preceding chapter God had given Ahaz, the idolatrous King of Judah, as a sign of the stability of the kingdom of Judah, viz., the birth of the virgin's Son, namely, Immanuel, Isa. vii. 14; Matt. i. 22, 23, at the same time informing him (Isaiah) that before his son Shear-jashub (whom he had been directed to take with him to meet Ahaz) should know to refuse the evil and choose the good, Syria and Israel should be forsaken of both her kings. Ahaz was warned at the same time of the judgments which should come upon him, although not from the quarter he dreaded. The birth of another son to the prophet, which he had predicted, is then recorded, chap. viii. 1; and he is informed that, before the child was able to speak, the spoil of Damascus and Samaria should be taken away by the King of Assyria. Judah, however, is reminded that they should not escape the same scourge. They are, however, encouraged to trust in God,—to fear Him; and it is predicted that Christ should be the sanctuary of his people, but a stumbling-stone and rock of offence to both houses of Israel.

This passage is frequently applied in the New Testament to Christ. The prophecy is, no doubt, obscure; but Shear-jashub and Maher-shalal-hash-baz, the sons of the prophet,

were for signs and wonders in Israel from the
Lord of Hosts; and as Isaiah and all the other
prophets were types of Christ, the great Prophet so long predicted, he and his children
were for signs and wonders.

The Apostle does not finish the quotation;
what remains was not to his purpose. He
intended to prove that Christ and His people
were all of one family; and this is established
by His first acknowledging them as His brethren, and declaring that in the midst of the
great congregation He will lead their praises,
and then representing them as His children,
who, along with their glorious Head, shall be
God's witnesses to the ends of the earth.
Acts i. 8; Rev. i. 5.

*V. 14, 15.—Forasmuch then as the children are par-
takers of flesh and blood, he also himself likewise took part
of the same; that through death he might destroy him
that had the power of death, that is, the devil; and deliver
them who through fear of death were all their lifetime
subject to bondage.*

Having shown that Christ and His people
were all of one family—that they were represented as His brethren and His children—the
Apostle goes on to prove the incarnation of
Christ as essential to perfect the unity which
was to subsist between them. The children
were partakers of flesh and blood, and he,

therefore, took part of the same. As the
Captain of their salvation it behoved Him
to be made perfect through sufferings. As
the great High Priest of His people it was of
necessity that He should have somewhat to
offer. Chap. viii. 3.

God had declared that He had no pleasure
in the burnt-offerings and sacrifices enjoined
by the law, Heb. x. 6; but He prepared a
body for the incarnation of Jesus, who came
to do His will by offering up Himself. The
children whom God had given Him were partakers of flesh and blood, and He also Himself
likewise took part of the same, that He might
through death destroy Him that had the
power of death, that is, the devil.

Satan had introduced death, and Christ came
that He might despoil Him of His usurped
dominion; that He might bruise Him under
the feet of His people; and by magnifying the
law which they had broken and offering a full
atonement for their sins, He might deliver
them who were all their lifetime subject to
bondage, and give them the answer of a good
conscience through His resurrection.

Men are said to be, through fear of death,
all their lifetime subject to bondage. This
fear is natural to us. Children from their
earliest age show their apprehension of danger.

Indeed, since the fall it is necessary to our preservation. Man in innocence had no apprehension of danger; satisfied with favour and full with the blessing of the Lord,—all animals subject to him,—not liable to pain,—what should he fear? But fear, the inseparable companion of guilt, effected a lodgment in the heart of Adam the moment he sinned, which is conveyed to all his posterity. The mind recoils from death; but in the atonement for sin, offered upon the cross, Christ has given His people the victory. They look to the empty grave of Jesus, and there they see the pledge of their resurrection. "This," says the Apostle, "is the victory that overcometh the world, even our faith;" and here he describes the victory of believers over the god of this world — thus are his plans defeated. His success issued in his destruction. Perhaps he imagined that the death of the Son of God secured the permanence of his dominion; but Christ being crucified in weakness, was the means of the utter subversion of his usurped power.

Now, Christ's people are enabled to say,— " It is God that justifieth, who is he that condemneth? it is Christ that died; yea, rather, that is risen again, who also liveth to make intercession for us." He committed His spirit to God when about to quit His body; and God showed Him the path of life, and set Him as the first of many brethren at His own right-hand, where there are pleasures for evermore. He has received power over all flesh, that He might give eternal life to as many as His Father had given Him; in other words, to all who by faith should enter His family—thus proving themselves vessels of mercy.

V. 16.—For verily he took not on him the nature of angels; but he took on him the seed of Abraham.

Angels as well as men had fallen, but Christ took not hold * of angels, they are reserved in everlasting chains under darkness to the judgment of the great day; but the Lord hath showed light to the seed of Abraham. It has arisen from the sacrifice being bound to the horns of the altar, from the atonement of Jesus Christ. He took not hold of angels, but of the seed of Abraham. Why is there this limitation? Why is it said the seed of Abraham instead of the seed of Adam? Because He took part in flesh and blood only for the sake

* In our version "the nature of" is supplied, but it is unnecessary and improper; both angels and men had fallen into a fearful pit. He who is mighty to save passed by the former and took hold of the latter; not, indeed, of all the natural seed of Adam, but of the seed of Abraham, as the father and representative of all the faithful.

of the heirs of salvation, the children whom
God had given Him, whom He is not
ashamed to call brethren. Others, it is true,
were also partakers of flesh and blood, but
He never knew them. They belong to another
family. He calls them not brethren. Abraham was chosen that in his seed a multitude,
whom no man should be able to number, might
be eternally blessed. The Saviour sprang from
Abraham; and in God's dealings with Abraham's
descendants he exhibited a pattern of His dealings with his spiritual children, with those who
are of faith, who are blessed with faithful Abraham. Israel after the flesh were redeemed from
bondage, were taken into covenant, guided
through the wilderness, fed with the emblem
of the body of Christ, made to drink from
the smitten rock, which the Apostle tells us
was Christ, 1 Cor. x. 6, and were brought to
the promised land flowing with milk and honey.
And thus God's love and care of the true Israel,
who are Christ's and heirs according to the
promise, Gal. iii. 29, were strikingly exhibited.
The whole plan of salvation is embodied in the
history of the descendants of Abraham. Every
doctrine of the Gospel is exhibited in God's
dealings with them. God's chosen Israel sprang
from an idolater; they were a perverse and
crooked generation. They were separated from
all other nations by the blood of their cove-

nant; God's Spirit remained among them.
He chastened them as a man chasteneth his
son; and, at length, wrath came upon them to
the uttermost, and God cast them off. But
they have not stumbled that they should fall;
they shall be restored to the favour of God,
and serve Him in the land He gave to their
fathers. Such is the parable.

The interpretation of it is God's unchanging
love to the true Israel, whom He hath loved
with an everlasting love, and with lovingkind-
ness hath drawn unto Himself; whom He
guides by His counsel, and will afterwards
receive to glory.

The wisdom of God is apparent in representing spiritual and eternal things in types
and figures, thus bringing the truth down
to our capacity. By the folly of mankind
this has been the grand means of corrupting
the Gospel and carnalizing the doctrine of
Christ. The spiritual ordinances of the New
Testament have been changed into a system of
external observances, which give an utterly
fallacious view of the character of the religion
of Christ.

*V. 17.—Wherefore in all things it behoved him to be
made like unto his brethren, that he might be a merciful
and faithful high priest in things pertaining to God, to
make reconciliation for the sins of the people.*

Having taken hold of the seed of Abraham,

it behoved Him to be in all things made like
unto his brethren, in order that He might be a
merciful and faithful high priest. Brethren are
of the same family, their hearts are fashioned
alike, Ps. xxxiii. 15; and in order to Christ
being a merciful and faithful high priest, He
must in all things be made like unto His brethren, and thus it was with our Lord Jesus
Christ. He not only, as the Apostle had
already stated, took part with them in flesh
and blood, Heb. ii. 14, but was touched with
a feeling of our infirmities, and was in all
things tempted like as we are, yet without sin.
Chap. iv. 15. The prince of this world came
to Him in all his malignity and in all his
power. He attempted to prevail over Him
through hunger, to which He was subject in
common with His brethren; he held out to
Him the prospect of admiration; he proposed
to Him the sovereignty of the world, but by
the Word of God's lips He kept Himself from
the paths of the destroyer. Ps. xvii. 4. He
not only baffled the adversary, but, in doing
so, He taught His people how they might suc-
cessfully resist the devil by opposing truth to
falsehood. But he was also to make reconciliation for the sins of the people,—that is, to
expiate the sins of the people; and this
could only be done by the sacrifice of Himself.
The sin-offering under the law must be perfect

to be accepted. Now, Jesus was holy, harmless, undefiled, separate from sinners; he was a lamb without spot or blemish, under the law, which was the figure of good things to come—without shedding of blood there was no remission. Now, Christ reconciled His Church unto God by His own blood. The word "reconcile," in Scripture, means "to make atonement." Lev. vi. 30; xvi. 20; viii. 15. 2 Chron. xxix. 24. Ezek. xlv. 15. Daniel ix. 24. Rom. v. 10. 2 Cor. v. 19. Now, Christ, by the sacrifice of Himself, made reconciliation, or atonement, for the sins of His people; they are all covered by His blood, and, when sought for, shall not be found.

V. 18.—For in that he himself hath suffered being tempted, he is able to succour them that are tempted.

Chap. v. 2. Now though Christ had no sin, yet, as we have seen, He was in all things tempted as we are. He was truly man, and therefore had all those inclinations and dispositions which His brethren have, although in entire subjection to the will of His heavenly Father.

Chap. iv. 15. As God, He knew all things, all our pains and sorrows; but by assuming our nature, by being tempted like as we are, yet without sin, He has become a merciful and faithful High Priest.

In God being manifested in the flesh, we

have an exhibition of the full restoration of man
to the favour of God, and learn how we may
pour out our hearts before that sympathizing
One who knoweth our frame, and remembereth
we are dust, and how we can thus put our case
into the hands of Him who, although perfect
and almighty, yet experienced the temptations
to which we are subject, and triumphed over
them all, when He put His foot on the neck of
our adversary, in proof of that complete victory
which He achieved, and in which all His people
shall participate.

When entering on His last conflict, He said
to His persecutors, " This is your hour, and the
power of darkness."   His soul was exceeding
sorrowful, even unto death.   He met with no
sympathy, even from his chosen disciples ; they
were overcome with sleep.   His agony is described in Psa. lxxxviii. 13—18 : " But unto
thee have I cried, O Lord ; and in the morning
shall my prayer prevent thee.   Lord, why
casteth thou off my soul ? why hidest thou thy
face from me ?   I am afflicted and ready to die
from my youth up : while I suffer thy terrors I
am distracted. Thy fierce wrath goeth over me ;
thy terrors have cut me off.   They came round
about me daily like water ; they compassed me
about together.   Lover and friend hast thou
put far from me, and mine acquaintance into

darkness." At length He exclaimed, "My God, my God, why hast thou forsaken me!" proving that He was tasting all the bitterness of death, that He felt the sword of justice entering His soul; but still His confidence in His Father's love was unshaken; with His dying breath He exclaimed, " Father, into thy hands I commit my spirit;" and, at its departure, Satan fell as lightning from heaven. His power was broken, whilst the resurrection and exaltation of Immanuel to the throne of the universe, as the supreme Judge of men and angels, showed the magnitude of the work which He had accomplished, and the perfection of that sacrifice which had finished transgression, made an end of sin, made reconciliation for iniquity, and brought in everlasting righteousness. Truly His glory is great in having accomplished this salvation. Honour and majesty are laid upon Him; and, because He humbled Himself, took on Him the form of a servant, and became obedient unto death, God hath highly exalted Him, and given Him a name that is above every name; "that at the name of Jesus every knee should bow, of things in heaven, and things in earth, and things under the earth; and that every tongue should confess that Jesus Christ is Lord, to the glory of God the Father." Phil. ii. 10, 11.

CHAPTER III.

V. 1.—Wherefore, holy brethren, partakers of the hea-
venly calling, consider the Apostle and High Priest of our
profession, Christ Jesus.

FROM the considerations which he had suggested, the Apostle urges the Hebrews to fix
their attention upon Christ Jesus, under the
character of the Apostle and High Priest of our
profession. The considerations alluded to are
His superiority not only to the prophets but
also to the angels, inasmuch as He was " over
all, God blessed for ever." Rom. ix. 5. By
Him the Gospel was first promulgated. He
ruled the new dispensation in the character of
the Son of man, having been for the suffering
of death crowned with glory and honour.

He was not the Saviour of angels, but of
sinners, of mankind, with whom He united
Himself in the closest bonds, becoming a member of the human family, taking part with them
in flesh and blood, that through death He
might destroy him who had the power of death,

that is, the devil, and thus free His brethren from the tyranny of the king of terrors. This unity with His brethren was necessary in order to His being a merciful and faithful High Priest, able to make atonement for their transgressions, and to make intercession for them, through His perfect atonement, which magnifies and makes honourable the law of God. Being Himself a man of sorrows and acquainted with griefs, He was also well qualified to sympathize with His afflicted people.

He addresses them as holy brethren; he had represented them as sanctified, chap. ii. 11; as separated from the rest of mankind by their union with Christ, who took part in flesh and blood with the children whom God had given Him. Believers are represented as sanctified by the blood of Christ, chap. xiii. 12, as Israel was sanctified or set apart as God's peculiar people by the blood of the Sinai covenant. There was, however, an essential difference: the latter was the blood of bulls and goats, and could never take away sin; the former was the blood of Immanuel, which cleanseth those for whom it was shed from all sin. Believers are also represented as sanctified by the Holy Spirit, of which they are all made partakers, 1 Pet. i. 2; 2 Thess. ii. 13; and as sanctified through the truth, John xvii. 17. In one sense they are at once all equally and completely sanctified, they are all washed in the blood of Christ, all partakers of His Spirit, and all are of the truth which dwelleth in them, which they have of God. Hence Christ is said not only to be made of God unto them righteousness, but sanctification. Every believer, from the first moment of his new life in Christ, has thus the germ of perfect holiness, although sanctification is also represented as a growth in holiness, and advancement in conformity to God, 1 Thess. iv. 3, 4; v. 23.

Believers are called to follow after holiness, Heb. xii. 14; to mortify their members which are upon the earth, engrossed with earthly objects, Col. iii. 15; and we are assured that all shall be judged according to their works, Rev. xx. 12; Gal. vi. 7, 8; 2 Cor. v. 10. So that, while all boasting is excluded, Christ's doctrine is manifestly according to godliness.

They are also represented as partakers of the heavenly calling. The privileges of the Sinai covenant were peculiar to Israel, Amos iii. 2; but the Gentiles were fellow-heirs, Eph. iii. 6; and therefore the Hebrew believers are described as partakers of the heavenly calling. It was not exclusively directed to them. In giving of the law God spoke on earth, but He now speaketh from heaven. Heb. xii. 25. Believers are frequently described as called, Rom. viii. 28; xvi. 7; 1 Cor. i. 24; and here described as partakers of the heavenly calling,

for it is a call to His kingdom and glory.
1 Thess. ii. 12.

They are exhorted to consider Jesus Christ
under the character of the Apostle and High
Priest of our profession. Christ is eminently the
sent of God. John vi. 29, 40; xvii. 18. Hence
He is termed the Apostle of our profession, and
is thus contrasted with Moses, whom God sent
to deliver Israel. Exod. iii. 10. While Moses
was in an eminent degree the Apostle of God
to Israel, Aaron was the High Priest; but
both these high offices were united in Christ,
and the Hebrews are here exhorted to consider
the Lord Jesus as uniting the offices both of an
Apostle and a Priest.

*V. 2.— Who was faithful to him that appointed him, as
also Moses was faithful in all his house.*

The Apostle was far from intending by the
contrast to lower the character of Moses; on
the contrary, he quotes the most honourable
testimony borne to him in the Scripture, that
he was faithful in all his house. He was not
only the lawgiver of Israel, but the laws were
executed under his direction; such was the
confidence with which the God of Israel was
pleased to treat his illustrious servant. Aaron
and his sister Miriam spoke slightingly of
Moses, specially condemning his marriage with
a woman who was not of the daughters of

Israel. It is to be observed that this marriage was
solemnized before the middle wall of partition
was set up between Israel and other nations;
and probably it was a prophetic intimation of
the Gentiles by union with Christ being admitted into the Church of God.

From the extraordinary meekness of Moses,
which is mentioned in connexion with their
speaking against him, it is probable that he
was disposed to pass over their presumption;
but the Lord was pleased at once to rebuke
any appearance of rivalry. He suddenly
commanded them to stand before the tabernacle, and, coming down in the pillar of the
cloud, informed them that He would communicate His will to the prophets by a vision or a
dream. Not so with His servant Moses; with
him He would speak mouth to mouth, and that
he should even behold the similitude of the
Lord. Probably there is here a reference to
the manifestation made to Moses on the occasion of the molten calf. Exod. xxxiii. 11, 21,
23. When this took place, no man was to be
with him, nor was any to be seen throughout
the mount. In the close of Deuteronomy we
are informed that there arose not a prophet since
in Israel like unto Moses, whom the Lord knew
face to face. Deut. xxxiv. 10. He was the
only lawgiver in Israel; but at length a prophet

was raised up unto him of their brethren, like unto Moses.   Deut. xvi. 15.

V. 3.—For this man was counted worthy of more glory than Moses, inasmuch as he who hath builded the house hath more honour than the house.

The Apostle, in contrasting the old and new dispensations, while he admits the glory of the old, observes that it had no glory in comparison of the new, 2 Cor. iii. 10; and here he illustrates the inferiority of Moses, as constituting a part of that house in the government of which he celebrates his faithfulness. Now a house may be very glorious, but it is evident that the builder has more honour than the house.   It owes its magnificence to his skill.

V. 4.—For every house is builded by some man : but he that built all things is God.

Every house is builded by some man ; it owes its existence to the skill of the architect; while God is the great architect of the universe, and the greater the glory of creation the greater the glory of the Creator.   Perhaps there is here a reference to chap. i. 8, and x. 12, in order to establish more fully the glory of the Son of God, as being the Creator and Proprietor of the house over which He presided.   This is confirmed by Ps. cxv. 5, 6.   He is the great

Shepherd, who feeds and nourishes His sheep.

V. 5.—And Moses verily was faithful in all his house, as a servant, for a testimony of those things which were to be spoken after.

And according to the testimony which he had quoted, Moses was faithful in all his house, " as a servant," as had been specifically noticed in the testimony borne to his faithfulness.

" My *servant* Moses is not so, who is faithful in all mine house." Numb. xii. 7. But the house in which Moses was "a faithful and wise servant" was erected for the purpose of bearing testimony to those things which were afterwards to be spoken. "For the law made nothing perfect, but the bringing in of a better hope did; by the which we draw nigh unto God." Chap. vii. 19. It was a scaffolding for the erection of a building.

The Jewish dispensation was a "shadow of good things to come," of the spiritual kingdom which God was afterwards to establish. " The law and the prophets," says Jesus, " were until John : since that time the kingdom of God is preached, and every man presseth into it." Luke xvi. 16. " For had ye believed Moses, ye would have believed me : for he wrote of me." John v. 46. Moses and the Apostle taught precisely the same thing; only Moses taught with a vail on his face, and the Apostle used great plainness of speech.

V. 6.—But Christ as a son over his own house; whose house are we, if we hold fast the confidence and the rejoicing of the hope firm unto the end.

While Moses was faithful as a servant in the house of God, Christ was faithful as a Son over His own house. It was erected by His power. He is heir of all things, Col. i. 16; Heb. i. 2; He is Lord of all. Acts x. 36. " The Father loveth the Son, and hath given all things into His hand." John iii. 35. " For the Father judgeth no man, but hath committed all judgment unto the Son." John v. 22. All things, without exception, are put under Him, chap. ii. 8, whose house are we.

The house over which He rules is a spiritual house, composed of living stones, built upon the foundation of the apostles and prophets, He Himself being the chief corner-stone. Christ is the fountain of life to all His people, and this life is communicated through faith; in other words, by resting on Him, as the stones of a building rest on the foundation.

The loadstone communicates its properties to iron; had it pleased God, it might have done so to stone; and we might conceive of a loadstone so powerful as to impart its qualities to every stone in the building erected upon it.

The supposition is realized in the house of God ; it rests upon Christ ; and, by faith, Christ dwells in every heart. " Now," says one Apostle, " we are His house, if we hold fast the confidence and the rejoicing of the hope firm unto the end."

Faith, or confidence, and hope are inseparably connected, and, indeed, may be used interchangeably. Believers are " begotten again to a lively hope by the resurrection of Jesus Christ from the dead," 1 Pet. i. 3 ; and this hope is founded on the immutable promise of God, confirmed by His oath. Heb. vi. 17, 18.

" This is the promise that He hath promised us (believers), even eternal life." 1 John ii. 25. " This is the record, that God hath given to us eternal life, and this life is in His Son." 1 John v. 11. Now the Apostle says, " Whose house are we, if we hold fast the confidence and the rejoicing of the hope firm unto the end." As when a stone ceases to rest on the foundation, it is no longer a part of the building ; so, if a man abide not in Christ, he is no longer of the house of God. " The just shall live by faith : but if any man draw back, my soul shall have no pleasure in him. But we are not of them who draw back unto perdition, but of them that believe to the saving of the soul." Heb. x. 38, 39.

V. 7.—Wherefore (as the Holy Ghost saith, To-day if ye will hear his voice.

Wherefore.—From the consideration of the privileges connected with keeping the faith, the Apostle delivers a very solemn exhortation, in a quotation from Ps. xcv. In order more powerfully to enforce it upon the minds of the Hebrews, he describes it as the saying of the Holy Ghost.

We have here a conclusive proof of the plenary or verbal inspiration of the Scriptures. The words referred to are represented as spoken by the Holy Ghost, which exactly corresponds with what the Apostle says:—" Which things also we speak, not in the words which man's wisdom teacheth, but which the Holy Ghost teacheth." 1 Cor. ii. 13. The Psalm referred to was written by David, Heb. iv. 7 ; but " the Spirit of the Lord spake by him, and his word was in his tongue." 2 Sam. xxiii. 2. To this also our Lord testifies, in the question which He asked the Pharisees, how David called Messiah Lord. David might have spoken erroneously; but David, in or by the Spirit, called Him Lord. He is the Spirit of truth, and therefore must here, as on every other occasion, have spoken truth.

The words of the Holy Ghost, to which the Apostle directs the attention of the Hebrews, are, " *To-day if ye will hear His voice.*" In the Psalm there is a reference to Israel's rebellion in the wilderness. The account of their journey is calculated to be very useful to those who profess the faith of Jesus, and is therefore repeatedly referred to in the New Testament. 1 Cor. x. Jude, in foretelling the departure from the faith which should take place, puts those whom he addressed in remembrance " how that the Lord, having saved the people out of the land of Egypt, afterward destroyed them that believed not." Jude 5. They are described as having tempted the Lord ten times, and not hearkened to His voice. Num. xiv. 22. But, after they had got possession of the land, they are warned " to-day" to listen to the voice of God, which evidently implies that their entrance into Canaan did not supersede the necessity of the exhortation. We are taught that Israel's provocations and punishment are recorded for our admonition, on whom the ends of the world are come. 1 Cor. x. 11.

V. 8.—Harden not your hearts, as in the provocation, in the day of temptation in the wilderness.

Men not listening to the voice of God pro-

ceeds from the hardness of their hearts, which,
as appears from the conduct of the Israelites,
will too frequently neither be melted by kindness nor subdued by suffering. Israel's conduct
in the wilderness was a tissue of provocations.
The object which God had in view in all His
dealings with them was to humble them and to
prove them, and to know what was in their
hearts, whether they would keep his commandments or no. Deut. viii. 3. Now the Apostle
warns the Hebrew believers by their example
not to harden their hearts and provoke God, as
their fathers had done in the wilderness, in the
day of temptation.

*V. 9.—When your fathers tempted me, proved me,
and saw my works forty years.*

We have seen that God's object in his dealings with Israel was to prove them, and bring
out the hidden evil of their heart; but we are
warned against tempting the Lord. Israel had
many proofs of the longsuffering of God; but,
instead of its leading them to repentance, it
emboldened them in sin. Presuming upon His
longsuffering, they seemed to be trying how far
it would extend. Now we are particularly
cautioned against tempting the Lord. We are
to cherish the most entire conviction of His
perfection, and to place the most unlimited con-

fidence in Him, which necessarily implies our being guided in all things by His wisdom. The day of temptation may refer to the whole period of their sojourning in the wilderness. During that period God was proving them, bringing out what was in their heart, while by their rebellion they constantly provoked Him.

V. 10.—*Wherefore I was grieved with that generation, and said, They do alway err in their heart ; and they have not known my ways.*

Here we have the result of Israel's provocations and temptations of God. He " was grieved with that generation, and said, They do alway err in their heart, and have not known my ways." They were so blinded by their love of sin, that they always erred in heart, and refused to be guided by Him. It is the character of the wicked that they know not God ; and such was the case with the generation whose carcases fell in the wilderness.

V. 11.—*So I sware in my wrath, They shall not enter into my rest.)*

So I sware in my wrath, &c.—In consequence of which, God sware in His wrath that they should not enter into His rest. We have a full account of what God said on this occasion, Num. xiv. 28—35. The expression here is elliptical, " If they shall enter into my rest."

Our translators have given the meaning correctly. It is an oath ; God swears by Himself. "I am not God if they shall enter into my rest."

V. 12.—Take heed, brethren, lest there be in any of you an evil heart of unbelief, in departing from the living God.

Upon the quotation which the Apostle had made from Ps. xcv., he founds an exhortation against there being in any of the believing Hebrews an evil heart of unbelief in departing from the living God. Israel were excluded from Canaan by unbelief. They had the promise of God on which to rely ; but, on hearing the report of the spies, respecting the fortified cities, and the prowess of the Canaanites, they determined to make a captain and return to Egypt.

There could not, therefore, have been a more suitable foundation for the exhortation against an evil heart of unbelief. The fears and apprehensions of Israel led them to disregard the promises of God, and to determine to act in direct opposition to their deliverer. The believing Hebrews stood by faith, and, if they let slip the truth, must necessarily fall.

V. 13.—But exhort one another daily, while it is called To-day ; lest any of you be hardened through the deceitfulness of sin.

They were not only each to mind his own

things, but every man also the things of others.
The Lord has commanded his people to associate together, that they may support and
strengthen each other. Eccl. iv. 9, 10. They
are not only individually to beware of an evil
heart of unbelief, but to exhort one another;
to be aware of the dangers to which they are
exposed, and to watch over one another in
love, and daily to exhort each other, lest they
should be hardened through the deceitfulness
of sin. Satan first entered the hearts of our
first parents in the form of a lie, and he in-
sinuated it in the most ensnaring manner. He
at first questioned whether our first parents
had rightly understood what God said. "Yea,
hath God said?" as if he said, It cannot be;
surely God could not lay you under this re-
straint. Had Eve spurned the insinuation—
had she rested on the glorious perfections of
the Divine character—had she considered that
it was her honour and happiness to be implicitly
guided by her Creator in all things, Satan
would have been baffled, and would have fled
from her, James iv. 7; but she chose to argue
the matter, to explain to the tempter the
liberty bestowed on them to eat of the trees of
the garden with one exception. This emboldened Satan directly to contradict the
Almighty, and to assure the woman that, in-

stead of dying, they should become as gods.
Thus was Eve hardened through the deceitfulness of sin; the tempter, by his subtlety, led
her not only to expect impunity, but an increase of rank and happiness; and thus, by the
hope of impunity, and the prospect of enjoyment, are men in every age hardened by those
lusts which are gendered by the deceitfulness
and desperate wickedness of the heart of fallen
man.   There is but one safeguard, to which
we have already alluded:—"Concerning the
works of men, by the word of thy lips I have
kept me from the paths of the destroyer." Ps.
xvii. 4.

V. 14.—*For we are made partakers of Christ, if we*
hold the beginning of our confidence stedfast unto the end.

The Christian life is compared to a race, a
warfare, in which we are exhorted to strenuous
exertion, while we habitually recollect that in
the Lord alone we have righteousness and
strength, and that, while we are called to work
out our own salvation with fear and trembling,
it is God who worketh in us to will and to do
of His good pleasure.   We are apt to err,
either by trusting in our own heart, which is a
sure proof of folly, or to think that we are
something, and that, by our resolutions and
exertions, we are able to overcome.   But, in

either case, we are hardened through the deceitfulness of sin, not holding the beginning of our
confidence firm unto the end. Faith worketh
by love ; it overcometh the world and its snares.
Hence this verse is connected with the preceding by the particle " for," reminding us how
prone we are to let slip the truth.

This verse is exactly similar to Heb. ii. 6 ;
in the former the Apostle says,—" Whose house
are we ; " in the verse before us,—" We are made
partakers of Christ "—of those benefits which
He bestows on His people, by their dwelling
in Him and He in them, communicating to
them of His fulness, leading them by His
counsel, and afterwards receiving them to
His glory. If we are Christ's house He dwells
in us, and thus we are made partakers of
Christ; so that the two verses express the
same idea, while, by the variation of the expression, our views of the mutual relationship of
Christ and His people are more fully exhibited.

The pronoun *our* is not in the original; it
is simply the beginning of the confidence
exactly corresponding with holding fast the
confidence. We may notice that the word
rendered " confidence," both in vers. 6 and 14,
are not the same in ver. 14 ; it is the same
word rendered " confidence in." " The *confidence* of things hoped for." The word, in ver. 6,

signifies boldness; openness, 2 Cor. vii. 4. It is connected with the rejoicing of hope. A bold avowal of the truth exposed the disciples to persecution; but this is the victory that overcometh the world, even our faith. 1 John v. 4.

When the Apostles were commanded by the Jewish rulers not to speak or teach in the name of Jesus, they replied, "for we cannot but speak the things which we have seen and heard;" and when they had been beaten for not complying with the commandment to hold their peace, " they departed from the presence of the council, rejoicing that they were counted worthy to suffer shame for his name." Acts v. 41. Here we have an illustration of the boldness, or confidence, and the rejoicing of the hope enjoined by the Apostle. Believers are begotten to a lively hope, but there are stony-ground hearers, who for a time appear to believe, and the Scriptures frequently speak of things according to their appearance; but he that endureth to the end shall be saved. In due season we shall reap if we faint not.

V. 15.—While it is said, To day if ye will hear his voice, harden not your hearts, as in the provocation.

The Apostle here recurs to the quotation already made from Ps. xcv., which demonstrates that the word of the Lord endureth for ever, and that its warnings and exhortations are applicable to every age; for the Psalmist says to the men of his generation, "To-day, if ye will hear his voice, harden not your hearts as in the provocation,"—referring to a transaction which took place hundreds of years before.

V. 16.—For some, when they had heard, did provoke: howbeit not all that came out of Egypt by Moses.

Some of the children of Israel, who had not only heard the commandments and promises of God delivered by Moses, but had heard the voice of God at Sinai, provoked him by their disobedience, although not all that came out of Egypt under the guidance of Moses; for, not only Caleb and Joshua, but all the tribe of Levi, all under twenty years of age, and, probably, many of the women, from not being numbered, were not excluded from Canaan. Numb. xiv. 29.

This illustrates the Apostle's doctrine, that there was a remnant according to the election of grace. Thus it was in the days of Elijah, in the days of Malachi (chap. iii. 16, 17), and also in the days of Paul. Rom. xi. 45.

V. 17.—But with whom was he grieved forty years? was it not with them that had sinned, whose carcases fell in the wilderness?

With whom was God displeased during

forty years? was it not with them whose
carcases fell in the wilderness? Numb. xxvi.
63—65.

*V. 18.—And to whom sware he that they should not
enter into his rest, but to them that believed not?*

And to whom did He swear that they should
not enter into His rest, but to them that believed not. Numb. xiv. 11. All the rebellions
of Israel sprang from unbelief. Their making
the calf, their murmuring against God and
against his servant Moses, and their refusing to
enter Canaan, all proceeded from unbelief.

*V. 19.—So we see that they could not enter in because of
unbelief.*

Thus we see that they could not enter the
promised land because of unbelief. Faith in God
was essentially necessary to their expelling the
Canaanites, who were by far more warlike than
themselves. They indeed quitted Egypt under
the assurance that they should inherit Canaan;
they followed the leader whom God had appointed through the sea, but they were at this
period escaping from the house of bondage,
where their lives had been embittered by
oppression; besides, Pharaoh's army was behind them, and to stop was certain destruction.
Such were the motives by which they were
induced to enter the path through the mighty

waters which God had opened for them. But
their circumstances on the borders of Canaan
were very different. They were, so to speak,
naturalized in the wilderness; albeit there was
neither earing nor harvest, all their wants were
richly supplied. The spies had given a description of the warlike condition of the
Canaanites; they represented it as certain
destruction to invade the land, so that every
natural principle forbade their making the
attempt. There was a lion in the way; and
thus it is that the conduct of men is often
ascribed to their faith, when, in fact, they are
walking by sight influenced by worldly motives, while they give themselves, and receive
from others credit for being actuated by confidence in God. Such was the case with Israel
at the Red Sea. There was, doubtless, a
remnant whose dread of the sea was overcome
by faith in God; but the great body of Israel
were children in whom there was no faith,
while their conduct on some occasions appeared
to result from this Divine principle.

CHAPTER IV.

V. 1.—Let us therefore fear, lest, a promise being left us of entering into his rest, any of you should seem to come short of it.

THE fear of God is often put for the whole of religion. Prov. i. 7. There are two kinds of fear; one is strongly inculcated on believers, and is necessarily produced by just views of the glorious majesty of God. "Sanctify the Lord of hosts himself; and let him be your fear, let him be your dread." Isa. viii. 13. It is opposed to hardening the heart. "Happy is the man that feareth alway: but he that hardeneth his heart shall fall into mischief." Prov. xxviii. 14. The other is condemned and represented as a characteristic of the wicked. The slothful servant feared his master, because he viewed him as an austere man. Luke xix. 21. The fearful are classed with the unbelieving. Rev. xxi. 8. David on one occasion, under the influence of fear, abandoned his purpose of bringing up the ark. 1 Chron. xiii. 12.

Here the Hebrews are enjoined to take warning from the example of their ancestors, and to beware lest, a promise of entering into rest being left on record, any of them should seem to come short of it. Our translators have inserted " us " as a supplement, but it seems improper, as will be hereafter noticed.

The Apostle had directed the attention of the Hebrews to their forefathers, who were excluded from Canaan through unbelief, and now he proceeds to make a more particular application of this circumstance.

Let us therefore fear. Fear is used both in a good and a bad sense in the Word of God. The Lord promises to put His fear into His people's hearts, that they may not depart from Him. The fear of God is the beginning of wisdom. Believers inhabit a world in rebellion against God, their hearts are deceitful above all things and desperately wicked; they are surrounded with temptation, and they have no strength to resist their numerous foes. The smallest temptation is sufficient to overcome them, and their only security is confidence in God. In this confidence there are two essential ingredients—a sense of our own weakness, and of the power and goodness of

God. If destitute of a sense of weakness, we
trust in ourselves; and the Scripture tells us,
" He who trusteth in his own heart is a fool."
If we trust in God, except as sinners saved by
grace, we trust in a lie. In Christ alone God
is revealed as just, and the justifier of those
who believe. Mercy flows in no other channel
than through the atonement of Christ. By
this the law was magnified and made honourable. He appeared as the substitute of His
people and bore their sins in His own body
upon the tree. With His dying breath He
proclaimed that the work of expiation was
finished, and the Father re-echoed the declaration from the bounds of the everlasting
hills by raising Him from the dead and placing
in His hands the reins of universal dominion,
and exalting Him at the right-hand of the
throne of God a Prince and a Saviour, to
give repentance to Israel and the remission of
sins.

They that are whole have no need of a
physician, but they that are sick; and, unless
we feel our own weakness, we shall not depend
on Christ. The Scriptures contain many precious promises and many solemn warnings.
By the promises we are encouraged to hope in
God, by the warnings we are cautioned against
those dangers with which we are surrounded.

Both ought to have an effect on our minds. The one exhibits Christ as a refuge from the storm—a hiding-place from the tempest; the other points out the dangers through which many have made shipwreck of faith and of a good conscience.

Our comfort and safety depend upon the due admixture of hope and fear. We read of those who feasted themselves without fear; and it is written, blessed is he that feareth alway. The principle of fear is implanted in our constitution, without it our natural life could not be preserved; we might from principle avoid what is dangerous, but dangers arise where there is no time for reflection, and we shrink from them instinctively. The same principle is applicable to the spiritual life. There is an instinctive fear implanted in the mind in the day of regeneration, which is as essential to our safety as the natural principle of fear is to the preservation of our life. In the fear of the Lord there is strong confidence. A sense of His glory and majesty, His purity and holiness, with our liability to fall into sin, necessarily produce circumspection and watchfulness, and lead to that fear which, so far from being opposed to the life of faith, are essential to its preservation.

It was well that the Israelites should be

aware of the power of their enemies, but they lost sight of the power of God. He who had opened the sea for them to pass through, who had given them manna and water from the rock, who had guided them through the pathless wilderness in a pillar of cloud by day and fire by night, could easily have given them the victory; but they walked by sight, they looked at the Canaanites and refused to attack them. They had the promise of God pledged to their fathers Abraham, Isaac, and Jacob, their own triumph over the Egyptians at the Red Sea to assure them of victory; but all the proofs of His power in the wilderness were forgotten, and they only thought of the prowess of the Canaanites, and, by refusing to enter the land, they came short of the promised rest.

God had said to Moses, " My presence shall go with thee, and I will give thee rest;" but, notwithstanding, they came short of it, and never obtained that rest.

On this the apostolic exhortation is founded; Canaan was a shadow of the better country, and Israel after the flesh, at least that generation, could not enter because they believed not God, nor trusted in His salvation. This is an example for those who are travelling to the better country, the heavenly Canaan, which teaches them that although a promise is left that the people of God should inherit it, still all are to see to it that they do not even seem to come short of the rest presented to their view. The word *us* is inserted in our version improperly; a promise is left that certain persons shall enter into rest, and this promise must be fulfilled, but it is not made in the Word of God to individuals any more than it was to that generation of the Israelites, with the exception of Caleb and Joshua, who came out of Egypt.

The Lord knoweth them that are his; they shall inherit the land, the elect shall obtain it; but we are exhorted to fear lest we should seem to come short of it, lest the cares of this world and the deceitfulness of riches should choke the word; lest believers, being led away by the error of the wicked, should fall from their own stedfastness. Blessed is the man who is so convinced of his proneness to depart from God that he is ever stirring up his soul and all that is within him to trust in God, knowing that safety is only to be found in Him.

The exhortation is similar to that of using diligence to make our calling and election sure, and of using diligence to the full assurance of hope to the end, proving that we are of the truth, and assuring our hearts before him. The Apostle is far from giving encouragement to that fear which hath torment, which is cast out by perfect love. Here we see the analogy to which we have referred between the natural and spiritual life. In our social intercourse or relations, we may be so convinced of the love of a fellow-creature that we have the fullest confidence in him, while in the same proportion we are afraid of doing anything that should offend him, or prevent him from bestowing on us any kindness which we expected from him. In short, if the natural fear implanted in our constitution be excessive, it will render our life very uncomfortable; so if, from defective views of the truth and not knowing the things which are freely given to us of God, our apprehension of our future state be painful, we shall be kept in bondage, destitute of the joy of the Lord, which is our strength. The Apostle, who tells the Hebrews to fear lest a promise being left of entering into rest any of them should seem to come short of it, teaches the Philippians to rejoice in the Lord always, and again He says, Rejoice.

V. 2.—For unto us was the gospel preached, as well as unto them: but the word preached did not profit them, not being mixed with faith in them that heard it.

Literally, we were evangelized as well as they. That the Gospel was preached to the Hebrews

was undoubted, but it was not so palpable that
it had been preached to their progenitors.
Some render the passage, the same good tidings
were preached to us as to them : namely, of
entering into rest. In consequence of Israel's
making the golden calf God threatened to
forsake them ; but, at the intercession of Moses,
he promised them his presence, and that he
would give them rest. Exod. xxxiii. 14. This
promise was made to the nation of Israel, and
to the nation it was fulfilled, although that
generation fell in the wilderness ; the promise
was not made to any individual, but to Moses
in the character of mediator and representative
of Israel ; consequently there was no breach of
promise in that, the carcases of those who had
been numbered, fell in the wilderness. But all
God's dealings with Israel were a parable for
the time then present, a pattern of heavenly
things. Hence we might rather have expected
it to be said, unto them was the Gospel preached
as well as unto us. There could be no question of the Gospel being preached to us, but
although it was also declared to them it was
only in types and shadows. The Apostle's
assertion is, we were evangelized as well as
they ; the word evangelized denotes receiving
good news of any kind, although it has long
been appropriated to the glad tidings of sal-

vation. The meaning here obviously is, the same good tidings are preached to us, which were formerly preached unto them, namely, of entering into rest. When God threatened to disinherit Israel the intercession of Moses prevailed, and he obtained the promise, " My presence shall go with thee, and I will give thee rest." Exod. xxxiii. 14.

This is the promise to which the Apostle refers, v. 1. It had been left, not to any individual, but to Moses in the character of mediator and intercessor, and by him made known to Israel. So it is with the Gospel, all the promises of which are yea and amen in Christ. Eternal life is the promise which God has given to believers. This is the record that God hath given us eternal life, and this life is in his Son, and he who hath (the knowledge of) the Son hath life, and he who hath not the Son hath not life. But the word of hearing— the word which Israel heard—did not profit them, not being mixed with faith in the hearers. God brought his people to the borders of Canaan, and told them to go up and possess it, Deut. i. 20, 21; but having no confidence in the promise of the land which God had made them, in other words the promise not being mixed with faith, it did not profit them. A promise may be absolute altogether, independent

of faith in the person to whom it is made ; but
such is not the promise of which the Apostle
treats.

It was a promise which could only be fulfilled by Israel judging him faithful who had
promised, and in this confidence disregarding
all the power of the inhabitants of the land.
Such is also the case with the promise of the
heavenly country.   It can only be fulfilled by
our treading in the steps of the great Captain
of our Salvation.   He endured the cross despising the shame, and is now set down at the
right hand of God, girded with universal power,
to bestow eternal life on all who will receive it
as the gift of God through Christ.   Nothing
therefore can be more appropriate than the
illustration of the Apostle, of the people of
God entering into rest through faith.

*V. 3.—For we which have believed do enter into rest,
as he said, As I have sworn in my wrath, if they shall
enter into my rest : although the works were finished from
the foundation of the world.*

For we who have believed do enter into rest ;
this is apparent from the oath already adverted
to declaring that the unbelievers should not
enter into his rest.   We have already mentioned that chap. iii. 11, which is rendered in
our version " They shall not enter into my

rest," is in the original an elliptical expression,
if they shall enter into my rest. Our translators
would have done well to have retained the same
rendering when the expression recurs, but they
have here rendered it literally, If they shall
enter, which introduces confusion.

The Apostle, however, was proving that
Israel was excluded from God's rest; but it
might be objected that they did enter into God's
rest, for the work in which God was engaged
as Creator was finished from the foundation of
the world.

*V. 4.—For he spake in a certain place of the seventh
day on this wise, And God did rest the seventh day from
all his works.*

And God rested the seventh day from all his
works. Hence the seventh day might be considered as God's rest, and as such was strictly
enjoined on Israel; so that in one sense they
did enter into God's rest.

*V. 5.—And in this place again, If they shall enter into
my rest.*

Yet God sware that they should not enter
into his rest.

*V. 6.—Seeing therefore it remaineth that some must
enter therein, and they to whom it was first preached entered not in because of unbelief.*

God gave not his promise in vain; the

promise implied that some must enter it, and
they to whom it was first preached did not enter
through unbelief, as had been proved. Chap.
iii. 19. In verse 6 the Apostle only states the
premises without drawing the conclusion, which
is not mentioned till verse 9, " there remaineth
therefore a rest for the people of God." The
reason of not drawing the conclusion was, that
the Apostle intended to prove not only that the
Sabbath was not the rest referred to by the
Psalmist, but that the land of Canaan was not
that rest. Had he drawn the conclusion at the
end of verse 6 it would have been necessary to
draw it a second time, and this did not suit the
rapidity of his ideas. But the reader may draw
it for himself.

*V. 7.—Again, he limiteth a certain day, saying in
David, To day, after so long a time ; as it is said, To day
if ye will hear his voice, harden not your hearts.*

*Again, he limiteth a certain day, saying in
David, To day, after so long a time ; as it is said,
To day,* &c. This abundantly proves that as
the observance of the Sabbath was not the rest
from which unbelievers were excluded by the
oath, neither was the enjoyment of Canaan.
For so long a time, after speaking by David, he
says, to day, after Israel had so long dwelt in
Canaan, which not only excludes the seventh

day, but also the land of Canaan, as the rest referred to.

V. 8.—For if Jesus had given them rest, then would he not afterward have spoken of another day.

For if Joshua had given them rest, he would not afterward have spoken of another day, long after the rest had been obtained.

V. 9.—There remaineth therefore a rest to the people of God.

There remaineth, &c. Here is the conclusion drawn from the premises laid down, which are that neither the Sabbath, on which God rested from all his works, nor the land of Canaan, where Israel ceased from their wanderings, was the rest spoken of by the Psalmist, for that was still future after Israel had possessed the land for so long a period.

We must observe that the Apostle here changes the word he had hitherto used and substitutes the word *Sabbatism.* The reason is, that God having rested on the seventh day and blessed and sanctified it, admitted man to a participation with him in his rest. This privilege he lost by his rebellion.

There is no reason to doubt that the Sabbath-day was observed by those who feared God from Adam to Moses, although this is not recorded until God separated for himself a

peculiar people, and visibly placed a middle
wall of partition between them and all other
nations. He gave them his Sabbaths to be a
sign between him and them.

The rest of mankind were toiling through
the whole week for their daily food, but the
return of the Sabbath on which Israel were
commanded to abstain from all servile work,
reminded them of the restoration of fellowship
between God and his people. The same instruction was given them in the rest from their
journeying in the wilderness and possession
of the land of Canaan, the rest into which they
then entered was a shadow for the time then
present; but there still remains a rest for the
people of God, as is evident from the language
of David, who, after so long a period, cautions
the men of his generation against coming short
of God's rest, which is prepared for his
people.

*V. 10.—For he that is entered into his rest, he also
hath ceased from his own works, as God did from his.*

The Israelites enjoyed rest from labour on
the Sabbath, and when they reached the land
of Canaan they rested from the fatigues of their
journey through the wilderness, but still they
were subject to that labour and toil to which
man is doomed during his pilgrimage here

below; so that their fellowship with God in his rest was incomplete, but he that is entered into that rest which remaineth for the people of God hath ceased from his own works as God did from his. His fellowship with God is complete. As God rested on the seventh day from all his works, so does he that is entered into his rest cease not only from the sore travail which God hath given to the sons of men to be exercised therewith, but from the warfare in which the believer is engaged in journeying to the Heavenly Canaan. In short, his fellowship with God is complete, he hath ceased from his own works as God did from his; to the same purpose it is written: " And I heard a voice from heaven saying unto me, Write, Blessed are the dead which die in the Lord from henceforth: Yea, saith the Spirit, that they may rest from their labours." Rev. xiv. 13. Into this rest Christ hath entered as their forerunner, having finished the work which the Father had given him to do; the everlasting doors were thrown open, and he entered as the forerunner of his people, to prepare for them those mansions in which they shall for ever dwell, where each shall exclaim, with joyful lips, " Return unto thy rest, O my soul, for the Lord hath dealt bountifully with thee."

V. 11.—Let us labour therefore to enter into that rest, lest any man fall after the same example of unbelief.

This is the practical improvement of what had gone before, believers are exhorted to labour to enter into that rest which remaineth for the people of God, lest any should fall after the same example of unbelief—viz., of the generation of Israel which fell in the wilderness. They could not enter into God's rest because of unbelief, and thus the Apostle illustrates and enforces the exhortation previously given to the Hebrews, to give the more earnest heed to the things which they had heard lest at any time they should let them slip.

V. 12.—For the word of God is quick, and powerful, and sharper than any twoedged sword, piercing even to the dividing asunder of soul and spirit, and of the joints and marrow, and is a discerner of the thoughts and intents of the heart.

Here the Apostle intimates the impossibility of the unbelief of the heart escaping detection. Some by the Word of God understand Christ, who is the judge of all; but it rather seems to refer to the word, which he declares shall judge us. John xii. 48. It is described as living and abiding for ever. 1 Pet. i. 23. Thy word, saith the Psalmist, hath quickened me, Psalm cxix. 50; and Christ describes His words to be spirit and life. John vi. 63. It is powerful, mighty through God to the pulling down of strongholds, casting down imaginations, and every high thing that exalteth itself against the knowledge of God, and bringing into captivity every thought to the obedience of Christ. 2 Cor. x. 5. Where the word of a king is there is power, this is the word of the King of kings. It is sharper than a two-edged sword. It pierces even to the dividing asunder of soul and spirit, of the joints and marrow; a sword may be so sharp as to sever the joints and marrow, but the Word of God is of such ethereal temper as to sever even soul and spirit. Man is represented as composed of soul, body, and spirit. 1 Thess. v. 23. The body was made of dust, a living soul was given to it in common with those animals in whom was the breath of life; but besides this man has an immortal spirit, which raises him above all the creatures, and by which in his first estate he was capable of knowing and holding intercourse with his Maker. Now the Word of God is living and powerful, and discerns and discovers the secrets of the heart. It is compared to a refiner's fire and fuller's soap.

V. 13.—Neither is there any creature that is not manifest in his sight: but all things are naked and opened unto the eyes of him with whom we have to do.

The Apostle had been treating of the Word
of God, but here he passes to God himself, and
declares that all things are naked and opened
unto the eyes of Him with whom we have to
do ; or, as some render it, to whom we must
give account.

*V. 14.—Seeing then that we have a great High Priest,
that is passed into the heavens, Jesus the Son of God,
let us hold fast our profession.*

*V. 15.—For we have not an High Priest which cannot
be touched with the feeling of our infirmities ; but was in
all points tempted like as we are, yet without sin.*

*For we have not a High Priest who cannot
be touched with* or cannot sympathize with *our
infirmities ;* for, having assumed our nature,
He was in all things tempted like as we are,
yet without sin.   The Lord Jesus was truly a
man, born of a woman, and consequently had
all the feelings of a man ; but these were
under such entire subjection to the will of
God, that He had no sin, but was entirely conformed to the will of God.   In every situation
He did the. things which pleased His heavenly
Father.   He suffered, being tempted, for instance, when He was hungry ; the devil tempted
Him to change the stones into bread.   His
hunger prompted him to comply ; but, while
His Father had given Him power to accomplish

many mighty works, in proof of His having come forth from God, had He employed that power for the supply of His own wants, it would have interfered with the example which He has left us of confidence in God, being assured that He will withhold from us no good thing. We cannot imitate the signs and wonders which He wrought. These were peculiar to Himself, and to those upon whom He thought fit to bestow them, for the confirmation of the word of the truth of the Gospel; but He was in all things conformed to His brethren, so that He hath afforded us a perfect pattern for our conduct during our pilgrimage; and, had He not in all things been made like unto His brethren, this could not have been the case. In all things, therefore, " it behoved Him to be made like unto His brethren, that He might be a merciful and faithful High Priest in things pertaining to God, to make reconciliation for the sins of the people. For in that He Himself hath suffered being tempted, He is able to succour them that are tempted." Chap. ii. 17, 18. Christ's entire submission to His Father's will, and not pleasing Himself, may be represented as inconsistent with His supreme divinity; but on the contrary it was His Divinity that enabled the man Christ

Jesus thus to glorify His Father. He thought
it not robbery to be equal with God; but,
having taken on Him the form of a servant,
He was in all things obedient to the will
of His Father. It was His meat and His
drink to do His will; and at last, in obedience
to the commandment which He had received,
He laid down His life and took it again.
A sin-offering must be perfect to be accepted;
and He offered Himself without spot or
blemish; and although He had no sin, yet
was He made sin for His people, that they
might be made the righteousness of God in
Him; that, having by His blameless life
and meritorious death, as the Head and
Surety of His people, atoned for their sins,
and brought in everlasting righteousness, that
righteousness might belong to all the seed
of the woman, with whom He took part in
flesh and blood. Thus God's eternal purpose
was accomplished by His own Son manifest in
the flesh. The Son of God made His soul
an offering for the sins of an unnumbered
multitude, who were chosen in and given to
Him by His Father; and thus grace reigned
through righteousness unto eternal life, by
Christ Jesus. Had His people broken the holy
law? He obeyed it in all its extent, and

endured its penalty. Had they come under the curse? He redeemed them by being made a curse for them, and opened a new and living way for their entering into life through His obedience unto death.

CHAPTER V.

*V. 1.—For every high priest taken from among men
is ordained for men in things pertaining to God, that he
may offer both gifts and sacrifices for sins.*

THE Apostle had said that under the Gospel
believers have a great High Priest who is
passed into the heavens, Jesus the Son of God,
chap. iv. 14; and, referring to the institution
of the Jewish law, he says, " Every high priest
taken from among men." That reference is
here made to the Jewish law, appears by the
Apostle speaking of a high priest. This was
peculiar to Israel. Previously to the giving of
the law, the head of each family seems to have
acted as its priest. Thus we read of Noah,
Abraham, Job, and Jethro, chap. xiii., Exod.
xviii. 2, offering sacrifices; but it does not
appear to have been confined to them, for Cain
and Abel both offered; and we read, " And he
sent young men of the children of Israel, which
offered burnt-offerings, and sacrificed peace-

offerings of oxen unto the Lord." Exod. xxiv.
5. Here the *young men* were the offerers; but,
after the giving of the law, Aaron and his
family were exclusively appointed to the priesthood. They alone were permitted to enter the
tabernacle, or house of God, and to burn incense, and sprinkle the blood of the sacrifices.
The tabernacle was divided by a vail into two
compartments—the holy, and holiest of all.
Into the former the priests had daily access.
The chief or high priest alone was admitted
within the vail, and that only upon one day of
the year, when he made an atonement for all
Israel, and sprinkled with blood the mercy-seat
which covered the ark, and which was the
throne of the God *of Israel*, intimating that
mercy could only flow to sinners through an
atoning sacrifice.

The first time the priesthood is mentioned in
Scripture is in the case of Melchisedec, who, as
the Apostle afterwards teaches us, was a remarkable type of Christ, who is said to be a priest
for ever after the order of Melchisedec, for the
priesthood of Aaron was but temporary. Even
among the heathen the office of priest was
known. Thus we read of the Egyptian priests,
Gen. xlvii. 22; and of the priest of Midian,
Exod. ii. 16.

The Lord took Israel to be his peculiar

people, and he chose Aaron and his sons to be
His priests. The great object of the institution
was that they might offer gifts and sacrifices,
and for this purpose they were selected and set
apart. The office of the priesthood was also an
intimation that fallen man could have no immediate access to God, but that he required a
daysman, an intercessor. He was to offer gifts
and sacrifices; this is repeated, chap. viii. 3.
Gifts, as distinguished from sacrifices for sin,
were expressions of gratitude to God for His
goodness in general, or for any manifestation of
it on a particular occasion.

*V. 2.—Who can have compassion on the ignorant, and
on them that are out of the way; for that he himself also
is compassed with infirmity.*

Being himself a man, he could have compassion on the ignorant and erring, being conscious
that he was compassed with infirmities.

This is probably mentioned by the Apostle,
because no sacrifice was appointed or accepted
for presumptuous sin. Ps. li. 16. This is one
of the many proofs of the inferiority of the
Jewish to the Christian dispensation—of the
shadow to the substance.

The man who sinned presumptuously was to
be taken from God's altar and put to death; of
this we have an example in the case of Joab;

but the blood of Jesus cleanseth the believer from all sin. However aggravated our guilt, pardon is proclaimed to us through faith in Jesus.

V. 3.—And by reason hereof he ought, as for the people, so also for himself, to offer for sins.

Since the high priest was himself compassed with infirmities, it was necessary that he should offer sacrifices not only for the people but for himself.

V. 4.—And no man taketh this honour unto himself, but he that is called of God, as was Aaron.

The office of the priest, more especially of the high priest, was peculiarly honourable; he stood between God and the people. He was, as it were, brought nigh to God. This was indeed the case with the whole tribe of Levi, who are described as brought near to God. Numb. xvi. 9. They alone had access to the Tabernacle, the royal pavilion.

They were, so to speak, the household servants of the King of Israel, but the High Priest was the head servant, so far as the worship of God was concerned; he was the chief, the ruler of all God's house, and no man took the honour to himself. What should we say of a man who entered the palace of an

earthly king, and assumed authority to give
directions to the servants ? Such conduct would
not be tolerated, and how much less that any one
should assume the office of High Priest in Israel,
without a special call similar to that given to
Aaron ? Exod. xxviii. 1. His appointment
to the office was conducted in a very solemn
manner. He was distinguished by a peculiar
dress emblematic of his office, and minute directions were given him as to the mode of executing his office. In causing his rod to bud, to
bring forth blossoms, and bear almonds, God
confirmed his appointment; and again, by consuming Korah and his company, who dared to
burn incense, and whose censers were made
broad plates for a covering of the altar. Numb.
xvi. 39, 40. This was a standing memorial
that no stranger, who was not of the seed of
Aaron, should come near to offer incense before
the Lord.

*V. 5.—So also Christ glorified not himself to be made
an high priest ; but he that said unto him, Thou art my
Son, to-day have I begotten thee.*

This, like all the other ordinances of Moses,
had its fulfilment in the Kingdom of God, for
Christ did not glorify Himself by assuming un-
called the office of High Priest. He received
this high office from Him who declared him to

be His only begotten Son, and thus setting Him far above all principality and power, and every name that is named not only in this world but in that which is to come.

V. 6.—As he saith also in another place, Thou art a priest for ever after the order of Melchisedec.

And in another place he pronounces him to be a priest for ever, after the order of Melchisedec. This is taken from Psalm cx., and is applied by the Lord to himself, and by his Apostle, Acts ii. 34, 35 ; and also in a previous part of this Epistle, Heb. i. 13, under Melchisedec.

V. 7.—Who in the days of his flesh, when he had offered up prayers and supplications with strong crying and tears unto him that was able to save him from death, and was heard in that he feared.

In the days of his flesh, during his abode in this world, John i. xiv., he offered up most earnest supplications and prayers to him with whom are the issues from death, Ps. lxviii. 20, with strong crying and tears, as we find in the Garden of Gethsemane, and was heard in that he feared ; hearing prayer implies receiving a favourable answer. 1 John v. 16, 18.

No man took the life of Jesus from him, he laid it down of himself. To the last he asserted his power to rid himself of his enemies. His death was an act of obedience to his Father, as indeed was every action of his life and every word that he spoke. John xii. 49. My doctrine, says he, is not mine, but His that sent me. In John viii. 16 it is said, To Him that was able to save him from death. If we understand this to mean to prevent him from dying, the Lord's prayer was not heard, for he actually tasted death. When he said, " Now is my soul troubled; and what shall I say ? Father, save me from this hour," he adds, " but for this cause came I unto this hour." John xii. 27. He knew that he came forth from God and was going to God, and that the Son of Man was to be glorified and that his death was essential to this consummation, for he says : " Verily, verily, I say unto you, Except a corn of wheat fall into the ground and die, it abideth alone : but if it die, it bringeth forth much fruit." John xii. 24. When, therefore, we read of his supplications and tears to be delivered from death, we cannot understand him as meaning that he might not die, for the Father heareth him always, and had not his death been perfectly voluntary he would not have died; but his being saved from death refers to his resurrection, being brought from the fearful pit and miry clay. Ps. xl. 2. He knew that his soul

was not to be left in Hades, nor was the Holy
One of God to see corruption.   In the regions
of death, the path of life was to be shown him,
and at his Father's right hand he was to enjoy
pleasures for evermore.

We have an account of his agony in the
garden, and the supplications and prayers
which he offered up, but these are to be found
more fully in the Book of Psalms,—a book by
which we are admitted into our Redeemer's
closet and learn his entire submission to his
Father's will, together with the keenness of his
feelings when, as the surety and representative
of his people, he bore the sins of his people,
which, as a heavy burden, were too heavy for
the man Christ Jesus, and brought him to the
dust of death.   But he could not be held under
the power of death, and his resurrection to the
power of an endless life was the pledge of his
having magnified the law and made it honourable, having finished transgression, made an
end of sin, made reconciliation for iniquity,
and brought in everlasting righteousness.

With his dying breath he exclaimed, it is
finished or perfected, and his Father re-echoed
the declaration by raising him from the dead
and crowning him with glory.

His resurrection is ascribed sometimes to
the power of the Father, sometimes to his own

power, and sometimes to the power of the
Spirit. These three are one in operation, whatever is done by one is done by all. We
especially see their unity in the plan of salvation, each taking a share : " Now there are
diversities of gifts, but the same Spirit. And
there are differences of administrations, but the
same Lord ; and there are diversities of operations, but it is the same God which worketh all
in all." 1 Cor. xii. 4—6.

While the subsistence of the Eternal Jehovah in three persons, who are one, is an unfathomable mystery, it is essential to the right
understanding of the plan of salvation, which
indeed is founded upon it. The Father chooses
his people and gives them to the Son, whom he
sends to deliver them from condemnation, and,
as their head and representative, to communicate to them a new and endless life. The
Son takes part with them in flesh and blood,
thus becoming a member of Adam's fallen race,
and having the right of redemption as the near
kinsman of the children whom God has given
him. The Spirit is given to him without
measure, and as the precious oil poured on the
head of Aaron ran down to the skirts of his
garments, so the Spirit is through him communicated to all whom he is not ashamed to call
brethren. They are all accepted in the beloved,

are saved with an everlasting salvation, and thus the eternal purpose of God, the manifestation of his manifold wisdom, is accomplished.

V. 8.—Though he were a Son, yet learned he obedience by the things which he suffered.

Though he were a Son, yet learned he, &c. He was the Son of God, the object of the worship and adoration of the angels of God, the Creator of the ends of the earth, yet he learned obedience, &c. In all things it behoved him to be made like unto his brethren, and therefore, like them, it was necessary that he should yield obedience to the law which they had broken, and thus he practically learned obedience by suffering the just for the unjust, that he might bring them to God.

From them obedience to the holy law of God was required ; but from him it was obedience unto death. He received a commandment to lay down his life, and he was not disobedient.

V. 9.—And being made perfect, he became the author of eternal salvation unto all them that obey him.

Christ was absolutely perfect, holy, harmless, undefiled, separate from sinners. The prince of this world came, and found nothing in Him. The perfection here spoken of refers to His priesthood. The Apostle had previously spoken of Him as the Captain of His people's salvation, being made perfect through sufferings, chap. ii. 10. How else could He atone for sin? Thus we are taught that it was necessary that He whom God gave as a leader and commander of the people should be fully qualified for the office through sufferings. Under the law there was no remission of sins without shedding of blood. Now the blood of bulls and goats could never take away sin. The Church could only be ransomed by the blood of Christ. The wages of sin is death; and, in order to show to His people the path of life, it was necessary that He should tread the path of death, and give His life a ransom for many.

In this passage we are taught that, as our great High Priest, He was made perfect, that is, His consecration was completed. There is a reference here to the process of the consecration of the Jewish high priest. In the first place, the holy garments were to be prepared and put upon Aaron and his sons, after they had been washed with water. They were then to be anointed with oil. A bullock was next to be brought, on which they were to lay their hands, which was then to be killed, and the ram was to be burned upon the altar. The ram completed the consecration of Aaron, and therefore was called the sacrifice of consecration or of perfection, because by it the consecration of the priest was perfected or completed. So the consecration of the great High Priest being completed by His death, and the pouring out of the blood of the everlasting covenant, He became the author of eternal salvation to all them that obey Him.

To obey and to believe are synonymous; for Christ saves all believers from their sins; He writes the law upon their hearts; and, under the constraining influence of His love, they deny ungodliness and worldly lusts, walking in newness of life. Eternal salvation is here mentioned in contrast with the temporal salvation of Israel from the land of Egypt, from the house of bondage.

V. 10.—Called of God an high priest after the order of Melchisedec.

In His discourse with the Pharisees, Matt. xxii. 43, 44, the Lord Jesus applies the 110th Psalm to Himself. In it He is described as a priest for ever after the order of Melchisedec. This appellation was given Him by God. It may be observed that in the Psalm it is said, " Thou art a priest for ever." The Apostle gives Him the title of High Priest because, although all the Levitical priests were types of Christ, yet the high priest was the most eminent. And as there is but one priest in the kingdom of God, the Lord Jesus is here and in many other parts of this epistle described as a High Priest for ever after the order of Melchisedec. The Apostle afterwards points out the superiority of the priesthood of Melchisedec to that of Aaron. Here he merely quotes from Psalm cx., where the priesthood of Christ is said to be after the order of Melchisedec, which implies what is afterwards fully stated, that our Lord's priesthood was far superior to that of Aaron.

V. 11.—Of whom we have many things to say, and hard to be uttered, seeing ye are dull of hearing.

The Apostle, however, does not immediately enter upon the subject of the difference of the order of the priesthood of Aaron and Melchisedec, but takes occasion to rouse the attention of the Hebrew believers by informing them that he had much to say concerning Melchisedec which was not easily explained, not so much from the difficulty of the subject, as from their slow apprehensions of spiritual things.

V. 12.—For when for the time ye ought to be teachers, ye have need that one teach you again which be the first principles of the oracles of God ; and are become such as have need of milk, and not of strong meat.

Considering the time during which they had been in the school of Christ, they ought to have been capable of teaching others, but they required to be taught the first principles of the oracles of God. This appears to refer to their ignorance of the types and shadows of the Mosaic dispensation, which are termed by the Apostle rudiments or elements, the misunderstanding of which prevented many from discerning the truth. The Mosaic ordinances were a kind of hieroglyphic, having a hidden meaning. They are termed weak and beggarly elements, and the elements of the world, because they were only the shadow of heavenly things.

The whole Mosaic dispensation was a parable for the time then present, in which spiritual and heavenly things were represented by earthly things. But the carnality of men's minds led them to rest in the shadow and overlook the substance.

We see in the history of the beginning of the Gospel, and in Paul's Epistles, especially that to the Galatians, the pernicious consequence of not understanding the nature of the Mosaic dispensation. It was a parable for the time then present, in which spiritual and heavenly things were set forth under the emblems of those which were carnal and earthly, with which we are most conversant.

To those by whom this was fully understood
the old dispensation was a prophetic, and consequently obscure, intimation of the establishment of the spiritual and eternal kingdom of
Messiah, together with the ordinances to be
observed by its subjects.

The observance of the laws of Moses was
calculated to maintain the expectation of the
appearing of Christ, and thus preserve Israel in
a state of separation from all other nations, as
well as to present spiritual things in a palpable
form to men in every age ; and not only so, but
to remain, till the consummation of all things, a
conclusive evidence of the truth of the Scriptures, by the perfect correspondence of the two
parts into which they were divided, which appeared at first sight very dissimilar.

But while the wisdom of God strikingly
appears in his dealings with Israel, this has
been in every age the great stumblingblock in
the way both of the Jews and of the followers
of Christ. The Jews have adhered with an
unaccountable obstinacy to the shadow, disregarding the substance ; while the great body
of nominal Christians, and many of the true
disciples of Christ, have blended Judaism with
Christianity ; and to this we owe the great
apostacy, in which Heathenism, Judaism, and
Christianity are blended together, and by which

the pure and holy doctrine of Christ has been converted into a system of gross superstition and idolatry.

The apostles foresaw the revelation of the man of sin, and prescribed the only infallible preservative from his wiles: " Therefore, brethren, stand fast, and hold the traditions which ye have been taught, whether by word or our epistle." 2 Thess. ii. 15. But the false principle that, while in regard to the great doctrines of the Gospel we are bound to abide by the rule of Scripture, we are at liberty, in what are termed external things, to be guided by circumstances, has induced the generality even of Protestants to go back to the weak and beggarly elements of Judaism. This system will continue till the great overturning predicted by the Word of God, Ezek. xxi. 27, shall take place. The Lord will then "turn to the people a pure language, that they may all call upon the name of the Lord, to serve Him with one consent." Zeph. iii. 9.

The object of this Epistle is to preserve believers to the end of the world from this snare of the devil, as well as to check the apostacy which it appears had taken place among many of the Jews who had professed the faith to which the Apostle repeatedly alludes. To the misunderstanding of this subject the Apostle attributes the little progress which the Hebrews had made, and that they had become as those that had need of milk, and not of strong meat.

V. 13.—For every one that useth milk is unskilful in the word of righteousness : for he is a babe.

Every one that feeds on milk is unskilful in the word of righteousness : for he is a babe. The Apostle uses similar language to the Corinthians. 1 Cor. iii. 1, 2. They are thus characterized on account of their disposition to follow different leaders. Sometimes the term babes, or little children, is used in a good sense. We are commanded, as new-born babes, to desire the sincere milk of the word. In malice we are to be children, but in understanding to be men. If we do not receive the kingdom of heaven as little children we cannot enter therein. Our high imaginations must be cast down and our thoughts brought into subjection to Christ.

But here the word babes is not used in a good sense. The Apostle charges the Hebrews with being weak in the faith, babes in understanding. There is, probably, a reference to their attachment to Jewish observances, and their desire to remain under the bondage of the Jewish observances, which he elsewhere terms the elements of the world, Gal. iv. 3, weak and beggarly elements.

V. 14.—*But strong meat belongeth to them that are of full age, even those who by reason of use have their senses exercised to discern both good and evil.*

As grown up persons do not feed upon milk, but are able to digest strong meat; so those who are perfect,* well instructed, who have their senses exercised to discern good and evil, view the ordinances of the Mosaic dispensation in their true light, as what they really are, shadows; as shadows of good things to come, chap. x. 1, and thus discern the wisdom of God in a mystery, even the hidden wisdom which God ordained before the world unto our glory. 1 Cor. ii. 7.

* The word rendered " of full age" is, literally, *perfect,* a word which is very frequently used in this Epistle, and means well instructed. The Apostle uses the same word Phil. iii. 15, where it has probably a reference to those who were initiated in the heathen mysteries. They were termed perfect.

CHAPTER VI.

V. 1.—Therefore leaving the principles of the doctrine of Christ, let us go on unto perfection; not laying again the foundation of repentance from dead works, and of faith toward God.

THE Apostle had said that he had many things to say concerning Melchisedec, which were hard to be uttered, in consequence of the Hebrews being dull of hearing. As it is difficult to speak to a deaf man, so it was difficult to explain to them the mystery contained in his history. This was not owing to the subject being new to them, for, considering the time they had been in the school of Christ, they ought to be teachers, and yet they required to be taught again the elements or first principles of the oracles of God, and needed to be fed with milk, and not with strong meat; as milk is suitable for babes, and strong meat for grown up persons. Now the Hebrews, from the advantages which they had enjoyed, ought to have their senses exercised to discern true and false doctrine.

But, considering the advantages which they had already enjoyed, and the progress they ought to have made, he would leave the elements or principles of the doctrine of Christ (literally the word of the beginning of Christ, which seems to be the same as what is termed the first principles of the oracles of God, chap. v. 12, literally the elements of the beginning of the oracles of God), he would go on to perfection: that is the explanation of what had been darkly shadowed forth in the Old Testament. He would not again lay the foundation of repentance from dead works* and of faith in God, which were so frequently inculcated by Moses and the prophets.

V. 2.—Of the doctrine of baptisms, and of laying on of hands, and of resurrection of the dead, and of eternal judgment.

It may seem strange that the doctrine of baptism and laying on of hands should be introduced along with repentance and faith. But repentance and faith were enforced in the Jewish economy, in which there were divers baptisms, Heb. ix. 10, signifying the necessity of repentance. In like manner, the laying on of hands on the sacrifice about to be offered, represents faith. The worshipper, by laying

* Dead works, mean works deserving death.

his hands on the victim, confessing his sins,
expressed his faith of remission through the
shedding of blood.   Heb. ix. 22.*

V. 3.—And this will we do, if God permit.

This, therefore, was the course, which, by
Divine permission, he intended to follow.

*V. 4.—For it is impossible for those who were once
enlightened, and have tasted of the heavenly gift, and were
made partakers of the Holy Ghost,....*

It appears from this and other parts of the
Epistle that there had been a great apostacy
among the Hebrews who had professed the

* The *baptisms* here spoken of cannot refer to the
ordinance of Christ, for there is but *one* Christian baptism.
Eph. iv. 5.   The resurrection of the dead, which is a
most prominent part of the doctrine of Christ, was
plainly taught by Moses and the prophets, and generally
believed by the Jews.   Acts xxiv. 15; John xi. 24;
Acts xxiii. 6; Mark xii. 23, 27; while the Sadducees
denied it.   Acts xxiii. 8.   The faith of the resurrection
implied the future judgment.   Indeed the future judgment
was implied by mankind after the fall being divided into
two classes, while all were to return to the dust.   The
separation must be made after death, so that the resurrection and the judgment were clearly taught from the
beginning.   All go to one place whatever be their character, the grave receives them all; in dividing mankind
into two classes after the fall, God clearly intimated the
general judgment.   It is called eternal judgment, because
its decisions will never be reversed.

faith of Christ, but had returned to Judaism, and their case was so hopeless that the Apostle would not occupy time by addressing himself to them. They are described as having been once enlightened. When the Lord divides the hearers of the Gospel into four classes, one class is represented as receiving the word with joy, but having no root, and therefore only enduring for a time. The same persons are described—" For if after they have escaped the pollutions of the world through the knowledge of the Lord and Saviour Jesus Christ, they are again entangled therein and overcome, the latter end is worse with them than the beginning. For it had been better for them not to have known the way of righteousness, than, after they have known it, to turn from the holy commandment delivered unto them." 2 Peter ii. 20, 21. See also Heb. x. 26, 27. Whence it appears that a great external reformation may be produced by the Gospel, and the feelings of the hearers may be greatly excited while they are destitute of saving faith. This is the gift of God, and the gifts and calling of God are without repentance. Rom. xi. 29.

There may, however, be a temporary impression made by the Gospel, whence some are described as believing for a time, Luke viii. 13; which is explained in next clause, *and have been made partakers of the Holy Ghost.* This refers to the miraculous gifts conferred by the laying on of the Apostle's hands. Men thus receiving the Holy Ghost did not imply that they were truly converted. Hence our Lord says: " Many will say to me in that day, Lord, Lord, have we not prophesied in thy name? and in thy name have cast out devils? and in thy name done many wonderful works?" Matt. vii. 22. And the Apostle supposes the case of men possessing a faith by which they might remove mountains, 1 Cor. xiii. 2, while destitute of love, and therefore ignorant of God. 1 John iv. 8.

V. 5.—And have tasted the good word of God, and the powers of the world to come.

Tasted the good word of God, felt somewhat of its sweetness: " How sweet are thy words unto my taste! yea, sweeter than honey to my mouth!" Ps. cxix. 103. " More to be desired are they than gold, yea, than much fine gold: sweeter also than honey, and the honeycomb." Ps. xix. 10. " Thy words were found, and I did eat them; and thy word was unto me the joy and rejoicing of mine heart: for I am called by thy name, O Lord God of Hosts." Jer. xv. 16. The persons referred to have tasted somewhat of this excellence and the power of the world to come. What is rendered the

Everlasting Father is in the LXX. the Father of the age to come, and we read of the world to come, that is the Gospel dispensation. Heb. ii. 5. Now the power of the world to come means the diversity of miraculous gifts under the new dispensation, referred to by the Apostle. 1 Cor. xii. 4, 10. We are unable accurately to distinguish these, because we do not possess miraculous gifts; but there are the powers conferred under the Gospel dispensation. What is rendered in our version working of miracles, 1 Cor. xii. 29, is working of powers. Again in Matt. vii. 22, 23, wonderful works, is in the original, powers.

V. 6.—If they shall fall away, to renew them again unto repentance; seeing they crucify to themselves the Son of God afresh, and put him to an open shame.

There is no *if* in the original; it is " and having fallen away;" for it is coupled with the preceding participles, enlightened, tasted, made partakers of, after all had fallen away.* While

* This does not imply that the people of God shall ever fall away. We have already seen that the gifts and calling of God are without repentance; indeed this must be the case, because believers were chosen in and given to Christ. Eph. i. 4; John xvii. 6; and shall never perish. John x. 28, 29. Where God begins a good work he will carry it on till the day of Christ; but believers as well as others require cautions and warnings, and it is not

this is a solemn warning to him who thinketh
he standeth, to take heed lest he fall, 1 Cor.
x. 12, it throws no doubt upon the perseverance of the saints, although we can only know
that such is our character by holding fast the
truth.   It is evident from this and many other
passages that men's natural feelings may be
much excited, and such a change in their habits
and sentiments produced as may strikingly
resemble the fruits of the Spirit, while they
are imposing on themselves and others.

But it may be asked, why is it impossible to
renew such persons again to repentance ? It is
not impossible for God thus to renew them, for
with Him all things are possible.   The impossibility appears to be the same as for a rich man
to enter the kingdom of God.   " It is easier,"

improbable that there may be here an intentional obscurity in regard to the feelings excited by the truth as it is
in Jesus, which is intended to serve as a beacon against
any tendency to backslide from God. Our comfort ought
not to be derived from our past feelings or fancied
acquirements, but from the habitual contemplation of
Christ as our Saviour. We can only enjoy the assurance
of hope by the contemplation of the glory of the sacrifice
of Christ, and the absolute freeness of the great salvation. Let the apparent genuineness of our Christian
experience be what it may, we can only have proof of
our being living members of Christ by abiding in him
and holding fast the truth.

says the Lord, " for a camel to pass through the
eye of a needle than for a rich man to enter
the kingdom," and adds, " with man it is impossible, but not with God; for with God all
things are possible."   However, their case was
so very hopeless that the Apostle would not
attempt to recover those who had apostatized,
since by that act they had justified the conduct
of the Jews in reviling and crucifying the Son
of God as a blasphemer and an impostor, and
thus, as it were, putting him to an open shame,
or making him a public example.   Matt. i. 19.
They, as it were, set their seal to all the insults
and injuries which were heaped on Jesus, and
that after the fullest evidence had been given
of his divine character and mission, not only
by his resurrection but by the outpouring of
the Spirit, of whose miraculous gifts they had
been made partakers.   Acts ii. 33.   We find
a parallel passage in chap. x. 26, 29, where
apostates are represented as treading under foot
the Son of God, and counting the blood of the
covenant wherewith he was sanctified* an un-

* " Sanctified " may either apply to Christ, who says,
" For their sakes I sanctify myself, that they may be
sanctified through the truth."   He was set apart, like the
paschal lamb, that his people might be set apart through
the truth ; or it may refer to the apostate, for the Scripture often speaks of them as they appear, for instance
Simon Magus is said to have believed.

holy thing; and, having done despite to the
Spirit of Grace, by rejecting the testimony he
bore to Jesus. These passages confirm the
observation already made that many of the
Hebrews who had professed the truth had
returned to Judaism; and the Apostle wrote
this Epistle with a view of putting a stop to
the apostacy by teaching the Hebrews the
nature of the Mosaic law, by the misunderstanding of which they had been misled, and
showing them that it was a temporary dispensation, a shadow of good things to come.

*V. 7.—For the earth which drinketh in the rain that
cometh oft upon it, and bringeth forth herbs meet for them
by whom it is dressed, receiveth blessing from God.*

The Scriptures both of the Old and New
Testament frequently illustrate spiritual by
temporal things, and not uncommonly by a
reference to the operations of husbandry. See
John xv. 1, 2. Here we are taught that the
fertility of the earth proceeds from the blessing
of God, Gen. i. 11 and xxvii. 27; Psalm
lxv. 9, 11. This does not, however, preclude
the labours of the husbandman, which is essential to the production of the fruits of the earth,
Gen. iii. 19; but all man's labour is vain
without the blessing of God, Psalm cxxvii. 1,
to which alone we are taught to look for
success. When he crowns the year with his
goodness, causing the grass to grow for the

cattle and herb for the service of man, bringing forth fruit out of the earth, Psalm civ. 14, we see the effect of his blessing.

V. 8.—But that which beareth thorns and briers is rejected, and is nigh unto cursing; whose end is to be burned.

But that which beareth thorns and briers is given up by the husbandman, who finds it vain to waste his strength without obtaining any return, and therefore lets it alone, only removing the surface as fuel. We have a beautiful representation of God's dealings with sinners, of mankind, in that striking parable in which Israel is compared to a vineyard on which the greatest care had been lavished, Isaiah v. 1, 2, but it produced wild grapes, on which account the Lord declared his intention of laying it waste, so that it should only produce thorns and briers. We have another illustration of this passage in the prophecies of Ezekiel. He describes the waters which flowed from the threshold of the house, which gradually augmented. The water was at first to the ankles, then to the knees, afterwards to the loins, and then a river which could not be passed over. In these waters there were exceeding many fishes, and fishermen spreading their nets: " And it shall come to pass, that every thing that liveth, which moveth, whithersoever the

rivers shall come, shall live : and there shall be
a very great multitude of fish, because these
waters shall come thither : for they shall be
healed ; and every thing shall live whither the
river cometh. And it shall come to pass, that
the fishers shall stand upon it from En-gedi
even unto En-eglaim ; they shall be a place to
spread forth nets ; their fish shall be according
to their kinds, as the fish of the great sea,
exceeding many. But the miry places thereof
and the marishes thereof shall not be healed ;
they shall be given to salt." Ezek. xlvii. 9—11.
Ezekiel's vision of the temple is very obscure,
but it is evident that the waters issuing from
the house of God denote the Gospel, and the
fishers the Apostles and those who succeeded
them as preachers of the Gospel.

Every thing lived whither the waters came,
but the miry places and the marshes thereof
were not healed: " They shall be given to salt,"
ver. 11.

The Gospel is not only the savour of life
unto life, but of death unto death, and of such
it will prove to apostates of whom the Apostle
treats. To such we may apply the words of
the prophet respecting Jerusalem: " In thy
fithiness is lewdness ; because I have purged
thee, and thou wast not purged, thou shalt not
be purged from thy filthiness any more, till I

have caused my fury to rest upon thee." Ezek.
xxiv. 13; and again, " But my people would
not hearken to my voice; and Israel would
none of me. So I gave them up unto their
own hearts' lust: and they walked in their own
counsels." Ps. lxxxi. 11, 12.

*V. 9.—But, beloved, we are persuaded better things of
you, and things that accompany salvation, though we thus
speak.*

Having delivered this solemn warning the
Apostle proceeds to encourage his brethren who
had stood fast in the faith. He was persuaded
better things of them, although he thus spoke.
It was necessary for him to set before them the
awful state of those who had apostatized, but
he had confidence in those whom he addressed.
He was persuaded better things of them, even
things that accompany salvation, although he
had found it necessary to use the language he
had done. It may be asked, What are the better
things to which he refers? and he answers the
question, Things which accompany salvation,
which are the evidence of our union with Christ,
and which are therefore far superior to these
gifts to which he had referred, and to which
apostates may attain. We have here an instance
of the wisdom and tenderness with which the
Apostle addressed his brethren. He had set
before them the awful doom of apostates, and

he now returns to the strongest expressions of
confidence and brotherly love.   Of this we have
another instance, 2 Thess. ii. 13.   There also
he speaks of apostates, whom in righteous
judgment God gave up to strong delusion, that
they should believe a lie, but adds: " But we
are bound to give thanks alway to God for you,
brethren beloved of the Lord, because God
hath from the beginning chosen you to salvation
through sanctification of the Spirit and belief
of the truth." 2 Thess. ii. 13.   So also Eph.
iv. 20.   He had described the wickedness of
the Gentiles, who had abandoned themselves to
all uncleanness with greediness, but adds:
" Till we all come in the unity of the faith,
and of the knowledge of the Son of God, unto
a perfect man, unto the measure of the stature
of the fulness of Christ."   Eph. iv. 13.

V. 10.—*For God is not unrighteous to forget your work
and labour of love, which ye have shewed toward his name,
in that ye have ministered to the saints, and do minister.*

Here, as elsewhere, brotherly love is described
as far superior to all spiritual gifts, which the
Apostle had shown might be possessed by
hypocrites and apostates.   " Beloved," says
another Apostle, " let us love one another : for
love is of God ; and every one that loveth is
born of God, and knoweth God.   He that loveth
not knoweth not God ; for God is love.   In

this was manifested the love of God toward us, because that God sent his only begotten Son into the world, that we might live through him. Herein is love, not that we loved God, but that he loved us, and sent his Son to be the propitiation for our sins. Beloved, if God so loved us, we ought also to love one another. No man hath seen God at any time. If we love one another, God dwelleth in us, and his love is perfected in us." 1 John iv. 7—12. Christ condescends to acknowledge what is done to his brethren as having been done to himself, Matt. xxv. 45, and here the Apostle says God is not unrighteous. He acknowledges himself as having been laid under an obligation by their work of faith and labour of love, which he will not forget, in having in time past ministered, and still continuing to minister, to his saints. We can have no claim upon God, we have nothing but what we receive from his bounty ; but he has engaged to reward the services of his people, and he is faithful who hath promised and will also do it. 1 Thess. iv. 23, 24. The same line of argument is pursued by the Apostle: " Though I speak with the tongues of men and of angels, and have not charity, I am become as sounding brass, or a tinkling cymbal. And though I have the gift of prophecy, and understand all mysteries, and all

knowledge ; and though I have all faith, so that
I could remove mountains, and have not charity,
I am nothing.   And though I bestow all my
goods to feed the poor, and though I give my
body to be burned, and have not charity, it pro-
fiteth me nothing." 1 Cor. xiii. 1—3. Hence we
learn that gifts, however great, are inferior to
love ; and we may observe that the Apostle supposes a man to give his goods to feed the poor
and his body to be burned, for attachment to
the profession which he has made, and yet to be
nothing because destitute of love; he then
proceeds to describe the love which he so highly
commends.   1 Cor. xiii. 4—7.   It is the very
Spirit of Christ; God is love.   There is no
inconsistency in this declaration with our God
being a consuming fire.   The God of love is
described as being jealous, and revenging, and
being furious ; his fury is poured out like fire.
Nehem. i. 3—6.   Sin has brought misery and
confusion into his universe ; and, as he sware
that he would have war with Amalek from
generation to generation, he hath sworn irrecon-
cilable war with sin.   But this, so far from
being inconsistent with God's being love, is
essential to the perfection of his character as the
God of love.   It is in his righteous indignation
against sin that his character is fully brought
out.   He is indeed angry with the wicked

every day, he will in no wise clear the guilty;
but the full manifestation of the love of God
consists in his sending his only begotten Son
into the world that we might live through him.
1 John iv. 9.

The Hebrews had shown great liberality in
ministering to the saints in the beginning of
the Gospel, Acts ii. 48, iv. 34, and they had
compassion of himself in his bonds, Heb. x. 34,
ministering to him when he was prisoner at
Cæsarea, and, not only so, but they still per-
severed in the same course.

*V. 11.—And we desire that every one of you do shew
the same diligence to the full assurance of hope unto the
end.*

Yet they required to be admonished not to
be weary in well doing, and the Apostle speaks
to them as it were individually, *every one of you.*

This was much calculated to impress their
minds and to teach them the importance of the
exhortation. Attention to this precept was
intimately connected with their possessing the
full assurance of hope unto the end. Faith and
hope may be distinguished, but are inseparable.
If we believe the Gospel, in proportion to our
faith will be our hope of the enjoyment of
eternal life. The Gospel exhibits a sure foundation of hope to the most unworthy. It is a
proclamation of pardon through faith in the
Lord Jesus. By it we are begotten to a lively

hope of the enjoyment of the eternal inheritance. The moment we perceive the truth
concerning the perfection of the atonement
connected with the freeness of the Gospel
invitation, we must be filled with joy and peace.
Thus it was with the eunuch, Acts viii., and
with the jailor, Acts xvi. The Lord manifested
himself to them in a way he doth not to the
world, and they felt themselves safe in the
everlasting arms. But it is essential to the
continuance of this comfort that we be fruitful
branches of the true vine. The truth works
effectually in all that believe, and if our faith is
genuine such will be the case with us. Hence
it is evident that although the full assurance of
hope is not based on our bringing forth the
fruits of righteousness, these are essential to
its continuance. It is a part of the testimony
of God that Christ saves his people from their
sins, and consequently that sin shall not have
dominion over those who are under grace. If
we experience the sanctifying influence of the
truth it is a proof that it is the true grace of
God in which we stand; and while, as we have
observed, the full assurance of hope may be
enjoyed totally independent of the consideration of our conduct, in order to its continuance
it is absolutely necessary that our conduct
should correspond with the precepts of Christ.

Faith worketh by love, it purifieth the heart

and overcometh the world ; and, if our faith is
genuine, such will be its effect on us. Hence
the Apostle, while commending the Hebrews
for their liberality to their brethren, exhorts
them to show the same diligence to the full
assurance of hope unto the end. Some would
render it *in* the full assurance of hope, &c. ;
and, perhaps, the preposition will bear this
signification, but the rendering in our version
is borne out by parallel passages, 2 Peter
i. 10, 11 ; here the brethren are exhorted to
give diligence to make their calling and election
sure, by abounding in courage, knowledge,
temperance, patience, godliness, brotherly kindness, and love, that they might not be un-
fruitful in the knowledge of our Lord Jesus
Christ, at the same time representing those
who lack these things as blind and short-sighted,
and as having forgotten that they were purged
from their old sins. This does not seem to
refer to unbelievers, but to those who had
backslidden.

We say of a person who is very shortsighted,
that he is blind,—not absolutely, but comparatively.

Another Apostle, after exhorting the believers not to love in word and in tongue, but
in deed and in truth, adds : " And hereby we
know that we are of the truth, and shall assure

our hearts before him," 1 John iii. 19. This exactly corresponds with the passage under consideration, that we should use diligence to the
full assurance of hope unto the end. Our hearts
are deceitful above all things, and we are prone
to take comfort from considering ourselves as
believers; this is very common, and many substitute faith for the great object of faith. We
see people utterly destitute of the knowledge
of Christ shocked with the sentiments of in-
fidels; they believe that the Scriptures are true,
as king Agrippa believed the prophets; but as
he did not believe what the prophets testified,
neither do they believe the Gospel of Christ,
but a figment of their own brain. I may ask
a man the road to a particular place, with the full
assurance that he knows it well; but, if I mistake
his directions, this will not lead me to the place.
So we may believe that the Gospel is true,
while we substitute a fable for the truth as it is
in Jesus; and what will such faith profit us?
Now we are guarded against error, not only by
the great plainness of speech used by the Lord
and His Apostles, but by being informed what
effects the faith of the Gospel must necessarily
produce, and the more these effects are produced in us the greater evidence we have that
it is the true grace of God wherein we stand.
Nothing is more insisted on in Scripture than

brotherly love. It is Christ's new commandment, and the possession or the want of it is
represented as the decisive test of our belonging to him, or being of the world that lieth in
the wicked one. Matt. xxviii. 34, 40.

While the Word of God pours contempt on
our own righteousness, declaring that by the
deeds of the law no flesh living shall be justified,
it enforces the duty of obedience, declaring
that without holiness no man shall see the
Lord; and so inseparably connected are faith
and obedience, that all shall receive of the deeds
done in the body, whether they be good or bad.
The grace of God teaches the believer that,
denying ungodliness and worldly lusts, he
should live soberly, righteously, and godly;
and, while we are justified by grace through
faith, we are taught the inseparable connexion
of faith and works, by the declaration that
Abraham, the father of believers, James ii.,
was in one sense justified by works.

Hence we are commanded to examine ourselves, to prove ourselves, comparing our conduct with the fruit of the Spirit, as described
in the Scripture. While the Apostle gloried
only in the cross, having no confidence in the
flesh, he tells us our rejoicing is this, the
testimony of our conscience that, in simplicity
and godly sincerity, not with fleshly wisdom,

but by the grace of God, we have had our conversation in the world. Hence he urged the
Hebrews to continue diligently in their work
and labour of love, that they might continue to
enjoy the full assurance of hope unto the end.
Two things are essential to the full assurance of
hope; a clear view of the fulness and freeness
of the salvation of Christ, and walking humbly
with God, yielding obedience to His holy will.
The former cannot be enjoyed without the
latter. If we grieve the Holy Spirit by a
careless walk, we must lose in proportion
our perception of the glory of the truth. The
Spirit will no longer bear witness with our
spirit that we are born of God; and, instead of
knowing the things that are freely given to us
of God, we shall be brought under the spirit of
bondage.

*V. 12.—That ye be not slothful, but followers of them
who through faith and patience inherit the promises.*

Sin naturally engenders slothfulness, so
that we move slowly in the race set before us.
The constraining influence of the love of
Christ is wanting. We lose the joy of the
Lord, which is our strength. The word
" slothful " here is the same that is rendered
" dull," chap. v. 11. In opposition to slothfulness, he urges them to be followers of them

who through faith and patience are now inheriting the promises. The Old Testament
saints had finished their course, and were now
inheriting the promises. Abraham, Isaac, and
Jacob had fallen asleep, and, according to the
sentence pronounced on fallen man, had returned to the dust; but the spirit had returned to God who gave it. God is not the
God of the dead, but of the living. They were
absent from the body, but present with the
Lord. He assured the dying thief that he
should be with Him in paradise that night;
and although those who now inherit the promises have not entered on the full enjoyment
of what God has prepared for His people, still
they are with the Lord, and are enjoying the
fulfilment of those promises which from the
beginning were all yea and amen in Christ, all
wrapped up in the first parable—that declaration, " The seed of the woman shall bruise the
head of the serpent."

*V. 13.—For when God made promise to Abraham,
because he could sware by no greater, he sware by himself.*

The Apostle here refers to what took place
when, in obedience to the Divine commandment, Abraham offered Isaac upon the altar.
Never did faith triumph so remarkably as on
this occasion. Abraham, sustained by the pro-

mise of a numerous posterity, and of all the families of the earth being blessed in him, had left his father's house, having become an alien from his brethren.

For many subsequent years he had no child. At length, Ishmael was born of Hagar, the bond-woman; and, some years afterwards, Isaac, the child of promise, was born of Sarah. In consequence of Ishmael's mocking Isaac, he was put out of the family, so that all Abraham's hopes centred in Isaac. Yet, as a trial of his faith, God commanded him to offer his son for a burnt-offering, thus reducing him to ashes. Abraham well knew that upon the life of Isaac depended the fulfilment of the promises which had been his stay and support during all the days of his pilgrimage. Yet he did not hesitate; he set out for the place which God had said He would show him; and, leaving his servants, accompanied by his son, he proceeded to the mountain which God pointed out, which seems to have been Moriah, on which the temple was afterwards built, and the sacrifices offered. There he bound Isaac upon the altar, lifted up the knife to slay him, but was stopped by the angel of the Lord, who expressed his approbation of Abraham's conduct, at the same time renewing the promise, and confirming it with an oath. Thus, after

many years of patient endurance, he obtained
the irrevocable confirmation of the promise, by
the oath of Him who cannot lie.   He could
swear by no greater, and therefore He swore
by Himself.

*V. 14.—Saying, Surely blessing I will bless thee, and
multiplying I will multiply thee.*

Assuring Abraham of His blessing and a
numerous posterity.

*V. 15.—And so, after he had patiently endured, he
obtained the promise.*

Abraham is here exhibited as our pattern of
faith and patience.   He is the father of believers, who, like him, have need of patience.
They walk by faith, not by sight, and are
taught by the example of Abraham, though
the vision tarry, to wait for it, because it will
surely come, it will not tarry.   Hab. ii. 3.

*V. 16.—For men verily swear by the greater: and an
oath for confirmation is to them an end of all strife.*

Men swear by the greater, by some one
superior to themselves ; and, when other evidence cannot be obtained, an oath settles the
matter.   Israel were commanded to swear by
the name of the Lord, Deut. vi. 13, so that
the strife is brought to an end.   The example
of God, with the Apostle's observation, decides
the question of the lawfulness of oaths, which

has been denied. Can we for a moment suppose that God, in His transactions with men, should by His own example sanction what is unlawful, and direct the Apostle to speak of an oath as putting an end to strife? Strife arises now as formerly, and an oath for confirmation is as necessary now as it was before.

There are two passages in the New Testament which are alleged as a proof of the unlawfulness of oaths. In the sermon on the mount, the Lord says, " Swear not at all;" but it is more evident, from the connexion, that the Lord there condemns the confirmation of a vow by an oath. " Thou shalt not forswear thyself, but shalt perform unto the Lord *thy vows*.* But I say unto you, Swear not at all." We have an example of a vow without an oath in the history of Jacob at Bethel, Gen. xxviii. 20—22. The Apostle James likewise forbids swearing, chap. v. 12; but it is evident, from the connexion, that he is also treating of vows. Not only were oaths regulated by the Jewish law, but the Lord Himself, when questioned by the high priest, gave no answer till, put upon His oath, He heard " the voice of swearing." And not only so, but the Apostle Paul frequently appeals to God for the truth of

* There is no reference here to transactions between men.

what he asserts ; so that none of the followers of Jesus ought to hesitate, on proper occasions, to confirm their testimony by an oath.

V. 17.—Wherein God, willing more abundantly to shew unto the heirs of promise the immutability of his counsel, confirmed it by an oath.

Wherefore God, willing to give the heirs of promise (Rom. iv. 13—17; Gal. iii. 27) the fullest assurance of the unchangeableness of His counsel, confirmed His promise with an oath. Num. xiv. 22; chap. iii. 17; Isa. xlv. 23.

V. 18.—That by two immutable things, in which it was impossible for God to lie, we might have a strong consolation, who have fled for refuge to lay hold upon the hope set before us.

That by two immutable things, the promise and the oath of God, in which it was impossible for God to lie, we who have fled * for refuge to the hope set before us might have strong consolation.

The promise of God, which He confirmed by an oath to Abraham, is, that He would bless and multiply him. This was, no doubt, most

---

* The word refuge is not in the original. It is, literally, Who have fled away to lay hold. Probably the appointment of the cities of refuge—to which, indeed, there appears to be a reference, Num. xxxv. 11, 12—has led our translators to the insertion of the word.

satisfactory to the patriarch; but, although the promise may be considered to include the heirs of promise, they are not specifically mentioned, which may be accounted for by the Apostle directing the attention of the Hebrews to the promise, by quoting a part of it, and leaving them to supply the rest from the book of Genesis, in which the heirs of promise are particularly mentioned. " And in thy seed shall all the nations of the earth be blessed; because thou hast obeyed my voice." Gen. xxii. 18. So that the promise was confirmed to them as well as to their father Abraham.

V. 19.—Which hope we have as an anchor of the soul, both sure and stedfast, and which entereth into that within the veil.

The hope set before us is the blessing of Abraham, which has come upon the Gentiles (as well as Jews) through Jesus Christ, that we might receive the promise of the Spirit through faith, Gal. iii. 14, and thus be sealed to the day of redemption. This hope is compared to an anchor, and the figure is most appropriate and beautiful. The anchor, which holds the ship, and prevents her from drifting with the wind and tide, is out of sight, fixed in the ground by its form and weight. Thus it is with the believer; the Lord Jesus Christ, who has entered within the vail, is his hope, 1 Tim. i. 1, and this keeps him stedfast and immovable, preventing his being led away by the lying vanities of this present evil world. When about to remove from her anchorage, the ship is drawn forward to the anchor, which is then weighed, and comes into sight. In this world we hope for what we see not, and with patience wait for it; but, when we receive the adoption, to wit, the redemption of the body, our hope will be swallowed up in enjoyment; then we shall see what, while on earth, we only hoped for.

Besides preserving a ship from drifting, the anchor is used to remove her from one part of a river or harbour to another; and thus, while the hope of the believer keeps him stedfast, it at the same time serves to draw him nearer to the object of his hope, till he shall no longer see through a glass darkly, but face to face; and shall no longer hope for eternal glory, but enter on the full possession of it.

V. 20.—Whither the forerunner is for us entered, even Jesus, made an high priest for ever after the order of Melchisedec.

Christ, the great object of our hope, has, in the character of our forerunner, entered within the vail, thus taking possession, as it were, on our behalf, of the heavenly inheritance, and giving us the assurance of being with Him.

He is gone to prepare a place for His people, and He says, " And if I go and prepare a place for you, I will come again, and receive you unto myself; that where I am, there ye may be also." John xiv. 3. Having offered an all-sufficient sacrifice, and being brought again from the dead through the blood of the ever-lasting covenant, He has entered into the most holy place with His own blood, as the glorious head and representative of His body the Church. He is made for ever an high priest after the order of Melchisedec.

CHAPTER VII.

THE Apostle now proceeds to unveil the face of Moses in the account which he gives of Melchisedec. We have formerly adverted to the depth and fulness of the instruction contained in the Word of God. We have seen how much instruction our Apostle elicits from what is recorded of the oath in Psalm xcv. 11, and the same observation applies to the history of Melchisedec, respecting whom we may observe that we can know no more than what Moses records in the Book of Genesis, and the commentary on the account given by our Apostle. All conjectures which we may form on the subject are out of place. We must take the narrative of Moses just as it stands. The Apostle had repeatedly spoken of Christ as our high priest, chap. ii. 17, iii. 1, iv. 14, 15, v. 5, 6. To this effect he had been called of God, and his priesthood was after the order of Melchisedec, which is proved by a quotation from

Psalm cx. Chap. v. 6. This was a subject of
great importance, and is therefore repeated
v. 10. After some preliminary observations
the Apostle again describes Jesus as made an
high priest after the order of Melchisedec,
Chap. vi. 20, and at the same time enters more
fully into the account given of him, explaining
the mystery and what Moses records concerning
this very eminent personage.

Before entering upon this subject we may
advert to the opinion which has been advanced
that Melchisedec was the Son of God. This
notion is sufficiently refuted by his being
said to be made like unto the Son of God;
language which could not be employed if he
were actually such: a thing cannot be said to
be like to itself. Again, Christ was a high priest
after the order of Melchisedec; if then he
were Melchisedec he was made a high priest
after his own order. It is true Christ in the
character of the angel Jehovah, the angel of
the Covenant, appeared in the likeness of man
to the patriarch, but Christ was not incarnate
till he was born of Mary, and therefore could
not be a priest; for every high priest is represented as taken from among men, chap. v. 1,
and it " behoved him to be made like unto his
brethren, that he might be a merciful and
faithful high priest," chap. ii. 17, not merely

having the appearance of a man, but being actually such.

V. 1.—For this Melchisedec, king of Salem, priest of the most high God, who met Abraham returning from the slaughter of the kings, and blessed him.

Melchisedec, after whose order Christ had been declared to be a priest, was king of Salem. This was, probably, Jerusalem, but of this we can have no certainty, nor is it of the smallest importance in order to our entering into the meaning of the Apostle. He was also priest of the most High God, Gen. xiv. 19, so that he united in his own person the offices of king and priest; he was, therefore, a royal priest. He met Abraham and blessed him, after the slaughter of the kings who had taken Lot, his nephew, prisoner.

This was a part of the duty of a priest in Israel. He offered the sacrifices, burnt incense, and blessed the people. Numbers vi. 22, 27. The blessing which he pronounced on the patriarch is recorded. Gen. xiv. 19, 20.

V. 2.—To whom also Abraham gave a tenth part of all; first being by interpretation King of righteousness, and after that also King of Salem, which is, King of peace.

Abraham gave to Melchisedec tithes of all, viz., of the spoils of the kings whom he had slain. This is the first time that we read of tithes in the Scripture, and, no doubt, this was the example followed by Jacob when he vowed a vow at Bethel, Gen. xxviii. 22, although it does not appear to whom the portion devoted by him to God was to be given.

There is a mystery in the name of Melchisedec.* Its interpretation is king of righteousness. This is descriptive of the Son of God, Psalm xlv. 6, Hab. i. 8, Luke xix. 38, Isaiah xxxii. 1, John i. 49, xviii. 37. He was also king of Salem, which is by interpretation king of peace, which completed his resemblance to the Son of God. Psalm lxxii. 1, 3, and 7.

V. 3.— Without father, without mother, without descent, having neither beginning of days, nor end of life ; but made like unto the Son of God ; abideth a priest continually.

We have already observed that Melchisedec was a man ; he must, therefore, have had a father and a mother, but his priesthood was not by descent like that of the sons of Aaron, " having neither beginning of days nor end of

---

* Names in Scripture were frequently, if not always, given to denote something characteristic concerning them, such as Noah, Gen. v. 29 ; Isaac, Jacob, &c. ; and sometimes their names were changed in token of some favour vouchsafed to them, such as Abraham, Sarah, Israel, Solomon.

life." We may again observe that in the description given of Melchisedec no conjecture is admissible ; we must suppose nothing, but take the account given in Scripture as we find it, without addition or diminution. Now in regard to his parents the Scripture is silent, and it was not the intention of the Holy Ghost by the Apostle to add to the information already given. We read nothing of his father or mother, or of his descent. We read of Aaron and his sons being consecrated to, and entering on, the priest's office, and of their deaths, but nothing of this kind is related of Melchisedec. He appears in the Scripture as a royal priest executing his office, and there he remains a remarkable type of the Son of God whose priesthood is everlasting.

V. 4.—*Now consider how great this man was, unto whom even the patriarch Abraham gave the tenth of the spoils.*

Having directed the attention of the Hebrews to this royal priest, who in so many particulars was an emblem of the high priest of our profession, the Apostle pauses to consider how great this man was to whom even the patriarch* Araham gave the tenth of the spoils.

V. 5.—*And verily they that are of the sons of Levi,*

* The word patriarch means head of the fathers, and is so translated in the Syriac version.

who receive the office of the priesthood, have a command-
ment to take tithes of the people according to the law, that
is, of their brethren, though they come out of the loins of
Abraham.

The priests in Israel were of the tribe of
Levi and of the family of Aaron. By Divine
appointment they received tithes of their
brethren, who were, like themselves, descendants
of Abraham.

V. 6.—But he whose descent is not counted from them
received tithes of Abraham, and blessed him that had the
promises.

But he whose descent is not counted from
them, and who, consequently, did not derive
his title to receive tithes from them, *received*
tithes of Abraham, and blessed him, to whom
God had given the promises of being the
progenitor of Christ and the father of all
believers.

V. 7.—And without all contradiction the less is blessed
of the better.

Upon this there can be no question, a father
blesses his children, a priest blesses those for
whom he ministers, and Abraham, by receiving
Melchisedec, blessing and paying him tithes,
acknowledged himself his inferior.

V. 8.—And here men that die receive tithes ; but
there he receiveth them of whom it is witnessed that he
liveth.

Under the Jewish economy men that die receive tithes, but in the account of Abraham's intercourse with Melchisedec he received tithes, of whose death we have no account, it is only testified that he lived.* Of all the Jewish priests we read that they died and were succeeded by others, but we find Melchisedec engaged in the discharge of the duties of his office, and there we leave him.

V. 9.—*And as I may so say, Levi also, who receiveth tithes, payed tithes in Abraham.*

And indeed Levi may be said to have paid tithes in Abraham, the progenitor of the whole family of Israel.

V. 10. *For he was yet in the loins of his father, when Melchisedec met him.*

V. 11. *If therefore perfection were by the Levitical priesthood, (for under it the people received the law,) what further need was there that another priest should rise after the order of Melchisedec, and not be called after the order of Aaron ?*

We have already noticed that the word perfect occurs very frequently in this Epistle, it means the fulfilment, or completion, of an object.

* He *received them ;* this is a supplement, and should be in the imperfect tense, as likewise *lived* instead of liveth. The Scripture testifies of Melchisedec, as living and exercising his priesthood. It gives no hint of his death.

Here our Apostle argues the weakness and insufficiency of the Levitical priesthood, from the Scripture foretelling that another priest should arise after the order of Melchisedec and not after the order of Aaron.

V. 12.—*For the priesthood being changed, there is made of necessity a change also of the law.*

For the priesthood being changed, there is necessarily *a change also of the law.* Sacrifices were to be offered and incense offered only by the family of Aaron. Theirs was an everlasting priesthood coeval with the Mosaic dispensation, and therefore the change of the priesthood necessarily involved a change of the law.

V. 13.—*For he of whom these things are spoken pertaineth to another tribe, of which no man gave attendance at the altar.*

For he was declared a priest after the order of Melchisedec, ch. iii. 1, iv. 14, 15, and v. 4—10, and pertained to another tribe of which no man officiated at the altar. We have seen that the priesthood had been expressly limited to the family of Aaron, and the appointment was confirmed in a very remarkable manner. When Izhar, the son of Levi, and Dathan and Abiram, the sons of Eliab, and On, the son of Peleth, sons of Reuben, sought the priesthood, Num. xvi. 3—31, alleging that all the congre-

gation was holy, and complained that Moses
and Aaron lifted up themselves above the congregation of the Lord, they took their censers
and put fire in them, and laid incense thereon,
standing in the door of the tabernacle. The
earth opened her mouth and swallowed them
up, and of their censers were made broad
plates for a covering of the altar,—" To be a
memorial unto the children of Israel, that no
stranger, which is not of the seed of Aaron,
come near to offer incense before the Lord;
that he be not as Korah, and as his company :
as the Lord said to him by the hand of Moses."
Num. xvi. 40. And not only so, but by the
Lord's commandment the rods of the princes of
the congregation, twelve rods, were laid before
the Lord in the Tabernacle, and next day
Aaron's rod was budded and bloomed blossoms
and yielded almonds, Num. xvii. This settled
the matter; the children of Israel said,
" Whosoever cometh anything near unto the
tabernacle of the Lord shall die." Num.
xvii. 13.

*V. 14.—For it is evident that our Lord sprang out of
Juda; of which tribe Moses spake nothing concerning
priesthood.*

The language of the Apostle merits special
attention. We have seen that the priesthood in Israel was irrevocably limited to the

family of Aaron. Here we are told that
Moses spake nothing concerning priesthood in
the tribe of Judah.*   At first sight this may
appear but a negative proof, but the proof that
the priesthood was exclusively confined to the
family of Aaron was most positive. The family
of Aaron was expressly designated to this office,
and we have seen that the earth opened and
swallowed up 250 chief men of the congregation for presuming to burn incense, and that the
priesthood was further established in Aaron's
family by his rod blossoming and bearing
almonds.   Why then does this Apostle say that
Moses *spake nothing* concerning priesthood
in the tribe of Judah?   No doubt to show
the fallacy of the assertion that if such a
thing is not prohibited it may therefore be
practised.

Here we are guarded against this sophistry,
and taught that whatever is not enjoined in
the worship of God is virtually forbidden.
There are two ways in which any religious
observance is enjoined, precept and example.
When we have an express precept nothing
more is necessary; but apostolic example is
equally binding. The Apostles delivered the

---

* One of the greatest of the kings of the same tribe
presumed to offer incense, and was struck with leprosy
to the day of his death. 2 Chron. xxvi. 21.

same directions to every church, 1 Cor. iv. 17, vii. 17; of this we have conclusive evidence in what is written on a comparatively unimportant subject. In the Church at Corinth some of the women, probably from the false principle that there was neither male nor female in Christ Jesus, and that therefore there should be no distinction in the Church, prayed and sang praises with their heads uncovered. The Apostle showed that this was improper, and concludes his argument,—" But if any man seem to be contentious, we have no such custom, neither the churches of God." 1 Cor. xi. 16. It is impossible for language more clearly to prove that we are to be guided by the recorded example of the apostolic churches. This is all that is necessary to put a stop to the endless divisions which prevail among the disciples of Christ.

But it has happened to them, as to mankind after the fall, God revealed himself in the seed of the woman, that is Christ, and appointed ordinances of worship. This is evident from the sacrifices of Cain and Abel. Through faith Abel offered a more excellent sacrifice than Cain, and faith must have respect to the Divine testimony; but when they thus knew God they glorified him not as God, by receiving and acting upon the instructions which he was

pleased to deliver.   They professed themselves
to be wise, and capable of discovering the most
acceptable mode of worshipping God, and their
wisdom issued in their changing the image of
the incorruptible God into an image made like
unto corruptible man, and birds and beasts and
four-footed things; and as the meet reward of
their folly and wickedness God gave them up
to every moral abomination.

Precisely the same course has been adopted
since the promulgation of the Gospel, and this
has issued in the manifestation of the man of
sin, and the innumerable divisions of the people
of God, fully realizing the description of what
took place when there was no king in Israel;
every man did what seemed right in his own
eyes.   Now as Moses, speaking nothing concerning priesthood in the tribe of Judah, pre-
cluded our Lord from acting as a priest under
that dispensation, so the Lord and His apostles,
speaking nothing of any ordinance of worship,
is tantamount to a positive prohibition.

Here we may observe the directions given by
the Apostle to guard the Thessalonians against
being involved in this mystery of iniquity :—
" Therefore, brethren, stand fast, and hold the
traditions which ye have been taught, whether by
word or our epistle." 2 Thess. ii. 15. This is a sufficient, and, in fact, the only security against their

being involved in the apostacy. It originated
in the fancied liberty of introducing into the
worship of God ceremonies He had not enjoined, but which appeared calculated to have
a good effect on the worshippers. This principle, once introduced, opened the floodgates of
corruption. The doctrine of Christ is embodied
in the few and simple ordinances which He has
appointed; but, when these ordinances were
changed, a new and false doctrine was exhibited,
and gradually the Gospel of Christ was transformed into a system of will-worship and
idolatry. The only remedy for this state of
things was to adhere, without addition or diminution, to what is prescribed by the apostles,
or exhibited in their practice, as recorded in
their epistles.

*V. 15.—And it is yet far more evident: for that after
the similitude of Melchisedec there ariseth another priest.*

It is still more evident that another priest was
to arise after the similitude of Melchisedec.
This was plainly declared in the 110th Psalm. In
chap. v. 6 the Apostle describes the Lord Jesus
as a Priest after the order of Melchisedec, here
He is said to be after the similitude of Melchisedec. The resemblance holds in a variety
of particulars. He united in Himself the kingly
and priestly offices; He did not succeed to them
by birth, nor had He any successor. There

are also other particulars of resemblance to which the Apostle adverts.

V. 16.—*Who is made, not after the law of a carnal commandment, but after the power of an endless life.*

The Aaronic priesthood was made after the law of a carnal commandment, the son succeeding his father as death opened the succession; but the priesthood of Christ was after the power of an endless life, enduring in immortal strength.

V. 17.—*For he testifieth, Thou art a priest for ever after the order of Melchisedec.*

For He (the Father) testified of Him, Thou art a priest for ever after the order of Melchisedec, which the Apostle had proved was altogether different from the order of Aaron.

V. 18.—*For there is verily a disannulling of the commandment going before for the weakness and unprofitableness thereof.*

For there is verily a disannulling of the commandment going before, which the Apostle had described as a carnal commandment, and, consequently, weak through the flesh. Rom. viii. 3. This, however, is applicable to the whole law, the stability or removal of which depends on the continuance or abolition of the priesthood, which we have seen was to be coeval with the dispensation, of which it formed the most important part.

V. 19.—For the law made nothing perfect, but the bringing in of a better hope did ; by the which we draw nigh unto God.

The Apostle had previously inquired if perfection were by the Levitical priesthood, under which the people had received the law—they were closely and inseparably blended—why another priest was foretold after a different order? Here he says the law made nothing perfect, it was merely the introduction of a better hope,* by which we draw near to God. It was no more than a shadow of good things to come, chap. x. 1, and of that glorious dispensation under which believers draw nigh to God, having access by one Spirit to the Father. Eph. ii. 18; iii. 12; Rom. v. 2.

V. 20.—And inasmuch as not without an oath he was made priest.

Here the Apostle proceeds to another point of superiority of the priesthood of Christ, proceeding still to comment on Ps. cx. The Apostle's object is to prove the superiority of the priesthood of Christ to the Levitical priest-

---

* Our translators have inserted the supplement *did*, but it evidently should be *was*. This passage generally corresponds with chap. x. 1.

hood, from the description given of the former in Ps. cx. He had shown that Christ's priesthood was everlasting, while the Levitical priesthood passed from father to son; and here he proceeds to another argument for its superiority—it was made with an oath. Our translators have inserted a supplement, " He was made a priest," which is necessary for completing the sense.

V. 21.—(*For those priests were made without an oath; but this with an oath by him that said unto him, The Lord sware and will not repent, Thou art a priest for ever after the order of Melchisedec.*)

This is a parenthesis, and contains a proof of the superiority of the priesthood of Christ from the Levitical priesthood, which was made without an oath, because it was only temporary; but the priesthood of Christ with an oath, which rendered it, and, consequently, the covenant with which it stood connected, everlasting.

V. 22.—*By so much was Jesus made a surety of a better testament.*

By so much Jesus was made the surety of a better covenant.—The word rendered "surety" does not occur in any other passage of the New Testament; it is derived from the word *near,* and is equivalent to mediator—one through whom we draw near. Israel drew near to God through the Levitical priests; but the Apostle had shown that the Mosaic dispensation was temporary, and merely introductory to a better, even an eternal covenant, of which Jesus is the Mediator. It had been previously proved that the continuance of the law depended on the continuance of the Aaronic priesthood, ver. 12. Aaron had four sons, two of whom died immediately after they had entered on their office; so that the continuance of the Jewish dispensation depended on the lives of the survivors, and their leaving male children. The priests might, therefore, with great propriety, be called the sureties of the Sinai covenant; while Jesus, whose priesthood is everlasting, is the Surety of a better covenant. Our translators have rendered the word διαθηκη in this place *testament*. The LXX.* uniformly translates the Hebrew word *Pruth*, by covenant, and in the Old Testament they are followed in our version.

It occurs thirty-one times in the New Testament, and is translated covenant, excepting in seven places; and it would have been much better if it had been uniformly translated covenant, and there is no good reason for this not having been done.

* The Septuagint translation of the Old Testament into Greek was made about three hundred years before Christ.

V. 23.—And they truly were many priests, because they were not suffered to continue by reason of death.

The priesthood of the house of Aaron comprehended many individuals, because they were mortal, which implied the temporary nature of the Sinai covenant, to which they were attached, and of which they were the sureties.

V. 24.—But this man, because he continueth ever, hath an unchangeable priesthood.

But this man, because, according to the oath, he continueth ever, hath an unchangeable priesthood, which, in like manner, implies the stability of the covenant of which He is the Surety.

V. 25.— Wherefore he is able also to save them to the uttermost that come unto God by him, seeing he ever liveth to make intercession for them.

In consequence of His unchangeable priesthood, He is able to save to the uttermost, or for evermore, those that come unto God by Him, seeing He ever liveth to make intercession for them. The intercession of Christ is founded on His atonement, whereby He hath magnified the law of God, and made it honourable, restoring what He took not away. He bore the sins of His people in His own body on the tree. He once suffered for sins, the just for the unjust, that He might bring them to God. "Forasmuch, then, as the children are par-

takers of flesh and blood, he also himself likewise took part of the same; that through death
he might destroy him that had the power of
death, that is, the devil; and deliver them who
through fear of death were all their lifetime
subject to bondage." Heb. ii. 14, 15. "He
gave himself for them, an offering and a sacrifice unto God of a sweet-smelling savour."
Eph. v. 2.

Had it so pleased God, the whole race of
mankind might doubtless have been saved by
His death. It was a sacrifice of infinite value;
and, had it so pleased God, might have expiated the sins of all men. Had such been the
case, however, it might have been alleged that
mankind had been hardly dealt with; but a
part of them, like the rebel angels, perished,
while an innumerable multitude of our fallen
race chosen in Christ before the foundation
of the world, are washed in His blood, and
created anew in Him who is to them the
spring and source of their spiritual, as the first
Adam was of their natural life; and as their
first father's death was the death-knell of the
whole family, so the eternal life to which
Christ has risen is the assured pledge of all
His people, even those whom He is not ashamed
to call brethren, in contradistinction to those
to whom He will declare, "I never knew

you," living and reigning with Him for ever and ever.

V. 26.—For such an High Priest became us, who is holy, harmless, undefiled, separate from sinners, and made higher than the heavens.

The Apostle then proceeds to describe the character of our High Priest. " Such an High Priest became us." We have the same expression, chap. ii. 10, " For it became him, for whom are all things, and by whom are all things, in bringing many sons unto glory, to make the captain of their salvation perfect through sufferings." It corresponded with and necessarily resulted from His character, that the Captain of our salvation should be fully qualified for His office through sufferings. In exercising mercy, God could not cease to be just and true. There could be no jarring of His glorious attributes. He had denounced death as the wages of sin, and fallen man must die after a life of sorrow and suffering. When He constituted His only-begotten Son the Head of the seed of the woman, it was necessary that this second Adam should take part with the children whom God had given Him in flesh and blood ; that He should be a man of sorrows and acquainted with grief ; and not only so, but that He should be made free among the dead, because the wages of sin is death.

The full penalty was exacted of Him. The first man had violated the law of God, as if its burden was too grievous to be borne; and it behoved the second Adam, the surety and representative of God's chosen family, to wipe off the foul aspersion by cheerfully obeying that law; although now, in consequence of sin, his obedience was connected with self-denial and suffering. He tasted all the bitterness of death, as the expiator of the guilt of His brethren, and as the reward of His obedience unto death, receiving a new and endless life, which He communicates to all His brethren.

In the passage under consideration, we are taught that it necessarily resulted from our circumstances that our High Priest should be holy; not merely separated from His brethren, to stand between them and God; not only free from any bodily defect or blemish; but holy, perfectly and absolutely holy, as God is holy, harmless, and undefiled even in passing through this polluted world. *

* The priests under the law were liable to contract defilement, both by contact with anything unclean, and by bodily infirmities; but our High Priest is undefiled. He was purity itself; nothing could render Him unclean. It is remarkable that our Lord proved this by laying hands on lepers, and touching the dead. Matt. viii. 2, 3; Luke vii. 14. Temptation proved like the application of fire to an incombustible substance.

The prince of this world came, but he found
nothing in Jesus on which his venom could fix;
neither the pangs of hunger, the desire of admiration, nor the possession of power led Him
for a moment to swerve from that undeviating
obedience which the holy law required. He
could challenge His enemies to convict Him of
sin, and He could appeal to His Father for His
love to the law. It is exceeding broad; it ex-
tends to the thoughts and intents of the heart;
but He felt no wanderings of desire that the
obedience it required should be less extensive.
Being Himself infinitely holy, as Immanuel,
God with us, the image of the invisible God,
an image so exact that he who saw Him saw
the Father, the law was in His heart on account
of its perfect purity. Ps. cxix. 140.

Another qualification essential to our High
Priest was, that He should be made higher
than the heavens. The Apostle had already
proved the superiority of Christ to the angels.
He had by inheritance obtained a more excellent name than they, Heb. i. 4; nay, had been
described as God seated on His eternal throne,
Heb. i. 8. He had ascended far above all
heavens, that He might fill all things. Eph.
iv. 10. In delivering their commission to His
Apostles, He informed them that all power was
committed to Him in heaven and in earth.

Matt. xxviii. 18. As God over all, He ever possessed this power; but, in the passage referred to, he speaks of it as given to Him in the character of Mediator. Power was given Him over all flesh, that He might give eternal life to as many as the Father had given Him. John xvii. 2. As the Father raiseth the dead, and quickeneth them, so the Son quickeneth whom He will. John v. 21. All that are in the grave shall hear His voice, and receive from Him their irreversible sentence. Such is the matchless glory of our High Priest, and such an high priest became us. It is the property of wisdom in the use of means neither to employ such as may prove insufficient, nor such as are redundant. This is exemplified in the character of our High Priest; all His power and glory are essential to the discharge of His office. Such an high priest became us.

We see, then, in our great High Priest every necessary qualification; unspotted holiness, to meet the utmost demands of the law. We are taught that the heavens are not clean in the sight of God, but He is ever well pleased in His beloved Son. He sees all His own perfections fully reflected by Him. Those whom He came to deliver were dead; the curse of God lay heavy on them; and so great was the work of redeeming His people, that the whole

creation was, so to speak, put in motion for
their recovery; and therefore angels, principalities, and powers were made subject to Him,
and thus He was made higher than the heavens.

*V. 27.—Who needeth not daily, as those high priests,
to offer up sacrifice, first for his own sins, and then for
the people's: for this he did once, when he offered up
himself.*

It follows that he had no occasion, like the
Jewish high priests, to offer many sacrifices;
first, for his own sins, and then for those of the
people. Sins he had none; his hands were
clean, his heart was pure, and he fully expiated
the sins of his people by once offering himself
as a Lamb without spot or blemish.

The grave had not ceased to cry, Give, give,
and those who entered its gloomy chambers
mouldered to dust; but the Holy One of God
could see no corruption, the earth cast forth
her dead, thus declaring that the dominion of
death was at an end; that, in fact, it was abolished, being deprived of its sting, and the
grave converted into a bed of rest from which
all the redeemed shall come forth, that in one
body they may occupy those mansions which
the Firstborn is gone before to prepare.

*V. 28.—For the law maketh men high priests which
have infirmity: but the word of the oath, which was since
the law, maketh the Son, who is consecrated for evermore.*

The law constitutes men high priests which
have infirmity, and who, by reason of death,
cannot continue in their office; but the word
of the oath, which was uttered since the law,
Thou art a high priest for ever after the order
of Melchisedec, constitutes the Son of God a
priest for evermore.

CHAPTER VIII.

THE Apostle had proposed to leave the elements, or first principles, of Christian doctrine, (chap. vi.,) which we have interpreted of the types and figures of the Mosaic law. That such was his meaning is evident from the course he actually pursues; in the first place proving the security of the heirs of promise, from the oath by which the blessing was secured to Abraham and his seed; then proceeding to unveil the mysteries of the priesthood of Melchisedec, and to show its accomplishment in the everlasting priesthood of Christ, together with the benefits derived from him by those to whom he stands in the relation of their High Priest. He now sums up what he had previously taught, by giving a comprehensive view of the superiority of the new covenant over the covenant of Sinai.

V. 1.—Now of the things which we have spoken this is the sum: We have such an high priest, who is set on the right hand of the throne of the Majesty in the heavens.

The sum of what he had said of the priesthood of Christ was that believers have an high priest, who is set on the right hand of the throne of God, according to the promise in the cxth Psalm, which he had so fully illustrated.

V. 2.—A minister of the sanctuary, and of the true tabernacle which the Lord pitched, and not man.

He was a minister of the holy places, τῶν ἁγίων, in distinction to the tabernacle, or royal tent, in which the God of Israel represented himself as dwelling among his chosen people, first in the wilderness, and then in the land of Canaan.

The true tabernacle may either be understood of heaven, or of the body which was prepared for the incarnation of Christ, which was essential to his unity with his people, chap. ii. 11, and being qualified to act as their high priest, chap. v. 1. The tabernacle was the habitation of the God of Israel, and we find Jesus, when the Jews desired a sign, saying, " Destroy this temple and in three days I will raise it up, but he spake of the temple of his body," John ii. 18—21, or, perhaps, it rather means heaven itself, in distinction from the worldly sanctuary. He afterwards teaches that Christ is not entered: " For Christ is not entered into the holy places made with hands, which are the figures of the true; but into heaven itself, now to appear in the presence of God for us," chap. ix. 24.

V. 3.—For every high priest is ordained to offer gifts and sacrifices: wherefore it is of necessity that this man have somewhat also to offer.

As every high priest is ordained to offer gifts, free will offerings, and propitiatory sacrifices, it is therefore necessary that this High Priest have somewhat to offer.

V. 4. For if he were on earth he should not be a priest, seeing that there are priests that offer gifts according to the law.

For if he were on earth he could not be a priest, seeing an order of priests were already constituted who offered gifts and sacrifices according to the law.

V. 5.—Who serve unto the example and shadow of heavenly things, as Moses was admonished of God when he was about to make the tabernacle: for, See, saith he, that thou make all things according to the pattern showed to thee in the mount.

The services of these priests were an example and shadow of heavenly things, which was intimated to Moses by the charge given him to make all things according to the pattern showed him in the mount. Some suppose that we are here taught that not only minute directions were given to Moses respecting the tabernacle and the services of the Levitical priesthood, but that he received an explanation of the mystery or parable which he was employed to communicate to Israel, and this interpretation receives countenance from what the Lord said on the occasion of the difference which arose between Moses and Aaron and Miriam: " Hear now my words: If there be a prophet among you, I the Lord will make myself known unto him in a vision, and will speak unto him in a dream. My servant Moses is not so, who is faithful in all mine house. With him will I speak mouth to mouth, even apparently, and not in dark speeches; and the similitude of the Lord shall he behold: wherefore then were ye not afraid to speak against my servant Moses?" Numbers xii. 6—8. Now it may be alleged that if Moses only beheld a pattern of the tabernacle and the vessels of the ministry of Aaron and his sons, the Lord only made his will known to him in a vision. From the language employed, however, that he was to make all things according to the pattern showed to him in the mount, it would appear that he did not see the reality, but simply a pattern, namely, the tabernacle complete in all its parts, and the priests performing their various services, which was " an example and shadow of heavenly things." This interpretation appears to be confirmed by what the Lord said to his servant when he besought the Lord to show him his glory:

" And he said, Thou canst not see my face: for there shall no man see me, and live. And the Lord said, Behold, there is a place by me, and thou shalt stand upon a rock : And it shall come to pass, while my glory passeth by, that I will put thee in a clift of the rock, and will cover thee with my hand while I pass by : And I will take away mine hand, and thou shalt see my back parts : but my face shall not be seen." Exod. xxxiii. 20—23. Had it been given to Moses to behold the true tabernacle, and our great High Priest ministering therein, he would have seen God's face, or, in other words, the glory of the Lord in the unveiled face of Jesus Christ; 2 Cor. iii. 18; according to our Lord's words, " He that hath seen me hath seen the Father," John xiv. 9. Hence we conclude that a vision of the tabernacle and its services was given to Moses in the Mount, and that, as in the case of David, all this the Lord made him, understand in writing by His hand upon him, even all the works of this pattern. 1 Chron. xxviii. 19.

If it be asked, how Moses was admonished of God that what was enjoined was an example and shadow of heavenly things, by being charged to make all things according to the pattern showed to him in the Mount? it is replied, that the care enjoined not to deviate in any par-

ticular from the pattern shown to him evidently
implied that it was an emblem of heavenly
things, for how otherwise would God have
enjoined such minute attention to services
which, considered in themselves, were unworthy
of his notice ?

*V. 6.—But now hath he obtained a more excellent
ministry, by how much also he is the mediator of a better
covenant, which was established upon better promises.*

The Apostle had shown that it behoved our
great High Priest to have somewhat to offer,
since the very object of the priestly office is to
offer gifts and sacrifices for sins, ch. v. 1. He
also argues that this offering could not be made
upon earth, because priests were already appointed exclusively to offer gifts according to
the law, whose services are an example and
shadow of heavenly things, as had been plainly
intimated to Moses. He therefore concludes
that our great High Priest hath obtained a
more excellent ministry, being the mediator of
a better covenant, which was established upon
better promises. He thus introduced what
he intended to say of the new covenant, the
difference between which and the Sinai covenant is the grand object of the Epistle.

Jesus is here described as the mediator of a
better covenant. We are taught that the first
covenant was ordained by angels in the hand of

a mediator, Gal. iii. 19, referring to Moses, who stood between God and the people Israel, went up to the mount with God, and received the instructions which he was pleased to deliver. But the Apostle is here speaking of the priesthood of Christ, and although Moses was the mediator of the Sinai covenant, yet when he was removed the high priest acted as mediator, for he presented the gifts and sacrifices which were enjoined, burned incense, and blessed them, and inquired of God upon any emergency which arose; but Jesus had obtained a more excellent ministry, being the mediator of a better covenant, established upon better promises.

The better promises of the new covenant are salvation from sin and eternal life. The promises of the Sinai covenant were all earthly, such as long life in the land of Canaan, plentiful harvests, victory over their enemies, and national prosperity. This may be ascertained by consulting Lev. xxvi., Deut. xxviii., and therefore that covenant was ratified with the blood of bulls and goats which can never take away sin, and only sanctifies to the purifying of the flesh. The new covenant, as has been already stated, is established upon better promises and was ratified with the blood of Christ, which cleanseth the children of the covenant

from all sin. They shall all be presented
faultless before the presence of God's glory
with exceeding joy.

V. 7.—For if that first covenant had been faultless,
then should no place have been sought for the second.

Had the first covenant been faultless there
would have been no place for a second. It has
been already observed, ch. vii. 19, that God
does nothing in vain. In his dealings with
mankind there are no works of supererogation.

V. 8.—For finding fault with them, he saith, Behold,
the days come, saith the Lord, when I will make a new
covenant with the house of Israel and with the house of
Judah.

In God's dispensations towards Israel we
perceive the highest wisdom. The misunderstanding of it has been indeed the great means
of corrupting the religion of Jesus. The folly
and wickedness of man perverts and abuses the
goodness of God. " All the words of his
mouth are in righteousness, there is nothing
perverse or froward in them." Prov. viii. 8.
The Sinai covenant was very glorious, and this
was signified by the glory of Moses' countenance, but this glory not enduring, imported
the vanishing away of the glory of the first
covenant, when it had answered the purpose of
introducing the second. The first covenant
fully attained its Divine end, namely that of

introducing the second covenant; but it was never intended to give eternal life, and therefore, considered in itself, it was not faultless nor adequate to the exigencies of fallen man. Hence the Lord, finding fault, says to the Israelites,* " Behold the days come when I will make a new covenant with the house of Israel and with the house of Judah." The first covenant was made with Israel after the flesh, the seed of Abraham, Isaac, and Jacob; the new covenant is made with those that are Christ's, who are Abraham's seed and heirs according to the promise. Gal. iii. 29. God adopted Israel after the flesh to be his peculiar people, in virtue of their being the seed of Abraham, and consequently related to Christ; but it was a carnal relation; hence Israel were blessed with all carnal blessings in earthly places, namely, the land flowing with milk and honey. But the true Israel, in virtue of their spiritual relation to Christ, are blessed with all spiritual blessings in heavenly places in Christ Jesus. Eph. i. 3.

* When the Lord promised to make a new covenant, he was not finding fault with Israel. Jer. xxxi. 31. The Apostle had said, if the first covenant had been faultless, then no place should have been found for the second. The promise of a new covenant was virtually finding fault with the old, declaring its insufficiency.

V. 9.—Not according to the covenant that I made with their fathers in the day when I took them by the hand to lead them out of the land of Egypt ; because they continued not in my covenant, and I regarded them not, saith the Lord.

Here we have a characteristic of the new and better covenant. It is first described negatively. It was not to be according to the covenant that God made with their fathers,* when He took them by the hand to lead them out of the land of Egypt. †

Before forty days had elapsed since they trembled under the voice of God, they broke the covenant by bowing to the golden calf ; and their whole history was a continued course of rebellion. Hence the judgments executed on them, and their present state of dispersion among all nations. They refused to hearken to their covenant God, who had distinguished them above all other nations ; and therefore they largely experienced the curses denounced against disobedience, until they were cast out of their inheritance.

* Although the believing Gentiles were not descended from Israel after the flesh, yet they are here spoken of as their children. We find the Apostle using the same language, 1 Cor. x. 1.

† The redemption of Israel was temporal, from the bondage of Egypt, as were all their temptations in the wilderness.

V. 10.—For this is the covenant that I will make with the house of Israel after those days, saith the Lord; I will put my laws into their mind, and write them in their hearts: and I will be to them a God, and they shall be to me a people.

Here the covenant is described positively. God engages to put His laws into their minds, and write them upon their hearts. The law delivered to Israel was written on tables of stone, plainly showing them their duty, saying, " This is the way; walk ye in it; " but it gave no strength, no disposition to obey, and is, therefore, described by the Apostle as the letter, or writing, which killeth. The children of the new covenant, on the other hand, are described as the epistle of Christ, written with the Spirit of God in fleshly tables of the heart. They are exhorted to work out their own salvation with fear and trembling, for it is God that worketh in them to will and to do of His good pleasure.

They are chosen unto obedience through sanctification of the Spirit and sprinkling of the blood of Jesus Christ. 1 Pet. i. 2. They are God's workmanship, created in Christ Jesus unto good works, which God had before ordained that they should walk in them. " Moses describeth the righteousness which is of the law, That the man which doeth those things shall live by them. But the righteousness which is of faith speaketh on this wise, Say not in thine heart, Who shall ascend into heaven? (that is, to bring Christ down from above:) or, Who shall descend into the deep? (that is, to bring up Christ again from the dead.) But what saith it? The word is nigh thee, even in thy mouth, and in thy heart: that is, the word of faith, which we preach; that if thou shalt confess with thy mouth the Lord Jesus, and shalt believe in thine heart that God hath raised him from the dead, thou shalt be saved." Rom. x. 5—9. The children of the old covenant were under the law, and were a stiff-necked people; but the children of the new covenant were under grace, and therefore sin shall not have dominion over them. They are the temple of the Holy Ghost which dwelleth in them, which they have of God. "The law," says the Apostle, "was given by Moses; but grace and truth came by Jesus Christ." John i. 17.

And I will be to them a God, &c.—By the Sinai covenant God proclaimed Himself the God of Israel, and required their obedience; but they broke the covenant, by making the golden calf; and although the tables were renewed, still they were rebellious, and brought upon themselves many severe judgments; and not only so, but their rejection

was foretold. " Ye are not my people, and I
will not be your God," Hosea i. 9 ; and again,
" The Lord God shall slay thee, and call his
servants by another name." But, amidst all
their rebellions, there was a remnant according
to the election of grace; and " as the new wine
is found in the cluster, and one saith, Destroy
it not, for a blessing is in it ; so the Lord did
for his servants' sakes, that he might not destroy
them all." Isa. lxv. 8. But when they filled
up the measure of their iniquities, by not only
killing the Lord Jesus, but rejecting the evidence of His resurrection and ascension, in the
outpouring of the Spirit on the day of Pentecost, wrath came upon them to the uttermost;
the Lord, according to His threatening, slew
them, and called His servants by another name.
Acts xi. 26.

By the new covenant God is the God of His
people, in a higher sense than He was to Israel
after the flesh. The privileges which the children of both covenants enjoyed were in virtue
of their relation to Christ. The one was a
carnal relation ; of them, according to the flesh,
Christ came, and, in consequence, they were
blessed with all carnal blessings in earthly
places.

They were redeemed from Egyptian bondage;
they were fed with manna, preserved in the

wilderness, put in possession of a land flowing with milk and honey. Thus were they blessed with all carnal blessings in earthly places. The children of the new covenant are spiritually related to Christ, and are consequently blessed with all spiritual blessings in heavenly places. Their redemption is spiritual; their citizenship is in heaven; their inheritance is incorruptible, undefiled, and fadeth not away.

V. 11.—And they shall not teach every man his neighbour, and every man his brother, saying, Know the Lord: for all shall know me, from the least to the greatest.

This is another part of the blessing bestowed on the children of the new covenant. They all know the Lord, from the least to the greatest. This knowledge is not communicated by every man teaching his neighbour. " It is written in the prophets," says our Lord, " They shall be all taught of God. Every man, therefore, that hath heard and hath learned of the Father cometh to me." John vi. 45. And in exact correspondence with this, the Apostle John says, in writing to believers, " I have not written unto you because ye know not the truth, but because ye know it, and that no lie is of the truth;" and again, " These things have I written unto you concerning them that seduce you. But the anointing which ye have received of him abideth in you, and ye need

not that any man teach you : but as the same
anointing teacheth you of all things, and is
truth, and is no lie, and even as it hath taught
you, ye shall abide in him." 1 John ii. 21, 26,
27. It is unnecessary to add, the expression,
" They shall not teach every man his neighbour,
and every man his brother, Know the Lord,"
does not mean that believers are not to teach
and admonish one another, which is so frequently enjoined by the apostles; the passage
means that the knowledge of the Lord, which
all the children of the new covenant possess, is
not derived from human instruction, but from
the Spirit of Christ taking of the things of
Christ, and showing them unto us. All the
children of the new covenant have received, not
the spirit of the world, but the Spirit that is of
God, that they might know the things that are
freely given to us of God. 1 Cor. ii. 12.

God commanded Moses to make a covenant
with the children of Israel in the land of Moab,
besides the covenant which He made with them
in Horeb. Deut. xxix. 1. In this covenant
He not only warned them against disobedience
by denouncing the awful consequences which
would follow, but informed Israel that when all
these things, the blessing and the curse, had
come upon them, they should be brought into
the land which their fathers possessed, and that

He would circumcise their hearts, and the hearts of their seed, to love the Lord their God. Deut. xxx. 1, 6. Part of this chapter is quoted by the Apostle, who describes it as the language of the righteousness which is of faith, in contrast with the righteousness which is of the law. Rom. x. 5, 9. It is here the Apostle uses greater plainness of speech than Moses, who taught with a vail upon his face; but still he tells us that in the words quoted from Moses there is the language of the righteousness of faith, obscurely communicated by the Jewish lawgiver, but clearly taught under a more glorious dispensation. The account of the new covenant is taken by our Apostle from Jeremiah; but the same truth had been more darkly intimated by Moses, before Israel entered Canaan.

V. 12.—For I will be merciful to their unrighteousness, and their sins and their iniquities will I remember no more.

The sacrifices offered by the law only brought sin to remembrance. Heb. x. 3. They could not remove it; but the prophet, as quoted by the Apostle, foretells that, under the new covenant, God would be merciful to the unrighteousness of His people, and no longer remember their sin. This refers to the perfection of the atonement of the Son of God. The sins of

His people are for ever buried in their Saviour's
grave, and when they are sought for they shall
not be found.   Jer. l. 20; Col. ii. 14.   Thus is
fulfilled the prediction that our great High
Priest should finish transgression, make an end
of sin, make reconciliation for iniquity, and
bring in everlasting righteousness.   His salvation shall be for ever, and His righteousness
shall not be abolished.   Isa. li. 6.   Such is the
superiority of the new dispensation, to which
the old was merely preparatory.   Moses and
the apostles of Christ spoke the same things,
only Moses taught in parables, representing
spiritual and heavenly things under the vail of
things which were carnal and earthly.   The first
covenant was made with the posterity of Abraham, in the line of Isaac and Jacob; the second
with those that are Christ's, who are Abraham's
seed, and heirs according to the promise.

*V. 13.—In that he saith, A new covenant, he hath made
the first old.   Now that which decayeth and waxeth old is
ready to vanish away.*

We have had occasion to notice how much
instruction the Apostles deduce from words
and statements in the Scriptures which we
should be very apt to overlook.   For instance,
from Psalm xcv. 11; and from the account
of Melchisedec, chap. vii. 1—3.   Here we
find another instance of the same thing.

God had promised a *new* covenant, and from
this the Apostle draws the palpable conclusion
of the abolition of the first, or old covenant.
Should it be asked, Is it worthy the character
of the unchangeable God to establish a temporary dispensation ?   Does He not know the
end from the beginning ?   Certainly He does.
But in the establishment and abolition of the
Sinai covenant, there was no change of purpose.
The Mosaic economy was intended as an introduction of the new covenant ; and, instead of its
establishment and abolition being derogatory to
the wisdom of God, like every other part of the
Divine providence it is a striking manifestation
of His manifold wisdom, and affords the most
satisfactory evidence of the truth of revelation.

Had the Scriptures consisted only of one
part, it would naturally have been committed
to one class; and it might have been alleged
that it had been tampered with, and the recorded events been made to suit the predictions
which went before. But this cavil is completely
cut off.

By choosing the seed of Abraham, Isaac,
and Jacob as His peculiar people, of whom,
as concerning the flesh, Christ came, and
committing to them the living oracles which
testify of Christ, and afterwards rejecting them
on account of their unbelief; taking the king-

dom of heaven from them, and giving it to those who, by faith, were spiritually united to Christ; to whom the New Testament was committed; every possibility of collusion was prevented, and an unimpeachable proof given that the prophecies which went before were not the word of man, but that holy men of God spake as they were moved by the Holy Ghost; and not only so, but all the burdensome rites of Jewish worship, and, indeed, the whole history of that singular people, had their fulfilment in the kingdom of God.

In promising a new covenant, the first was made old; for when anything is said to be *new* in comparison of another thing, that must be *old* in comparison of it; and it is self-evident that what decayeth and waxeth old is ready to vanish away.

We have seen that a new and better covenant was made known to Israel by Moses, a covenant of which the token was not circumcision of the flesh, but of the heart, which is explained by Jeremiah, of writing His law in their hearts, and being to them a God in a higher sense than He was to Israel. Jer. xxxi. 33.

The same thing was made known by the prediction that the Lord would raise up to them a prophet like unto Moses, to whom they must hearken, on pain of condign punishment. Deut.

xviii. 18, 19. Now we are taught that "there
arose not a prophet since in Israel like unto
Moses, whom the Lord knew face to face."
Deut. xxxiv. 10. This was ·fulfilled in the
manifestation of the Son of God. Acts iii. 22,
23. Thus we find the abrogation of the Mosaic
economy clearly and repeatedly made known
to Israel. Indeed, how could it be otherwise,
when the blood with which the Sinai covenant
was ratified was that of bulls and goats, which
can only sanctify to the purifying of the flesh ?
Now, as all flesh is grass, and all human glory
like the flower of grass, so all the splendour
of the Jewish worship, being carnal and
earthly, necessarily gave place to that kingdom
which cannot be moved, and, like its great
Author, is the same yesterday, to-day, and for
ever.

The everlasting doors have been thrown open
for the entrance of the King of Glory. He has
for ever sat down at the right hand of the
majesty of the throne in the heavens, and is
engaged in preparing mansions for all his blood-
bought sheep, whom He is successively receiving into everlasting habitations; and when the
mystery of God shall be finished, they shall all
be made perfect in one, and, enriched with the
spoils of death and the grave, shall surround

His exalted throne through the revolving ages
of eternity, reigning with Him in the new
heavens and new earth wherein dwelleth righteousness.

CHAPTER IX.

THE Apostle having proved that the establishment of the new and better covenant, of which Christ is the mediator, had been clearly predicted, proceeds to contrast the ordinances of the old with those of the new covenant.

V. 1.—Then verily the first covenant had also ordinances of divine service, and a worldly sanctuary.

Then verily, &c.—The word covenant is properly supplied by our translators, as in verses 7 and 13 in the preceding chapter. Some would supply tabernacle, but this would occasion an awkward repetition in the end of the verse, and also in verse 2. The ordinances to which the Apostle refers were enjoined by the first covenant. There were ordinances of Divine service, or, rather, of worship, and a worldly sanctuary, or holy place, not only made of worldly materials, but erected in this world, and, as it had been stated, chap. viii. 5, a shadow of heavenly things.

V. 2.—For there was a tabernacle made; the first, wherein was the candlestick, and the table, and the shew-bread; which is called the sanctuary.

For there was a tabernacle made, in the first compartment of which was the candlestick. The candlestick was beaten out of a talent of gold. It had seven lamps, and gave light to the tabernacle. In the vision with which John was favoured, he saw seven golden candlesticks, Rev. i. 12, which are said to be the seven Churches. Ver. 20. The people of God are the light of the world; and perhaps this was shadowed forth by the candlestick with its seven lamps enlightening the tabernacle. Zechariah also saw a golden candlestick with seven lamps. These were supplied with oil by two olive-trees, which are explained by the angel as signifying the supply of the Spirit, by which the truth is maintained in this dark world.

The table.—On this the shewbread was placed; it was of shittim wood, overlaid with gold, and had a cornice, which prevented the leaves from falling off. It was carried by staves of shittim wood, overlaid with gold. It was consecrated by sprinkling of blood, and anointed with oil.

*And the shewbread; * which is called the sanctuary,* or holy place. Exod. xxvi. 33, 35.

* The shewbread consisted of twelve loaves, according

V. 3.—And after the second vail, the tabernacle which is called the Holiest of all.

And after the second vail, &c.—The first vail was the hanging for the door of the tent. Exod. xxvi. 36, 37. The second vail, within which no man in Israel, with the exception of the high priest, was permitted to enter, separated the holy place from the holiest of all.

V. 4.— Which had the golden censer, and the ark of the covenant overlaid round about with gold, wherein was the golden pot that had manna, and Aaron's rod that budded, and the tables of the covenant.

In the most holy place was the golden censer. This was used by the high priest when he went into the holy of holies, for he was not to enter till the cloud of the incense covered the mercy-seat. As the Apostle tells us, it was within the second vail; and, as the high priest was required to burn incense, no doubt it must have been placed so that he could reach it without entering. This golden censer appears not to have

to the number of the tribes of Israel, which were placed on the table. They were renewed every Sabbath, and were eaten only by the priests in the holy place. The tabernacle was the royal pavilion in 'which the King of Israel represented himself as dwelling in the midst of his people. The shewbread seems to have been an intimation of the coming of the Lord Jesus as Immanuel. Human food was provided.

been used on any other occasion than when the high priest entered the holiest of all. In the temple we read of censers of pure gold. 1 Kings vii. 50.

And the ark of the covenant, &c.—The ark was a chest, and it is called the ark of the covenant because in it the two tables of the law, written with the finger of God Himself, were deposited. It is also called the ark of the testimony, because it was a witness of the covenant which God made with Israel, avouching Himself to be their God, and requiring of them obedience. The ark was overlaid round about with pure gold, and had a crown of gold round about it.

Wherein was the golden pot that had manna. —Moses, by Divine commandment, laid up in a golden pot an homer of manna, as a memorial of the bread with which Israel had been fed in the wilderness. The Apostle cannot mean that the pot of manna was within the ark; for it is written, " There was nothing within the ark, save the two tables of stone, which Moses put there at Horeb." 1 Kings viii. 9; 2 Chron. v. 10; and, therefore, "wherein," or " in which," must refer to a remote antecedent σχηνη, called the holiest of all. Ver. 3.

And Aaron's rod that budded.—We have already referred to the sedition of the sons of

Korah, who claimed a right to the priesthood, and were consumed, and noticed that the rod of the chief of each tribe was laid up before the Lord, to ascertain to which tribe the priesthood belonged. All the other rods were unchanged; but Aaron's rod put forth blossoms, and bore almonds, after which there was no further dispute about the priesthood. Moses, by Divine commandment, brought Aaron's rod before the testimony, to be kept for a token against the rebels, Numb. xvii. 10; and the Apostle here informs us it was placed in the holy of holies.

And the tables of the covenant.—We have already seen that they contained the two tables which contained God's covenant with Israel.

V. 5.—And over it the cherubims of glory shadowing the mercyseat; of which we cannot now speak particularly.

The mercyseat was the covering of the ark. Moses having been informed by God that Israel had made the golden calf, came down with the two tables in his hand; and, when he witnessed the idolatrous feast in which the people were engaged, cast down the tables, and broke them at the foot of the mount. This, no doubt, was done in anger, but it was a significant action, showing that the law of which Moses was the minister can only condemn the sinner. Rom. iii. 20.

When the covenant was renewed through the intercession of the mediator, Moses prepared two tables like the first, upon which God again wrote the ten commandments, for the law is unchangeable ; and, by God's commandment, prepared the ark for their reception, the covering of which was called the mercyseat, which was also of pure gold. It was the throne of the God of Israel, from which He spoke to Moses. Exod. xxxvii. 6. No covering had been provided for the first tables, and they were broken before they reached the camp. The ark being covered with the mercyseat, intimated that there was forgiveness with God, and that, while He would by no means clear the guilty, He was the Lord God, merciful and gracious. The tables being covered with the mercyseat, showed that, in God's dealings with His people, mercy and truth have met together, righteousness and peace have kissed each other. Hence we find the Psalmist, quoted by the Apostle, speaking of the blessedness of the man whose sins are *covered*, to whom the Lord will not impute sin.

Christ is the true propitiatory, or mercyseat, Rom. iii. 24, in whom God is revealed as just, and the Justifier of all who believe. Through faith in His blood, pardon is proclaimed to the chief of sinners ; while a more awful manifestation of the justice, purity, and holiness of God is given, than if all Adam's race had been turned into hell, and, like the rebel angels, reserved unto judgment against the great day.

Whether the cherubim, as some suppose, are an order of angels, we know not, although it seems probable; but the cherubim of glory, or the glorious cherubim, were of gold, beaten out of the mercyseat, one at each end. They overshadowed the mercyseat, spoken of by the Apostle, and their wings met in the middle. Their faces were turned towards each other, toward the mercyseat. There appears to be an allusion to their posture, 1 Pet. i. 12, " Which things the angels desire to look into." They are represented as contemplating the wonders of the love of God to sinners of mankind, which, in its height and depth, its breadth and length, passeth knowledge.

Of which we cannot now, &c.—The Apostle intended to go on to what these emblems shadowed forth, and therefore would not further insist on the patterns of things in the heavens.

V. 6.—Now when these things were thus ordained, the priests went always into the first tabernacle, accomplishing the service of God.

Now when these things were thus arranged, the priests went daily into the first tabernacle

or compartment, performing the appointed
service.

*V. 7.—But into the second went the high priest alone
once every year, not without blood, which he offered for
himself, and for the errors of the people.*

But the high priest alone entered the second
compartment, and he only once in the year, not
without blood. He then sprinkled the blood of
the sin-offering upon the mercyseat, and also
the blood of the goat. Thus he offered first for
his own sins, and then for those of the people.

*V. 8.—The Holy Ghost this signifying, that the way
into the holiest of all was not yet made manifest, while as
the first tabernacle was yet standing.*

By giving those directions, and excluding
every man in Israel from entering the most
holy place, the Holy Ghost, by whom all these
directions were given to Moses, 1 Chron.
xxviii., intimated that the way into the holiest
of all was not yet laid open. The truth was but
darkly intimated by these shadowy ordinances.

The word rendered here by our translators
" holiest of all," is των αγιων, literally
" holies," and this is the same word in chap.
viii. 2, and there rendered " sanctuary." This
is evidently the true sanctuary, even heaven
itself; and the holiest of all, or holy places, in
this verse, has evidently the same meaning. It

is placed in contrast with the first tabernacle. This expression is employed, verse 6, to signify the first compartment of the Jewish tabernacle; but here it must be understood of the whole of the tabernacle worship instituted by Moses. This exactly corresponds with what the Apostle says, verse 24, of Christ having entered into heaven itself, there to appear in the presence of God for us. Here the Apostle speaks of the first tabernacle as he had formerly done of the first covenant. While it stood, the way into the true sanctuary was not made manifest.

V. 9.—Which was a figure for the time then present, in which were offered both gifts and sacrifices, that could not make him that did the service perfect, as pertaining to the conscience.

The Mosaic tabernacle was a figure or parable for the time then present, in or during which time * both gifts and sacrifices were offered, which could not give the worshipper the answer of a good conscience, because the blood of bulls and goats could never take away sin; they only sanctified to the purifying of the flesh, removing ceremonial uncleanness, and

* *Which* may refer either to the time, or, as our translators appear to have understood it, to the tabernacle; but, by the gender of the pronoun, the former appears to be intended.

fitting the Israelites to unite in the Mosaic worship.

V. 10.—*Which stood only in meats and drinks, and divers washings, and carnal ordinances, imposed on them until the time of reformation.*

Our translators have added *which stood*, to connect this with the preceding verse ; but this is not necessary. The meats and drinks may be connected with the worshipper, or him that worshippeth (as, indeed, the words stand in the original), with meats and drinks. This has been objected to because the meats and drinks do not comprehend all the Mosaic institutions. But the gifts and sacrifices, verse 9, and the meats and drinks, and divers baptisms, and carnal ordinances, include the whole Mosaic system of worship. The breaking down of the middle wall of partition which separates Jews and Gentiles was intimated to Peter by the great white sheet let down from heaven, with all manner of beasts, and his being commanded to arise, and kill and eat. The Gentiles were now to be fellow-heirs, and of the same body, and partakers of His promise in Christ by the Gospel. The sheet being let down from heaven, and being received up again, might intimate that the Mosaic dispensation, although having no glory, by reason of the glory that excelleth, as exhibited in the new dispensation, was from

God, and should remain for ever, a proof of
His manifold wisdom, in giving a pattern of
spiritual and heavenly things, before the full
manifestation of His glory in the unveiled face
of Jesus Christ.

*V. 11.—But Christ being come an high priest of good
things to come, by a greater and more perfect tabernacle,
not made with hands, that is to say, not of this building.*

*But Christ being made an high priest of good
things to come.*—We have seen that the Gospel
dispensation is termed the world to come, chap.
ii. 5 ; and this appears to be the meaning of good
things to come.   All the blessings of the old
covenant were carnal ; they referred to this
world, as may be seen in the blessings promised for obedience, and the curses pronounced
for disobedience.   Lev. xxvi. ; Deut. xxviii.
But Christ is made an High Priest of a dispensation which conveys spiritual and eternal
blessings.

The comforts and the blessings of time
perish with the using ; the things which are
seen are temporal ; but the things which are
unseen are eternal, and such are the blessings
conveyed to us by our great High Priest.   He
is made an High Priest of good things to come
—an High Priest for ever, chap. vi. 2, and after
the power of an endless life.   Chap. vii. 16.
The Apostle had shown the superiority of our

great High Priest to the priests under the law; and here he contrasts the tabernacle in which he ministers, with that erected by Moses. It was a greater and more perfect tabernacle. The former was only a pattern, the latter was the thing represented. The one was of human workmanship, the other was made by God Himself. The Apostle explains, "Not made with hands," by not of this building, or, more literally, not of this creation. The Most High dwelleth not in temples made with hands. Acts vii. 48. "Thus saith the Lord, The heaven is my throne, and the earth is my footstool: where is the house that ye build unto me? and where is the place of my rest?" Isa. lxvi. 1.

Some consider the greater and more perfect tabernacle, in which Christ ministers, to mean His body, in which He ministers as a priest, in which all the fulness of the Godhead dwells bodily, and this receives some countenance from Christ terming His body a temple, John ii. 19, 20; and from His being charged with saying that He would destroy this temple made with hands, and build another made without hands, Mark xiv. 58; but still it cannot be said that Christ entered once into the tabernacle of His own body, or that he is the minister of His human nature, as He is said to be of the true tabernacle. He is set at the right hand of the majesty in the heavens. Heb. viii. 1. This is the sanctuary of which He is minister. This is the true tabernacle into which He has entered by His own blood. Chap. ix. 12. Heaven itself is, then, the sanctuary where Christ ministers.

V. 12.—*Neither by the blood of goats and calves, but by his own blood; he entered in once into the holy place, having obtained eternal redemption for us.*

In all respects the ministry of our great High Priest is superior to the service of the Mosaic high priest. Jesus is an High Priest of good things to come, not of things present which are seen and temporal, but of those which are unseen and eternal. He ministers in a greater and more perfect tabernacle, Heb. viii. 2; He entered once for all into the most holy place, even heaven itself, having obtained eternal redemption for us. So glorious is His sacrifice that it neither requires nor admits of being repeated. It secures eternal redemption for all for whom it was offered. The Jewish sacrifices could only remove ceremonial uncleanness. The most solemn sacrifice, that on the great day of atonement, had only respect to sins committed during the preceding year; but the sacrifice of Christ hath removed all our sin from us as far as East is distant from the

West. When the sins of those for whom the
sacrifice of our great High Priest was offered
are sought for, they shall not be found. He
offered one sacrifice which never can be repeated, because it hath fully satisfied justice,
answering all the demands of the law, so that
Jesus proclaimed on the Cross, " It is finished "
—eternal redemption is now secured to all the
Israel of God. As the Jewish high priest bore
the names of all the tribes on his shoulders and
breastplate when he entered with the blood of
the sin offering into the holiest of all, the names
of the true Israel are engraved on His heart,
and His intercession for them is founded on His
having magnified and made honourable the law
which they had broken. Such is the unity
between Him and them that they all died in
His death, rose in His resurrection, and are
seated with Him in heavenly places.

*V. 13.—For if the blood of bulls and of goats, and the
ashes of an heifer sprinkling the unclean, sanctifieth to the
purifying of the flesh.*

The Jewish sacrifices being that of bulls and
goats, could never take away sin, they could
only remove ceremonial uncleanness, sanctifying
to the purifying of the flesh ; but by the Divine
appointment they had this effect.

*V. 14.—How much more shall the blood of Christ, who
through the eternal Spirit offered himself without spot to*

God, purge your conscience from dead works to serve the living God?

How much more shall the blood of Christ purge the consciences of his people from dead works? *—The sacrifices appointed by Moses had in themselves no efficacy, but they did sanctify to the purifying of the flesh, they fitted the Israelites who had contracted uncleanness to come into the court of the tabernacle, and to unite in the tabernacle worship.

This was a parable for the time then present. It prefigured the efficacy of the sacrifice of Christ in giving the believer the answer of a good conscience that he might draw near to God with childlike confidence. He who appointed the legal sacrifices, and gave them efficacy to answer the end of their appointment, hath provided a better sacrifice, which gives the true Israel boldness and access with confidence to approach to God. Christ is said to have offered Himself without spot to God.

Reference is here made to the sacrifices offered by the law. A sin-offering must be perfect to be accepted. Lev. xxii. 21; Matt. xviii. 13, 14. This was an emblem of Christ's

* Dead works, or works which merit death. Chap. vi. 1. All are by nature dead in trespasses and sins, hence all their works are dead works. John xiv. 4.

spotless purity, chap. iv. 15. He is a lamb
without blemish and without spot, 1 Pet. i. 19.
Christ offered Himself through the eternal
Spirit. He was truly man born of a woman,
while all the fulness of the Godhead dwelt in
Him bodily. He was also the Father's servant
to "raise up the tribes of Jacob, and to rest
on the preserved of Israel;" and, as all Adam's
posterity received natural life from Him, which
was forfeited by sin, so all the people of God,
all whom He had chosen in Christ, were to
receive spiritual and eternal life from their
great Head. When He entered upon His
public work, and was manifested to Israel by
a figurative burial and resurrection, the Holy
Spirit descended upon Him in a bodily shape
like a dove, and abode upon Him. Thus was
He sealed as the Son of God, the source and
fountain of spiritual life. As the precious oil
poured on the head of Aaron ran down to the
skirts of his garments, so is the Holy Spirit
which he received beyond measure communicated to all His people, who were dead in
trespasses and sins, but are now made alive
through their glorious Head; hence their life is
said to be hid with Christ in God, and because
He lives, they shall live also. By one Spirit
they are all baptized into one body, and are all
made to drink of that one Spirit. All He did

and said was under the guidance of the Spirit.
He said, " My doctrine is not mine, but the
Father's who sent me." He represents Himself as casting out devils by the Spirit of God.
In short, all He did and said upon earth was in
obedience to His Father's will, communicated
through the Spirit; and the last scene of His
eventful life was consequently by the eternal
Spirit through which He offered Himself without spot to God. So entire is the unity of
the persons of the Godhead, that whatever is
done by one is done by all. For instance,
Christ rose from the dead by the glory of the
Father, He laid down His life and took it
again, and He was quickened by the Spirit.
Here we are told that through the eternal
Spirit He offered Himself without spot to
God, and the perfection of this sacrifice
cleanseth believers from all sin, and gives
them boldness and confidence before God.
" Who," they exclaim, " shall lay anything
to the charge of God's elect? It is God that
justifieth, who is he that condemneth? It is
Christ that died, yea, rather that is risen again,
who is even now at the right hand of God, who
also maketh intercession for us." The Father
heareth him always, for His intercession is
founded on that sacrifice of a sweet smelling
savour, in which His Father is ever well

pleased. The eternal covenant between the
Father and the Son ran thus:—" When thou
shalt make his soul an offering for sin, he shall
see his seed, he shall prolong his days, and the
pleasure of the Lord shall prosper in his hand."
Isaiah liii. 10. Never was a service so hard as
that which Jesus served, and never was reward
so glorious as that which He received in recompense. All things are put under His feet ; all
power in heaven and in earth is committed to
Him ; the Father judgeth no man, but hath
committed all judgment to the Son, in order
that His prayer may be fulfilled in all its
extent,—" Father, I will that those whom Thou
hast given me may be with me where I am, that
they may behold my glory, which Thou hast
given me ; " and thus, according to His own
declaration, is He preparing mansions for them,
even an eternal inheritance.

*V. 15.—And for this cause he is the mediator of the
new testament, that by means of death, for the redemption
of the transgressions that were under the first testament,
they which are called might receive the promise of eternal
inheritance.*

*And for this cause he is the mediator of the
new testament.*—The word διαθηκη is uniformly
rendered by our translators Covenant, except
in the account of the institution of the Supper,
and in 2 Cor. iii. 6, Heb. vii. 22, and in this

passage, verses 15, 16, 17, 18, 20, where, following the Vulgate, they have rendered it Testament. But certainly this is improper. The Hebrew word Berith is always rendered covenant by the translators of the Old Testament, and there ought to have been no deviation from this practice in the New Testament.

The first covenant was ordained of angels in the hand of a mediator, Gal. iii. 19. But there is no room for a mediator in a testament, or last will. On this passage a commentator inquires, " Was it ever known, in the practice of any nation, that a testament needed a mediator ? Or that the testator was the mediator of his own testament ? Or that it was necessary the testator of a new testament should die to redeem the transgressions of a former testament ? Or that any testament was made by sprinkling the legatees with blood ? These things, however, were usual in covenants. They had mediators who assisted at the making of them, and were sureties for the performance of them ; * they were commonly ratified with sacrifices, the blood of which was sprinkled on the parties. We know that if a former covenant was infringed by the parties, satisfaction was given by making a second covenant. By calling

* Hence, when Israel broke the Sinai Covenant, Moses, the Mediator, offered to die in their room.

Christ *the mediator of the new testament* our thoughts are turned away entirely from the view which the Scriptures give of His death as a sacrifice for sin. Whereas if he is called the Mediator of the new covenant, which is the true translation of διαθηκης καινης μεσιτης, that appellation directly suggests to us that the new covenant was procured and ratified by his death as a sacrifice for sin."

For this cause he is the Mediator of the new covenant, that by means of death for the redemption of the transgressions that were under the first covenant, they who were called might receive the promise of eternal inheritance. The sacrifices prescribed by the law could not take away sin, and therefore, and as God is of purer eyes than to behold iniquity, neither can evil dwell with Him, in order that those who had sinned might receive the promise of an eternal inheritance, it was necessary that their sins should be expiated by the death of the Mediator of the new covenant. So that, under every dispensation, sin has been pardoned only through the blood-shedding of Christ. To the same purpose, the Apostle having stated that all have sinned and come short of the glory of God, and are only justified by his grace, through the redemption that is in Christ Jesus, proceeds, " Whom God hath set forth as a propitiation," (or mercy seat,*) " through faith in his blood, to declare his righteousness for the remission of sins that are past, through the forbearance of God." Rom. iii. 25. Here we have a plain intimation that the sins which are past, namely those committed under the first covenant, are remitted only through faith in the blood of Christ. The forbearance of God had waited during that dispensation, although no sacrifice had been provided that could expiate sin, Rom. ix. 23, 24, or through which the people of God could receive the promise of eternal inheritance.

V. 16.—*For where a testament is, there must also of necessity be the death of the testator.*

Where a testament is, there is of necessity the death of the testator. It is true that a testament, or last will, is liable to be altered so long as the testator liveth; but there may be a valid testament executed and in force for years while the testator survives. But we have already seen, and shall find further proof, that the Apostle's reasoning does not apply to a testament. The word rendered in our version testator is a participle of the verb which signifies to appoint. It may be rendered the

* The word here used is that translated mercy seat in the law of Moses.

appointed (victim or sacrifice), or that by which the covenant is confirmed, which is the same.

That the Apostle is speaking of a covenant is certain, both from what goes before and what follows. We find instances in which a covenant was made without any sacrifice ; on the other hand, sacrifices were frequently offered. Thus we find the covenant made with Abraham. Gen. xv. By the Divine commandment, Abraham took an heifer, a goat, a ram, a turtle-dove, and a young pigeon, dividing them in the midst with the exception of the birds, and when it was dark a smoking furnace and a burning lamp, the emblem of the Divine presence, Heb. xii. 29, passed between the pieces. Thus God made a covenant with Abraham, to give his posterity the land of Canaan. The heifer, goat, &c., were the appointed victims, whose death was essential to the ratification of the covenant. It was confirmed by their death.

We have another striking instance in Jeremiah xxxiv. During the siege of Jerusalem the Jews made a covenant to let their servants go free, a calf was the appointed victim or sacrifice ; it was slain, and those who made the covenant passed between the pieces. When they considered the danger to be passed they again brought the servants into bondage, and

for this wickedness God denounces his judgments upon them ; they are described as having
" passed between the parts of the calf," thus
confirming the covenant. These instances fully
explain the language of the Apostle.

*V. 17.—For a testament is of force after men are dead:
otherwise it is of no strength at all while the testator
liveth.*

For a testament is of force when men are dead.
There is nothing in the original about men.
The assertion of the Apostle is that a covenant
is firm or confirmed upon the dead; for
instance, the sacrifices employed by Abraham,
and the calf by the inhabitants of Jerusalem.
Till the death of these sacrifices, or victims,
respectively, neither Abram's covenant, nor that
of the Jews, was ratified or confirmed. This
clearly illustrates the Apostle's meaning.

*V. 18.—Whereupon neither the first testament was
dedicated without blood.*

In perfect correspondence with this the first,
or Sinai covenant, was not dedicated, or ratified,
without blood.

*V. 19.—For when Moses had spoken every precept to
all the people according to the law, he took the blood of
calves and of goats, with water, and scarlet wool, and
hyssop, and sprinkled both the book, and all the people.*

When Moses had written all the words of
the Lord he builded an altar, and took the

blood of calves and bulls, with water, and
scarlet wool, and hyssop, and sprinkled both
the book, in which the words of the covenant
were written, and all the people. It may
be asked, how the blood could be possibly
sprinkled on such a multitude? The answer is,
the twelve pillars represented the twelve tribes,
and on them the blood was sprinkled. That
all of such a multitude should be individually
sprinkled appears impossible, but the twelve
pillars which represented *all* the people might
easily be sprinkled. There are some things
mentioned by the Apostle which are not recorded by Moses, who informs us that having
told the people all the words of the Lord and
all the judgments, they answered with one voice
and said, " All the words which the Lord hath
said we will do." He then wrote in a book all
the words of the Lord, builded an altar, and
offered burnt offerings and sacrificed peace
offerings of oxen unto the Lord. He then read
the book of the covenant in the audience of
the people, who said, " All that the Lord hath
said will we do, and be obedient." Half the
blood was sprinkled on the people and half on
the altar; and Moses said, " Behold the blood
of the covenant, which the Lord hath made
with you concerning all these words." Exod.
xxiv. 3—8. There is some variation in the

account given by the Apostle, although it is substantially the same.

The goats mentioned by the Apostle seem included under the burnt offerings mentioned by Moses; Moses does not mention the water nor the scarlet wool and hyssop; but the Apostle wrote under Divine inspiration as well as Moses, and there is an entire correspondence between the account given by the Lawgiver and the Apostle.

V. 20.—Saying, This is the blood of the testament which God hath enjoined unto you.

When Moses sprinkled the blood on the book and on the people, he said, " This is the blood of the covenant which the Lord hath enjoined upon you." We may observe the correspondence between the words of Moses and those employed by the Lord at the institution of the Lord's Supper, " This is my blood of the new testament, which is shed for many for the remission of sins." Matt. xxvi. 28. The blood of the old covenant was that of bulls and goats, by which the first covenant was ratified. The blood by which the new covenant was ratified was that of Christ. By the old covenant the nation of Israel became God's peculiar people, who dwelt among them and gave them a land flowing with milk and honey. God dwells in the hearts

of all the children of the new covenant, and
bestows on them an inheritance incorruptible,
undefiled, and that fadeth not away.

*V. 21.—Moreover he sprinkled likewise with blood both
the tabernacle, and all the vessels of the ministry.*

In the account given of setting up the
tabernacle only the anointing oil is mentioned,
but we find that the altar was sanctified with
blood, Lev. viii. 15; and the Apostle informs
us that both the tabernacle and all the vessels
of the ministry were sprinkled with blood, and
that under that dispensation there was no
remission without shedding of blood, which
clearly intimated that the wages of sin is death,
and that the blood maketh atonement. Lev.
xvii. 11.

*V. 22.—And almost all things are by the law purged
with blood; and without shedding of blood is no remission.*

Almost all, &c.—There were some excep-
tions; some things were purified with fire,
others with water and the ashes of the red
heifer, Numb. xxxi. 23, xix. 9, and without
shedding of blood there was no remission.
Hence the morning and evening sacrifices, and
on the great day of atonement, Lev. xvi. 30,
of which it is said, " On that day shall the
priest make an atonement for you, to cleanse
you, that ye may be clean from all your sins
before the Lord."

V. 23.— It was therefore necessary that the patterns of things in the heavens should be purified with these ; but the heavenly things themselves with better sacrifices than these.

Thus we see it was necessary that the patterns of things in the heavens, for the ordinances of the Mosaic dispensation were no more, should be purified with these ; but the heavenly things themselves were better sacrifices than these. The whole of the Mosaic dispensation was a shadow of good things to come. The covenant and all its ordinances was a parable for the time then present. The moral law, even the ten commandments, were uttered in the hearing of all Israel by God himself, and were written on tables of stone, intimating their perpetual obligation. Thus the unchangeableness of God was the foundation of the covenant into which God brought the children of Israel. Hence it is frequently called the covenant, and the ark in which the tables were kept was called the ark of the covenant or of the testimony, because they testified the peculiar relation into which Israel were brought by the covenant. The people, not being able to endure that which was commanded, besought that God would not speak to them any more ; accordingly, after the ratification of the covenant with the blood of bulls and of goats, God delivered to Moses the statutes and judgments, and the sacrifices and purifications which Israel was to observe.

That the whole system was figurative, appears,

1st. From its being delivered to one nation, although all nations are made of one blood, and with God there is no respect of persons.

2d. Their obedience was required from the consideration of the peculiar relation in which God stood towards them, and of the temporal deliverance vouchsafed to them. " I am the Lord thy God, that brought thee out of the land of Egypt, out of the house of bondage, therefore thou shalt have no other gods before me."

3d. From God, whom the heaven of heavens cannot contain, commanding the tabernacle to be erected as the royal tent, in which he represented himself as dwelling in the character of the King of Israel in the midst of the people, from which he directed all their movements by the pillar of cloud by day and of fire by night.

4th. From the sacrifices which were enjoined, which could not possibly take away sin, and were offered from year to year continually, thus bringing sin to remembrance, at once testifying the necessity of atonement, and showing the inadequacy of the legal sacrifices, by their constant repetition.

5th. From the purifications, which only sanc-

tified to the purifying of the flesh, removing
ceremonial uncleanness.

6th. From the system of religion enjoined
being evidently local. All the males in Israel
were required to appear three times in the year
at a particular place, which might be suitable
for one nation, but was impracticable as an
universal system.

7th. From all the promises and threatenings,
and the inheritance bestowed on Israel being
carnal and earthly, Levit. xxvi., Deut. xxviii.,
Exod. iii. 8.

The necessity of which the Apostle speaks
arose—

1st. From the design of God to exhibit a
pattern of that heavenly and eternal kingdom
which it was his purpose to establish, in order
to keep up the expectation of the appearance
of the great King.

2d. Of separating the family from which he
was to spring from all other nations; thus
manifesting his faithfulness, in the fulfilment
of his promise to Abraham, of affording a
demonstration of the truth of the Gospel, for
which so great preparations were made and so
exact a pattern prepared; and, finally, of illus-
trating all the great doctrines of the Gospel,
from their being embodied and placed before
us in a tangible form. But, considered in

themselves, these were all weak and beggarly
elements, having no glory by reason of the
glory that excelleth. By heavenly things we
are not to understand literally things in the
heavens, but those spiritual and eternal things
revealed without a vail under the new and
better covenant, ratified with the blood of the
Son of God, which reveals a complete atonement for sin, consequently not to be repeated.
During the old and introductory dispensation,
while all the perfection of the Divine character
was revealed, Jehovah appeared as the God of
one nation, but this was only to make way for
that glorious system by which all the families
of the earth are invited to the enjoyment of an
eternal inheritance by faith in Christ.

It is true that the religion of Jesus has been
corrupted by blending the institutions of the
new with those of the old dispensation, but by
means of the Gospel, which we possess un-
adulterated in the Scriptures of truth, the
kingdom of the man of sin shall be destroyed,
and the Church of Christ, extended over all
nations, shall appear fair as the sun, clear as the
moon, and terrible as an army with banners.

*V. 24.—For Christ is not entered into the holy places
made with hands, which are the figures of the true ; but
into heaven itself, now to appear in the presence of God
for us.*

The Apostle here returns to our great High Priest, who hath not entered into the holy places made with hands, which are but figures of the true, but into heaven itself, now to appear in the presence of God for us. The priest daily entered the holy place, where incense was burnt on the golden altar ; but on the great day of atonement the high priest entered the holiest of all, and sprinkled the mercy seat with the blood of the bullock for his own sins and of the goat for the sins of Israel. Our great High Priest had no sin, but has entered into heaven itself with his own blood shed for the remission of the sins of his people. There he appears in the midst of the throne as a Lamb that had been slain. And as the people of Israel watched for the high priest coming out from the most holy place that they might receive the blessing, so do believers wait for the second coming of the Lord Jesus, who shall then receive them into the everlasting mansions which he has prepared for them, saying, " Come ye blessed of my Father, inherit the kingdom prepared for you from the foundation of the world."

V. 25.—Nor yet that he should offer himself often, as the high priest entereth into the holy place every year with blood of others.

Nor yet *was it necessary* that he should offer

himself often, as the high priest entereth into the holy place every year with the blood of the sacrifice.

The Jewish worship was a shadow of good things to come. In order to keep up the expectation of the sacrifice by which Christ was to finish transgression, make an end of sin, make reconciliation for iniquity, and bring in everlasting righteousness, the high priest year by year, on the great day of atonement, entered the holiest of all with the blood of the sin-offering.

V. 26.—For then must he often have suffered since the foundation of the world: but now once in the end of the world hath he appeared to put away sin by the sacrifice of himself.

In that case He must often have suffered since the foundation of the world; but now once in the end of the world, 1 Cor. x. 11, He hath appeared to put away sin by the sacrifice of Himself. When the tabernacle was reared, and when Aaron and his sons were consecrated, fire came down and consumed the burnt-offering upon the altar. Thus the Lord testified his approbation of the conduct of Moses in obeying the instructions which he had received.

This fire was not to be extinguished. It alone was to be employed in consuming the sacrifices, and two of Aaron's sons were struck dead for using strange fire. Many sacrifices continued to be offered in Israel; but still the Lord's fire, and His furnace in Jerusalem, continued to demand its victims. It did not say, " It is enough; from day to day and from year to year," it still cried, " Give, give." Like the grave, it was not satisfied: but now once in the end of the world Christ appeared effectually to remove sin by the sacrifice of Himself. Thus the demands of justice were fully satisfied, and Christ by His resurrection abolished death and showed His people the path of life.

V. 27.—And as it is appointed unto men once to die, but after this the judgment.

And as it is appointed unto men once to die —·to return to the dust from whence they were taken—*but after this the judgment.*— This passage is generally misquoted. As it is appointed for *all* men once to die, but there is no such appointment. Enoch before the law, and Elijah under the law, did not taste death, and the Apostle tells us those who remain to the coming of the Lord shall not all sleep, but shall all be changed; * but it is appointed to

* This is the change for which Job says he will wait. It does not refer to death, but to the resurrection, when this corruptible shall put on incorruption, and this mortal shall put on immortality. This is evident from the

men once to die. It is the law of our fallen nature. The exception of Enoch and Elijah is a mystery which the Apostle explains, 1 Cor. xv. 51, 52, of the change which shall take place on those who are alive at the coming of the Lord.

The judgment was intimated immediately after the fall. Sentence was passed on fallen man that he should return to dust; but mankind were divided into two families—the seed of the woman and of the serpent. The former were to prove victorious over their enemy, and we see him who was born of a woman, in His resurrection, trampling on the neck of Satan, and giving those whom He is not ashamed to call brethren the assurance of sharing his victory.

V. 28.—So Christ was once offered to bear the sins of many; and unto them that look for him shall he appear the second time without sin unto salvation.

Christ was made in all things like unto his brethren, yet without sin. In exact corre-

context: "Thou wilt call, and I will answer thee; thou wilt have respect to the work of thy hands." When the body is cast into the grave, God appears to have no respect to the work of His hands; but after the leprous house has been cast into an unclean place, it will be raised spiritual and incorruptible, like Christ's glorious body.

spondence with the appointment that man should once die, Christ once suffered to bear the sins of many (even the children whom God had given Him). The Apostle Peter says,—" His own self bare our sins in his own body on the tree, that we, being dead to sins, should live unto righteousness: by whose stripes ye were healed." 1 Pet. ii. 24. Such is the unity between Christ and His people, that they all died in His death and rose in His resurrection; nay, they are represented as seated with Him in heavenly places. Eph. ii. 6. Their citizenship is in heaven, whence they look for the Saviour, the Lord Jesus Christ. He is the head, they are the members; His suffering is their suffering. They were created in Adam, who is the source of natural life. It is dried up; the Second Adam is the source of spiritual and eternal life, and He says,—" Because I live ye shall live also. Thus their life is hid with Christ in God; and when He, who is their life, shall appear, then shall they appear with Him in glory. Sin had doomed His people to death, but He descended into their prison-house. He felt the pillars by which it was supported—the justice and truth of God; but He so magnified and made honourable the law which they had broken, that mercy and truth met together, righteousness and peace kissed each other. Hence the Gospel is called the revelation of God's righteousness; for, by Christ's fulfilment of the law in all its extent, by the most perfect obedience and the perfection of His atoning sacrifice, He has brought in everlasting righteousness, arrayed in which the believer stands unrebukable, and can challenge the universe to lay anything to his charge. God is, in short, the just God and the Saviour, and in the salvation of an innumerable multitude of our fallen race has given a more awful proof of his hatred of sin and of the impossibility of its passing unpunished than if all had perished, like the angels who kept not their first estate.

He has entered heaven with His own blood, His people are waiting without for His second appearing; they are looking for Him, and He will appear the second time, not in the likeness of sinful flesh, but without sin;* which

* A sin-offering is sometimes called " sin," because the sin of the worshipper was in a figure transferred to it; but Christ, in taking part with His people in flesh and blood and becoming their substitute and surety, was responsible—the Lord laid on Him the iniquity of them all. Hence He says, " Mine iniquities have taken hold upon me, so that I am not able to look up; they are more in number than the hairs of my head; therefore my heart faileth me." Ps. xl. 12.

was once imputed to Him, but is now cast into the depth of the sea. The Lord laid on Him the iniquity of all His people, and when they are sought for they shall not be found. In the day of his second coming the Church will appear a glorious Church, without spot or wrinkle. Their robes will be so white that "no fuller on earth can white them," and they shall for ever drink of the river of God's pleasures. The Second Coming of Christ was typified by the high priest coming out of the holy of holies to bless the people.

CHAPTER X.

V. 1.—*For the law having a shadow of good things to come, and not the very image of the things, can never with those sacrifices which they offered year by year continually make the comers thereunto perfect.*

For the law, &c.—The law is here described as a shadow, and not an image. Here the law, as in many other places, denotes the whole of the Mosaic dispensation. It had been previously characterized as standing only in meats : " Which stood only in meats and drinks, and divers washings, and carnal ordinances, imposed on them until the time of reformation." Chap. ix. 10. Under these carnal ordinances, spiritual and heavenly things were concealed. The carnal ordinances constituted the vail on Moses' face, which concealed the glory of his countenance. There is an important distinction between a shadow and an image. A shadow is a mere outline, having only two proportions, length and breadth ; an image has three—length, breadth, and thickness, and gives an exact representation of the object. Should it be asked whether it would not have been better had the law been an image of the new and spiritual dispensation, the reply is easy, By no means. Had this been the case, the people to whom it was given must have been gathered from all nations; and this would have defeated one important end of the separation of Israel, that the faithfulness of God in fulfilling his promise to Abraham, that he should be the progenitor of Christ, might be manifest. Again, as believers under the Gospel have but one priest, there could only have been one under the law. There would also have been but one sacrifice, one baptism. Once more the law must have been written on the hearts of all the people of the old, because this is the privilege of all the children of the new covenant. In short, every purpose of the giving of the law would have been made void; and, long before the expiration of the two thousand years which elapsed between the call of Abraham and the coming of Christ, the promise of the appearing of the Saviour would have been forgotten.

But the wisdom of God, by the separation of the seed of Abraham, Isaac, and Jacob, redeeming them from bondage, feeding them in the wilderness, and putting them in possession of a land flowing with milk and honey, appointing a priesthood in the family of Aaron, and, in connexion with this, establishing the daily and yearly sacrifices, purifications, and festivals, kept up during the space of fifteen hundred years a memorial of the new and more glorious dispensation under which God's people should be made free by the truth, should go up through the wilderness, should pass through the valley of the shadow of death, and inherit the better country.

Can never.—The sacrifices which were constantly offered could never make the worshippers* perfect by removing their guilt and obtaining their acceptance with God.

V. 2.—For then would they not have ceased to be offered? because that the worshippers once purged should have had no more conscience of sins.

Here the reason is given why the legal sacrifices could not make the worshippers perfect. Had they done so, they would have ceased to be offered. Some copies omit the word *not*, thus rendering it a positive affirmation. The meaning is precisely the same.

For the worshippers, &c.—Had the legal sacrifices really cancelled guilt, there would have been no need of their repetition; for the worshippers being once purified, would have

---

* Those who are described as the comers thereto, ver. 1, are spoken of as worshippers, ver. 2.

had no longer a consciousness of guilt; their
hearts would have been sprinkled from an evil
conscience, ver. 22; and they would have had
boldness in approaching their heavenly Father.

It may be alleged, that since men do not
cease from sin, that, although their guilt had
been removed, fresh guilt would have been contracted, which, notwithstanding the efficacy of
the sacrifice by which their guilt had been removed, would have required a fresh sacrifice;
but this is fallacious, and that it is so is proved
by matter of fact. The blood of Jesus cleanses
the believer from all sin. It gives him the
answer of a good conscience. Christ was delivered for our sins, and raised again for our
justification. The believer can therefore say,
"It is God that justifieth; who is he that condemneth?" He can plead a full remission of
his sins through the blood of Jesus. They are
all buried in his grave, and shall never appear
against him. There is a fountain opened in
Zion for sin and uncleanness, to which we have
daily recourse. By one offering Christ hath
perfected for ever them that are sanctified.
This is illustrated in what follows.

*V. 3.—But in those sacrifices there is a remembrance
again made of sins every year.*

So far from removing a sense of guilt, the

legal sacrifices brought the guilt of the worshippers to their remembrance every year.
The sacrifice on the great day of atonement
might seem to remove the sins of Israel, and it
did so in one sense ; it sanctified to the purifying of the flesh, chap. ix. 13, removed ceremonial uncleanness; but the following year the
same process took place.   Thus we see how the
sacrifices did no more than bring the sins of
Israel to remembrance.   Every succeeding day
of atonement testified the inefficacy of what had
gone before.

*V. 4.—For it is not possible that the blood of bulls and
of goats should take away sins.*

For it is not possible.—God does nothing in
vain.   It results from His infinite wisdom that
the means which He employs are exactly
adapted to the object He has in view, neither
greater nor less.   We may prove our folly by
employing means inadequate to the end we
have in view, or we may apply more strength
than is requisite.   But God is perfect in wisdom,
and therefore the means He employs always
exactly correspond with the end He has in
view.   Now, for fifteen hundred years, the blood
of bulls and goats flowed on His altar, and their
constant repetition proved their inefficacy.
But, in the fulness of time, He sent forth His

Son, born of a woman, made under the law, to redeem His people from the curse of the law; and no other proof is requisite to confirm the Apostle's assertion, that it is not possible that the blood of bulls and of goats should take away sin. Had such sacrifices been sufficient, the Son of God would not have suffered, the just for the unjust, that He might bring sinners to God.

Here is a demonstration that it is not possible that the blood of bulls and goats could take away sin. God does nothing in vain; there is nothing superfluous in His conduct. Sacrifices bled on the Jewish altar fifteen hundred years, but still the fire burned as fiercely as ever. Should it, then, be asked, Did all the generations of Israel, from Moses to Christ, die in their sins? the reply is, By no means.

They had before them an account of Abraham's justification through faith in Him whose day he saw afar off, and was glad. Moses wrote of the same exalted personage; and there was always a remnant in Israel whose heart God had touched, who looked for the coming of the Saviour. As the virtue of the atonement of Christ extended not merely to those who believed during the days of His flesh, but to the end of the world, so it looked back to the fall of Adam, and, like righteous Abel, all who believed in Him who was to come were partakers of the great salvation. This is plainly declared by the Apostle. Speaking of the Saviour, he says, " Whom God hath set forth to be a propitiation * through faith in his blood, to declare his righteousness *for the remission of sins that are past,* through the forbearance of God ; to declare, I say, at this time, his righteousness, that he might be just, and the justifier of him which believeth in Jesus." Rom. iii. 25, 26. Believers who lived under the law were justified by faith in Christ, as well as those who live under the new dispensation.

So that, while there was in Israel a remembrance again made of sins every year, the efficacy of the great atonement extended from the fall to the consummation of all things.

V. 5.—Wherefore when he cometh into the world, he saith, Sacrifice and offering thou wouldest not, but a body hast thou prepared me.

Therefore when he (that is, Christ) *cometh into the world.*—Christ was known among the Jews as He who should come, Luke vii. 19 ;

---

* A propitiatory, or mercy-seat. There are two words rendered in our version " propitiation." The one which is used in this passage is that by which the " mercy-seat " is rendered in the Septuagint ; the covering of the ark, the throne of the God of Israel, who sat between the cherubim.

and He is thus described in the passage before us. Thus we are taught that the 40th Psalm is descriptive of Christ. It was written by David, but a greater than David is here. Indeed, the better we understand the Psalms the more clearly shall we see that they speak of Christ. The Lord, in discoursing with His disciples, divided the Old Testament into three parts ; the Law of Moses, the Prophets, and the Psalms. Luke xxiv. 44. Moses wrote of Him. He is the end of the law, and to Him give all the prophets witness. David, the sweet singer of Israel, who wrote the greater part of the Psalms, was a remarkable type of Him ; and, in the greater part of the Psalms, while he speaks in his own person, he describes the experience of Christ in the days of His flesh. In the Psalms we are admitted into the Redeemer's closet. We contemplate Him as a man of sorrows and acquainted with grief, bowed down under the load of His people's sins, and, in the days of His flesh, making supplication with strong crying and tears to Him that was able to deliver Him from death. Both He that sanctifieth and they that are sanctified are all of one family ; therefore He is not ashamed to call them brethren. In virtue of their unity, their sins are His sins, and His righteousness their righteousness. Hence we find Him groaning

under a load of sin, although He did no sin,
nor was guile found in His lips. At other
times we find Him describing Himself as holy,
and rejoicing in the complacency with which
His Father always viewed His righteous servant. The application by the Apostle of the
40th Psalm to Christ, in the passage before us,
gives us a key which opens to us the meaning
of many other Psalms.

Sacrifice and offering thou wouldest not, or
thou didst not desire, Ps. xl. 6.—This describes
God's weariness of all the sacrifices enjoined in
the law. Isa. i. 10—14. They were enjoined to
maintain the expectation of a better sacrifice ;
but, when they had answered their end, they
were offensive to God. Everything is beautiful
in its season ; the time of their abolition was
come, and he that killed an ox was as if he slew
a man, &c. Isa. lxvi. 3.

A body hast thou prepared me.—It is in the
Psalm, " Mine ears hast thou opened." Various
conjectures have been offered to account for the
difference, but none of them are satisfactory.
The words, as quoted by the Apostle, are found
in the Septuagint ; but there seems a difficulty
in the supposition of his quoting this version
when writing to the Hebrews.

There is, however, a substantial agreement
in these different renderings. The ear is the

organ by which we receive the communications made to us by others. Hence to hear frequently signifies to believe, or obey. John viii. 6, 7; x. 27; Deut. i. 43. " The Lord God hath opened mine ear, and I was not rebellious, neither turned away back." Isa. l. 5. Jesus came as His Father's servant, Isa. xlix. 6; not to do His own will, but the will of Him that sent Him. John v. 30. On becoming incarnate, He took upon Him the form of a servant, Phil. ii. 7; and it was His meat and His drink to do the will of His Father; and, therefore, " A body hast thou prepared me," is equivalent to " Mine ears hast thou opened."

V. 6.—In burnt offerings and sacrifices for sin thou hast had no pleasure.

Various sacrifices were enjoined by the law, two of which, burnt-offerings and sin-offerings, are specified by the Apostle. In neither of these had God any pleasure as an atonement for sin. He, indeed, approved of their being offered in obedience to His command, and severely punished their being neglected; but, for the removal of guilt, they were utterly worthless.

V. 7.—Then said I, Lo, I come (in the volume of the book it is written of me,) to do thy will, O God.

The volume or roll of the book refers to the

manner in which books of old were rolled up. Thus the book which John saw in the right hand of Him that sat upon the throne was written both within and on the back, and sealed with seven seals; consequently, when the first seal was opened, a part of the contents of the book were discovered, and so on with each successive seal, until the whole was exposed to view.

The book here mentioned is evidently the Scriptures, which testify of Christ. Moses wrote of Him; to Him give all the prophets witness; and the Psalms exhibit all the secret workings of His mind in the house of his pilgrimage. His love to the law was stronger than death. To magnify and make it honourable He submitted to every privation; He voluntarily endured every hardship; and, finally, laid down His life to restore what His people had taken away. He had received a commandment from His Father to lay down His life; " and how am I straitened," said He, " till it be accomplished." Luke xii. 50. *

* Jesus had been manifested to Israel by His baptism; He was buried in and raised from the waters of Jordan, on which occasion the voice from the excellent glory proclaimed Him to be the Son of God, and the Spirit descended and rested upon Him; but this was only a figurative burial. He was to descend into the lower parts of the earth, and to be declared to be the Son of God with power by His resurrection from the dead. Rom. i. 4.

He was impatient to fill up the measure of His expiatory sufferings. Thus He came to do the will of God, according to the prophecies concerning Him which had gone before ; and, in the 40th Psalm, quoted by the Apostle, He expresses the pleasure He had in the hard service which He had undertaken.

V. 8.—Above when he said, Sacrifice and offering and burnt offerings and offering for sin thou wouldest not, neither hadst pleasure therein ; which are offered by the law.

Above when he said.—The Apostle here resumes his exposition of the 40th Psalm, recapitulating what he had already quoted in proof of the insufficiency of the legal sacrifices, of which, as he had said of the priesthood, " there was a disannulling of the commandment going before for the weakness and unprofitableness thereof." Chap. vii. 18.

V. 9.—Then said he, Lo, I come to do thy will, O God. He taketh away the first, that he may establish the second.

Then he said (Ps. xl. 7, 8), *Lo, I come to do thy will, O God. He taketh away the first,* &c. —viz., sacrifice and burnt-offerings, and offerings for sin, which are offered by the law.

That he might establish the second—that is, the efficacy of the sacrifice of Christ, who came to do the will of God by finishing transgression,

making an end of sin, making reconciliation for
iniquity, and bringing in everlasting righteousness. The blood-shedding of the Lamb of God,
which taketh away the sin of the world, in
which God smelled a savour of rest, had only
been prefigured by the legal sacrifices. The
Apostle's argument here is precisely similar to
his reasoning respecting the priesthood in
chap. vii., when he proves the inferiority of the
priesthood after the order of Aaron to that after
the order of Melchisedec. It is, in fact, the same
subject presented to us under two different aspects; the one being the legal sacrifices, abolished
by the great sacrifice which they only shadowed
forth; the other the priesthood made after the
law of a carnal commandment, superseded by
the priesthood made after the power of an endless life.

*V. 10.—By the which will we are sanctified through the
offering of the body of Jesus Christ once for all.*

By the which will, &c.—The Apostle had
quoted from the 40th Psalm the words of
Messiah, that He came to do the will of God,
and here he describes the effect of His obedience. " Sanctified " does not here signify internal purity or holiness, although the sanctification spoken of is the foundation of all fallen
man's conformity to God. The first-born in

Israel were to be sanctified or set apart for God, and, in their stead, the Levites were taken, who alone were permitted to do the service of the tabernacle. The nation of Israel were sanctified by the blood of the covenant, whereby God engaged to be their God, and to take them for His peculiar people. This, however, did not prevent their wickedness being greater than that of Sodom. Ezek. xvi. 48. All their privileges flowed from their relation to Christ, and this was a carnal relation. "Of whom," says the Apostle, "according to the flesh, Christ came, who is over all, God blessed for ever. Amen." Rom. ix. 5. Hence the blood of the covenant, wherewith they were sanctified, was the blood of bulls and of goats, which could never take away sin ; it merely sanctified to the purifying of the flesh, Heb. ix. 13, removing whatever ceremonial uncleanness had been contracted. On the other hand, the relation of believers, the true Israel, with Christ, is a spiritual relation, 1 Cor. vi. 17 ; and the covenant through which they enter into this relation is ratified with the blood of Christ. Hence it is written, "Wherefore Jesus, also, that he might sanctify the people with his own blood, suffered without the gate. Let us go forth, therefore, unto him without the camp, bearing his reproach." Heb. xiii. 12, 13. His blood cleanseth believers from all their sin, cancels all their guilt. It purges their conscience from dead works to serve the living God. Heb. ix. 14. It reconciles them to God; and, as the necessary consequence, they are saved through His life. Rom. v. 10. He is both their atoning sacrifice and high priest. He appears in the midst of the throne as a lamb that had been slain. As their great High Priest, He offers their prayers, perfumed with much incense. He bears their names on His breast, and the voice of His intercession has reached our ears, "Father, I will that those whom thou hast given me be with me where I am." To Him the Spirit was given without measure, and by this one Spirit, communicated through Him, are they all baptized into one body; and although their conformity to their glorious head is very imperfect, while both Adam, the source of corruption, and Christ, the source of purity, dwell in them, their path is like the shining light, which shineth more and more to the perfect day.

Christ has given us repentance by manifesting Himself to us as He does not to the world; and although we now see but in part, and there is a law in our members warring against the law of our mind, and bringing us into captivity to the law of sin in our mem-

bers, we are gradually advancing nearer to
Christ, shall shortly see Him as He is, and then
the transformation begun in the day of our new
creation, when the Spirit first took of the things
of Christ and showed them to us, shall be con-
summated ; we shall be like Him, for we shall
see Him as He is. Thus, then, are believers
sanctified through the one offering of Christ.
They are holy brethren, partakers of the heavenly calling, sanctified through the offering of
the body of Christ, once for all. This is the
foundation of their conformity to God ; and the
more they are under the teaching of the Spirit the
more they know of the things that are freely given
to them of God; the more are they renewed in the
spirit of their mind, and the better they understand that they are complete in Christ, and
that He is made of God unto them wisdom,
righteousness, sanctification, and redemption.

*V. 11.—And every priest standeth daily ministering
and offering oftentimes the same sacrifices, which can
never take away sins.*

Every priest in Israel stood daily ministering
and offering oftentimes the same sacrifices,
which can never expiate guilt. The daily and
yearly sacrifices were appointed by Divine authority ; but, as it had been already proved by their
constant repetition, they could not take away
sins. Indeed, it is not possible that the blood

of bulls and goats could take away sin, and
nothing can satisfy the conscience but what
satisfies Divine justice.

*V. 12.—But this man, after he had offered one sacrifice
for sins, for ever sat down on the right hand of God.*

But this priest, having offered one sacrifice
for sins for ever, sat down on the right hand of
God. Christ having sat down at the right hand
of God, is repeatedly mentioned by the Apostle.
Chap. i. 3; viii. 1; xii. 2. This is the fulfilment of the 110th Psalm, previously quoted,
" The Lord said to my Lord, Sit thou at my
right hand, till I make thine enemies thy footstool." Christ sitting down at the right hand
of God, after having offered His atoning sacrifice, demonstrated its perfection. The Jewish
priests stood while fulfilling their service. It
would have been death for the high priest to
have sat down within the vail; but our great
High Priest having humbled Himself, and become obedient to death, even the death of the
cross, and thus redeemed His people from the
curse of the law, by being made a curse for
them, ascended up far above all heavens, and
sat down at the right hand of God, angels, principalities, and powers being made subject to
Him.

*V. 13.—From henceforth expecting till his enemies be
made his footstool.*

From henceforth, &c.—All power in heaven
and in earth is given to Him. He is exalted
a Prince and a Saviour, to give repentance to
Israel, and the remission of sins. The Father
judgeth no man, but hath committed all judgment to the Son. All the dispensations of Providence are under His complete control; all the
angels of God are subject to Him, and are employed as ministering spirits, sent forth to minister to them that shall be heirs of salvation.
Hence the Apostle says to believers, " All
things are yours." The unlimited power of
their elder Brother is the security of all things
working together for their good. They are
not, indeed, exempted from the troubles of
life. " Whom the Lord loveth He chasteneth,
and scourgeth every son whom He receiveth."
Never was sorrow like to that sorrow wherewith their elder Brother was afflicted while a
pilgrim upon earth; their afflictions are a part
of their fellowship with Christ. He drank of
the brook in the way; therefore He lifted up
His head; and they must suffer with Him, that
they may also reign with Him. The glory in
which He is enthroned is the pledge of their
sharing it with Him. He that sanctifieth and
they that are sanctified are all of one; and as
all Joseph's power in Egypt was employed for
the benefit of his brethren, so is the glory of

Christ in his exaltation, the prelude of the entrance of all His people into the everlasting mansions.

V. 14.—*For by one offering he hath perfected for ever them that are sanctified.*

See on ver. 10. Here, again, the word "perfect" occurs. The sanctified àre those who are chosen in Christ before the foundation of the world, that they might be holy and without blame before Him in love; who are redeemed, not with corruptible things, such as silver and gold, but with the precious blood of Christ, as of a lamb without blemish and without spot; whose sins are forgiven for His name's sake; who are brought within the bond of the new covenant, and who are going up through the wilderness, leaning upon Him who has undertaken to guide them by His counsel and afterwards receive them to His glory. His one offering has made them perfect. God sees no iniquity in Jacob, nor perverseness in Israel. He is well pleased for His righteousness' sake. They are washed, and sanctified, and justified in the name of the Lord Jesus, and by the Spirit of our God. Such are the effects of His one offering. He stood as the head of His body, the Church, and they are complete in Him. So glorious is His offering, that there is no spot in

His redeemed. They are clothed in a garment in which God's omniscient eye discerns no flaw. They are complete in Christ. They have washed their robes and made them white in the blood of the Lamb.

V. 15.—Whereof the Holy Ghost also is a witness to us; for after that he had said before.

The Apostle here confirms what he had said by the testimony of the Holy Ghost. This language merits our particular attention. It demonstrates the verbal inspiration of the Scriptures. The Apostles spoke not in the word which man's wisdom taught, but that which the Holy Ghost taught. He then proceeds to quote the words of the Holy Ghost which he had mentioned before.

V. 16.—This is the covenant that I will make with them after those days, saith the Lord, I will put my laws into their hearts, and in their minds will I write them.

The Apostle had already quoted from Jeremiah what is repeated in this verse. See chap. viii. 10.

V. 17.—And their sins and iniquities will I remember no more.

The new covenant is not so fully described here as it had been formerly. He omits what he had said, chap. viii. 11, and passes on to the declaration that God would no more remember their sins and their iniquities, on which he intended to reason.

V. 18.—Now where remission of these is, there is no more offering for sin.

Now where.—It had been previously shown that the repetition of the Jewish sacrifices proved their inefficacy, but God engages to remember no more the sins and iniquities of the children of the new covenant. Now, it is self-evident that where there is remission of sins no farther sacrifice is requisite. The object of the sacrifice is to cancel guilt; and, where it is cancelled, any further offering must be superfluous. The children of the new covenant are sanctified by Christ's one offering, verse 14; and to present another offering for sin virtually pronounces it insufficient, thus making God a liar. Nothing can more clearly prove how utterly unscriptural is the sacrifice of the mass.

It is held by Roman Catholics to be a real sacrifice, a repetition of what took place on Calvary; and thus they deny the efficacy of the death of Christ as an atoning sacrifice, for as the Apostle argues that the worshippers, once purged, should have no more conscience of sin. Chap. x. 2. They may allege that the mass is only a commemoration of the sacrifice of Christ, but the Council of Trent declares the sacrifice

of the mass to be a "true and proper propitiatory sacrifice for sin," which directly con-
tradicts the assertion of the Apostle, and pours
contempt on that finished work of which God
hath expressed His full approbation by raising
Christ from the dead, and giving Him glory,
that our faith and hope might be in God.
Those who pretend to offer a sacrifice for sin
deny the perfection of the sacrifice of Christ,
and are not entitled to the name of Christians.

It was the manner of the Apostle in all his
epistles to bring forward the great doctrines of
the Gospel as the foundation of those exhortations which he saw to be requisite for those to
whom he wrote.

Men admire the morality of the New Testament, but they turn with disgust from those
truths on which alone the morality rests.
Christian practice is as inseparably connected
with the truth as it is in Jesus as the fruitful
branch is with the stock of the tree. The
work of the law is written on men's hearts;
hence they admire the practice which proceeds from the faith of the Gospel, while that
Gospel is a stumbling block and foolishness to
them.

The verse which we have been considering
forms the conclusion of the doctrinal part of
this Epistle. In what follows, the Apostle

proceeds to the practical improvement of the truth which he had laid down.

V. 19.—Having therefore, brethren, boldness to enter into the holiest by the blood of Jesus.

Having therefore, brethren, boldness, &c.— In Israel the high priest alone durst presume to enter the holiest of all, and that but once in the year, with the blood of the sacrifices. He remained within the vail but for a short time. But our great High Priest hath for ever sat down at the right hand of the majesty in the heavens, and through Him we have access by one Spirit unto the Father, Eph. ii. 18. The place of worship is indeed changed. Believers, being made priests to God, have boldness to enter into the holiest by the blood of Jesus, not into the holy places made with hands, which were the figures of the true, but into heaven itself, chap. ix. 24, into which their great High Priest has entered as their forerunner. It is true, that till they are absent from the body they are not present with the Lord. The heavens have received Him till the time of the restitution of all things, but it is to appear in the presence of God for us He is gone to prepare a place for His people, and He will come again and receive them to Himself, John xiv. 2, 3; meantime, believers are encouraged to come boldly unto the throne of grace. The place of worship is now transferred from earth to heaven; and, instead of sitting at the feet of Moses, whose instructions were veiled in types and parables, we behold in the unveiled face of Christ the glory of the Lord, and experience the transforming influence of the truth delivered by His Apostles, who used great plainness of speech.

V. 20.—By a new and living way, which he hath consecrated for us, through the veil, that is to say, his flesh.

By a new and living way. The Lord teaches us that He is the way, the truth, and the life, no man cometh to the Father but through Him. This is the new and living way which He hath consecrated for us, that is to say His flesh, or his body, which he offered once for all. The vail separated between the holy and the holiest of all, but at the death of Jesus the vail of the temple was rent in twain from the top to the bottom, which signified that the way into the holiest of all was now made manifest by the event which had just taken place. But although he died he is the living one, Rev. i. 18, and believers have access to the throne of God through him that was dead and liveth for evermore. Many generations have passed away since the vail of his flesh was rent; but, like

the ark in the midst of Jordan, his empty grave
stands as a memorial that although believers
must have fellowship with him in his death
they shall not remain under the power of
death. Through him they all have access by
one Spirit unto the Father, and when he hath
gathered in all his blood-bought sheep he shall
call to the heaven from above and to the earth
that he may judge his people: " Gather my
saints together unto me; those that have made
a covenant with me by sacrifice," Psalm l. 5;
who have entered the new and everlasting
covenant by faith in the sacrifice which cleanseth
believers from all sin.

*V. 21.—And having an high priest over the house of
God.*

*And having a great High Priest, &c.** The
great object of the whole Epistle was to exhibit the connexion between the Jewish and
Christian worship, by showing that the former
was a figure of the latter, an earthly or carnal
exhibition of a heavenly and spiritual object.
The Apostle therefore dwells on the priesthood
of Christ. In the new and spiritual dispensation He is all in all: like God's servant
Moses, who was faithful in all his house; but
as a son over his own house, which is composed

---

* It is in the original a great priest.

of living stones resting upon the foundation of
the Apostles and Prophets, He himself being
the chief corner stone. He is described as a
living stone, and through their union with Him
all the stones of the building are quickened.
We know the power of a loadstone, which
communicates magnetism to iron. God might
have given it the power of communicating
magnetism to stone, so that the foundation
might communicate its property to the whole
building. Such is the case with Christ; all
the stones of the living temple rest on Him,
and to them all, does He communicate a life
which never ends, according to that which is
written : " As the Father hath life in himself,
so hath he given to the Son to have life in
himself,* and hath given him authority to
execute judgment also because he is the Son
of man." John v. 26, 7. Here we see that
He is the source of the life of His people, and

* This refers to Christ in his mediatorial character,
as the Father's servant, but as being Himself God,
" in him was life." Hence he is called, " The eternal
life which was with the Father, and was manifested to
us," 1 John i. 2 ; but as Immanuel, God manifest in the
flesh, He was the Father's servant, and that eternal life,
which is the gift of God, is communicated to us through
Christ. " He asked life of God and he gave it to him,
even length of days for ever and ever ; and of his fulness
we all receive, and grace for grace."

that He quickeneth whom He will. " For the Father judgeth no man, but hath committed all judgment unto the Son." John v. 21, 22. All His sheep are known to the Good Shepherd, and that individually and by name.

V. 22.—Let us draw near with a true heart in full assurance of faith, having our hearts sprinkled from an evil conscience, and our bodies washed with pure water.

Let us draw near.—We have seen that the Israelites drew near to God by the priests, and especially by the great high priest, who entered the holiest of all, the secret place of the Most High, on the great day of Atonement. We are invited to draw near, through our great High Priest, who hath for us, as our surety and representative, entered into Heaven itself. Another Apostle says, " Truly our fellowship is with the Father, and with his Son Jesus Christ. Through him we cry Abba, Father." Let us then draw near with a true heart. This is opposed to dissimulation or hypocrisy. It is illustrated by the Psalmist, " If I regard iniquity in my heart the Lord will not hear me, but verily God hath heard me," &c. In full assurance of faith, that is in the fullest confidence of acceptance in Christ. Faith is the substance or confidence of things hoped for. Chap. xi. The salvation of Christ is full and free, it is for the chief of sinners; and in the

Gospel a foundation is laid for the most assured confidence of acceptance in Christ.

It is well observed, by Archbishop Leighton, that the want of assurance of our salvation must proceed from one of two things; either that the atonement of Christ is insufficient to remove our guilt, or that we require some qualification which we fear we do not possess. The Scripture calls every sinner who hears the Gospel to trust in Christ, however aggravated his guilt. All who hear are invited to take of the water of life freely, to draw near with a true heart, not merely with our mouth, not merely with our lips to honour God, while we have removed our hearts far from Him, and our fear towards Him is taught by the precept of men, Isaiah xxix. 13; but drawing near with true hearts deeply feeling the reverence and love which we profess, and in the full assurance of faith. Having no confidence in ourselves, but the most unlimited confidence in Christ, the fullest assurance of our acceptance in the Beloved. On this passage a very unsound observation is made by one who, in many respects, possessed just and scriptural views. He says, " This full assurance is not, as many conceive, an absolute certainty of a man's own particular salvation; for that is termed the full assurance of hope, chap. vi. 11, and arises from faith and its

fruits ; but *the full assurance of faith* is the
assurance of that truth which is testified and
proposed in the Gospel to all hearers of it in
common, to be believed by them unto their
salvation, and is also termed *the full assurance
of understanding.* Col. ii. 2." We have already
observed, that the full assurance of faith and of
hope may be distinguished, but cannot be
separated. It is the testimony of God that in
trusting in Christ we shall be saved, and in
order to the full assurance of faith and of hope
nothing more is necessary than our receiving
that truth.   To mingle faith with its fruits in
regard to our hope of salvation is utterly
unscriptural. We are indeed commanded to
examine ourselves whether we be in the faith,
to prove our own selves. Thus we are guarded
against self-deception, against *saying* we have
faith, against an empty profession of knowing
God while in works we deny Him. Faith gives
us the answer of a good conscience, it purges
our hearts from an evil conscience, by con-
vincing us of the perfection of the work of
Christ. On the night on which he believed
the gaoler rejoiced in God with all his house.
The eunuch, having heard the Gospel, went on
his way rejoicing. The only fruit they had to
look to was their having been baptized, their
professing the glorious truth which they had

received. Let us ever keep faith and its fruits in their proper place. Faith receives Christ, and in him eternal salvation; fruits prove the faithfulness of Him who saves His people from their sins, and gives them the witness in themselves, by the change produced in them by their receiving the love of the truth.—We are accepted *in the Beloved,* and whether we owed five hundred pence or fifty, our sins are all cast into the depths of the sea.

Having our hearts sprinkled from an evil conscience. There is an allusion here to the sprinkling under the law for the removal of ceremonial uncleanness; but such sprinkling only sanctified to the purifying of the flesh; but the blood of sprinkling, chap. xii. 24, removes guilt from the conscience and gives the believer confidence in approaching God.

V. 23.—Let us hold fast the profession of our faith without wavering; for he is faithful that promised.

On this Pierce says, " Our translators were doubtless in the wrong in joining the clause (and our bodies washed with pure water) to the end of v. 22, which most of the Greek Testaments I have seen make the beginning of v. 23." See also Whitby, Macknight, and others.

This is evidently correct, and it is also plain that the Apostle here refers to baptism. The

Apostle had been speaking of believers having their hearts sprinkled from an evil conscience, or the consciousness of guilt being removed by the sacrifice offered upon Calvary, and themselves begotten to a lively hope of the resurrection of Christ. He then proceeds to the confession of their hope by being baptized. Our translators have said the profession of our faith, while the confession of our hope is in the margin; both meanings are good, in fact synonymous. " So many of us (says the Apostle) as were baptized into Jesus Christ were baptized into his death. Therefore we are buried with him by baptism into death: that like as Christ was raised up from the dead by the glory of the Father, even so we also should walk in newness of life." Rom. vi. 3, 4. The Apostle thus describes the Gospel which he preached. 1 Cor. xv. 3, 4. In baptism the believer in a figure goes down into the grave of Christ and is raised again. This represents his fellowship with Christ in His death and resurrection. We have observed that Christ was manifested to Israel by a figurative burial and resurrection, and that He says I have a baptism to be baptized with, referring to His actual burial and resurrection ; now His people are commanded to go forth to Him without the camp bearing His reproach. They are, in a figure, to go down into and come up from His grave; thus expressing their hope of a glorious resurrection through their union with Him, and during the remainder of their life they are to hold fast the confession of their hope without wavering. Assured of the faithfulness of the promise on which God hath caused them to hope, Ps. cxix. 49, knowing that He who raised up the Lord Jesus shall raise them up by Jesus. 2 Cor. iv. 14.

V. 24.—And let us consider one another to provoke unto love and to good works.

Let us consider.—This admonition shows the deep concern the disciples of Christ should feel in each other's welfare. They ought mutually to consider each other's welfare and circumstances, that they may provoke each other to love and good works, adapting their admonitions to the peculiar necessities of their brethren.

V. 25.—Not forsaking the assembling of ourselves together, as the manner of some is; but exhorting one another: and so much the more, as ye see the day approaching.

The disciples of Jesus are commanded to assemble on the first day of the week, at once to commemorate the death and resurrection of Christ. That a leading object of believers meeting was to commemorate the death of Christ is manifest from 1 Cor. xi. 20, " When

ye come together therefore into one place, this
is not to eat the Lord's supper," and Acts xx.
7, to "break bread;" but in times of persecution the disciples were laid under much temptation to forsake the assembling of themselves
together. They might agree that they could
pray and read the Scriptures at home, and no
doubt there might be situations in which a
believer might be justified in absenting himself.
God has said, " I will have mercy and not sacrifice," but our love is apt to wax cold, and we are
prone to neglect what only particular circumstances may warrant us to omit. We are not
only to believe, but to confess Christ before men.
" He that confesseth me before men," &c.—
The violent prejudices of the Jews against the
doctrines of Christ, and the affliction and
persecution to which the believers were exposed in Judea, was much calculated to prevent the brethren from making a bold and
open profession of the truth; and hence it
appears that some had forsaken the assembling
with their brethren, perhaps satisfying themselves by alleging that they worshipped Christ
in secret. Such conduct, however, was calculated to prevent the progress of the Gospel.
It was putting the light under a bushel, and
improperly endeavouring to shun the reproach
of the Cross. Yet some of the Hebrews acted

thus. It was their custom or manner to absent themselves from the meetings of the brethren, thus neglecting a part of the will of Christ, which is at once a great means of impressing the truth upon our minds, by our observance of those ordinances in which it is embodied, and of diffusing the truth in the world by exhibiting it to our brethren of men.

But exhorting.—One great object of believers assembling themselves together is to exhort one another. We have ample directions on this subject in the Epistle to the Corinthians, 1 Cor. xiv. It is true, there is a special reference to the exercise of spiritual gifts, which have now ceased, but we are taught, by the abundant manner in which they were bestowed, that it is not the Lord's will that His people should be exclusively instructed or edified by the elders or overseers, although this is a most important part of their office, and much conduces to the edification of the people of God; but that the brethren should from time to time also edify one another. Miraculous gifts were not bestowed on all: by which we are taught that all are not qualified to instruct and edify their brethren; but they were bestowed upon many for the benefit of the Church. And thus we are taught,—" As every man hath received the gift, even so minister

the same one to another, as good stewards of
the manifold grace of God.   If any man speak,
let him speak as the oracles of God; if any
man minister, let him do it as of the ability
which God giveth : that God in all things may
be glorified through Jesus Christ, to whom be
praise and dominion for ever and ever.   Amen."
1 Pet. iv. 10, 11.   The Apostle expresses his
confidence in his brethren at Rome,—"And I
myself also am persuaded of you, my brethren,
that ye also are full of goodness, filled with all
knowledge, able also to admonish one another."
Rom. xv. 14.   The same word is rendered
exhort and comfort, for in admonishing each
other the mutual exhortations of believers must
be based on the glorious doctrines of the Gospel.

And so much the more, &c.—This evidently
refers to the destruction of Jerusalem, which
had been foretold by the Lord with the greatest
clearness.   He described it as the coming of the
Son of man, Matt. xxiv. 30, and 37—39, which
has been the occasion of the unscriptural tenet
of the personal reign.   It is called the "great
and terrible day of the Lord," Joel ii. 31, Acts
ii. 19, 20.   While, as we have seen it was foretold, Hab. i. 5, 6, Acts xiii. 40, 41, and its
certainty confirmed in the most solemn manner
by the Lord, Mark xiii. 31, there is one very
striking circumstance connected with it, that,

while Christ gives His disciples various tokens of its approach, He informs them that no man, not the angels of heaven, knew of that day, but His Father only; and, what is still more remarkable, He says, " But of that day and that hour knoweth no man, no, not the angels which are in heaven, neither the Son, but the Father." Mark xiii. 32. How shall we reconcile this with Jesus knowing all things? John xxi. 17. Let us compare it with John v. 19,—" The Son can do nothing of himself, but what he seeth the Father do ; " and " I can of mine own self do nothing," John v. 30. Jesus came as the Father's servant : He spoke the words of God,—" I speak," said He, " to the world those things which I have heard of him," John viii. 26. " As my Father hath taught me, I speak these things," John viii. 28. " I speak that which I have seen with my Father," John viii. 38. " The Father which sent me, he gave me a commandment, what I should say, and what I should speak," John xii. 49. " Whatsoever I speak therefore, even as the Father said unto me, so I speak," John xii. 50. " The words that I speak unto you I speak not of myself," John xiv. 10. Now, the day and the hour of the destruction of Jerusalem was a striking emblem of the end of the world, and the language in which it is

described is, therefore, in many respects applicable to that event; and, as this was not a
subject of revelation, He, who was in the
bosom of the Father, intimately acquainted
with all His counsels, having taken on Him
the form of a servant, could do or say nothing
but what He was commanded. Hence He
tells us that even the Son knew not of that
day, Mark xiii. 32: it had not been communicated to Him in his official character to be
made known to His Church. In conclusion,
we may observe that the prediction of our Lord
to His Apostles, respecting the destruction of
Jerusalem, is eminently practical to us in regard
to the end of this world.

*V. 26.—For if we sin wilfully after that we have re-
ceived the knowledge of the truth, there remaineth no more
sacrifice for sins.*

All sin is wilful: no man can compel us to
sin. There were, indeed, sins of ignorance
under the law. A man might contract defilement without being aware, and when he
became so, he offered the appointed sacrifice.
Saul of Tarsus persecuted the saints in ignorance, but Peter denied his Lord deliberately.
Here, it is evident, sinning wilfully implies
apostasy, rejecting the only available sacrifice
for sin. It is connected with forsaking the
assembling of themselves together, which might

proceed either from the fear of man, or from letting the truth slip, chap. ii. 1, and departing from the living God through an evil heart of unbelief, chap. iii. 12. Forsaking the assembling of themselves together was a step in the direction of total apostacy. Now, if we apostatize from Christ rejecting His sacrifice, there remaineth no other sacrifice for sins. Under the law, there was no sacrifice for presumptuous sin, such as murder or blasphemy. Indeed, this could not have been the case, for, as the punishment of these sins was death, had a sacrifice for them been appointed, either the legal punishment could not have been inflicted, or the sacrifice must have been offered in vain. The Apostle, in a passage already considered, had given a very solemn caution against apostacy, chap. vi. 1—6, and here he repeats the warning.

V. 27.—But a certain fearful looking for of judgment and fiery indignation, which shall devour the adversaries.

Such is the case of the apostate, which is more fully described by the Apostle. The Lord Jesus shall be revealed from heaven with His mighty angels, " In flaming fire taking vengeance on them that know not God, and that obey not the gospel of our Lord Jesus Christ: who shall be punished with everlasting destruction from the presence of the Lord, and from the glory of his power." 2 Thess. i. 8, 9. Such is the awful doom of those who have rejected the counsel of God against themselves, and especially of those who have apostatized. They draw back unto perdition.

V. 28.—He that despised Moses' law died without mercy under two or three witnesses.

The Apostle illustrates the subject by a reference to the law of Moses ; he that despised Moses' law, such as Korah and his company, who despised what God had declared concerning the priesthood, which was limited to the family of Aaron, and determined to seize on it themselves, Num. xvi., or those who refused to go up against the Canaanites, and determined to make a captain and return to Egypt. Num. xiv. and xv. 30. Two witnesses were necessary to prove guilt. Hence our Lord says, It is written in your law that the testimony of two men is true. Doubtless it may be false, as in the case of those suborned against Naboth ; but it was to be held true, and sentence passed accordingly.

V. 29.—Of how much sorer punishment, suppose ye, shall he be thought worthy, who hath trodden under foot the Son of God, and hath counted the blood of the covenant, wherewith he was sanctified, an unholy thing, and hath done despite unto the Spirit of grace?

The Gospel was far more glorious than the

Mosaic dispensation; it bore to the law the relation of the sun to the moon, and consequently the guilt of those who rejected it, or apostatized from it, was far greater than that incurred by the breach of the law of Moses. The Israelites, indeed, like all mankind, were under the law to God, and they all received the deeds done in the body according to that they had done, whether good or bad; but the peculiar dispensation under which they were placed contained only temporal promises and temporal threatenings, Lev. xxvi., Deut. xxviii. Everything was temporal and figurative. The life promised to obedience was a long life in the land of Canaan; the death threatened was the separation of soul and body. But the promises and threatenings of the Gospel are eternal; a life which shall never end is held out to believers, and the threatening is being cast off with everlasting destruction from the presence of the Lord and from the glory of His power as the portion of all who reject it. The rebellious Israelites only trod under foot the blood of calves and goats, with which the Sinai covenant was ratified; but the apostate from Christianity trod under foot the blood of the Son of God, and hath counted, &c. The blood of the covenant is that by which it was ratified. It may be a question whether the blood of the covenant wherewith he was sanctified refers to Christ or to the apostate. The Lord says, " For their sakes I sanctify myself, that they may be sanctified through the truth." John xxvii. 19. Again, believers are sanctified in Christ Jesus, 1 Cor. i. 2, chap. xiii. 12, but how can this be said of apostates? " They went out from us, but they were not of us; for if they had been of us, they would no doubt have continued with us : but they went out that they might be made manifest that they were not all of us." 1 John ii. 19. It is replied that the Scripture frequently speaks of things as they appear to be. Thus we read that Simon believed. Acts viii. Apostates are said to have been once enlightened, and so they may be said to be sanctified. This seems to be the meaning of the passage ; but, if we suppose it refers to Christ, we must refer it to His separation at once as the victim and as the priest. Every family in Israel was commanded to take a lamb without blemish on the fourteenth day of the month ; it was to be kept till the fourteenth, and then to be killed in the evening. In exact correspondence with this law, Jesus, six days before the passover, came to Bethany, where Mary anointed His feet against his burying. John xii. 1—7. Thus was He sanctified, or set apart as our passover.

Again, it has been already observed that the
first part of the consecration of the priests was
their being washed with water, accordingly
when Jesus began to be about thirty years of
age, (the time when the consecration of a priest
took place in Israel,) He was baptized in Jordan.
The next step in consecration was the anointing with oil, and when Jesus came out of the
water the Holy Spirit descended on Him in a
bodily shape. Still the consecration was not
complete, and accordingly our Lord did not act
as a priest during his abode upon earth. Chap.
viii. 4. The last part of the consecration was
the blood of the sin offering and the burnt
offering, which completed the consecration,
when the priest entered upon the duties of his
office, and thus was our great High Priest
consecrated, and having offered Himself without
spot unto God, he ever liveth to make intercession for the true Israel. Thus the expression, the blood of the covenant wherewith he
was sanctified, may either apply to Christ or to
him who professed the faith and afterwards
apostatized, thus counting the blood of the
covenant wherewith he appeared to be sanctified an unholy thing, and did despite to the
Spirit of Grace by rejecting the testimony
which he bore to Christ. This is the sin
against the Holy Spirit, of which we elsewhere

read. Jesus performed the most astonishing miracles; He cast out devils by the Spirit of God, but the Pharisees attributed this to the power of Satan, which led to the solemn caution given to them by the Lord, who informed them that all manner of sin and blasphemy should be forgiven to men; that a word spoken against the Son of man should be forgiven, but whosoever speaketh against the Holy Ghost should not be forgiven. They might blaspheme the Lord Jesus, might condemn and crucify Him, yet pardon would be proclaimed to them through the blood which He had shed, and more abundant evidence given of His having come forth from God by the outpouring of the Spirit upon His disciples, bestowing on them the gift of tongues, of the cure of the sick, and raising the dead, but if they rejected the testimony of the Spirit, ascribing His miracles to the power of Satan, then it should not be forgiven them either in this world or in that which was to come. We have observed that the world to come was an expression employed by the Jews to denote the kingdom of Christ, and indeed is thus employed by the Apostle. Heb. ii. 5. The rejection of the Holy Spirit's testimony should be involved in all the miseries which befel the Jews previous to and in the destruction of Jerusalem, and should then have their portion in the lake of fire.

The Spirit is here termed the Spirit of Grace, because from Him proceedeth every good and perfect gift. He takes of the things of Christ and shows them to believers; by His grace and power they stand, holding fast the truth; and, finally, raises them from the dead.

V. 30.—For we know him that hath said, Vengeance belongeth unto me, I will recompense, saith the Lord. And again, The Lord shall judge his people.

For we know him, &c. This is a quotation from Deut. xxxii. 35. In this prophetic song, given out by Moses at the close of his ministry, the peculiar kindness of God toward his people Israel is celebrated, together with their ungrateful returns and the consequent vengeance which he would inflict upon them. Here, as elsewhere, He claimeth vengeance as His peculiar prerogative. We are not to avenge ourselves, Rom. xii. 19; and it appears that when Joseph's brethren, after their father's death, besought him to forgive them, the question he put, " Am I in the place of God ? " Gen l. 19, was intended to intimate that vengeance belongs to him alone. This prerogative, however, is, in a certain degree, delegated to the civil magistrate. " As the servant of God he is an avenger, to execute wrath on him that doeth evil." Rom. xiii. 4.

In Israel he that despised Moses's law died without mercy; but no power is given to civil magistrates to punish irreligion; on the contrary, while we are commanded to be subject to every ordinance of men, to obey magistrates, and taught that in resisting " the power we resist the ordinance of God," the Lord expressly prohibits our acknowledging any civil authority in religion. Here we have but one Master, even Christ. Matt. xxiii. 8—10. This is repeated in order to enforce it more powerfully, and thus a broad line of distinction is drawn between civil and religious obedience. The former we are commanded to render, under pain of the vengeance which God has delegated to the civil magistrate; the latter is absolutely prohibited. In Christ's kingdom He is the blessed and only potentate. It is the duty of believers to warn and to admonish each other, and the highest penalty which they are authorized to inflict for false doctrine, or a violation of the laws of Christ, is to turn away from the offender. " My kingdom," says Christ, " is not of this world," and therefore he commits to his servants no carnal weapons.

And again the Lord shall judge his people; the word judge is ambiguous, it signifies either to plead the cause of his people by delivering or defending them, Psalm xliii. 1, or taking vengeance on the disobedient, Gen. xv. 14, 2 Chron. xx. 12, Ezek. vii. 3. From the connexion, the words quoted by the Apostle appear to bear the former sense : " For the Lord shall judge his people, and repent himself for his servants, when he seeth that their power is gone, and there is none shut up, or left." As applied in the passage before us they refer to the punishment of apostates: " Vengeance belongeth to me, I will recompense saith the Lord ;" and again, " The Lord will judge his people." Perhaps the lesson inculcated by the Apostle is, that while sin is that bitter thing which God's soul hateth, He, to whom vengeance belongeth, will visit with stripes the shortcomings of His people; but although He cause grief yet He will have compassion, according to the multitude of His mercies. Lam. iii. 32.

V. 31.—It is a fearful thing to fall into the hands of the living God.

It is a fearful thing. God is called the living God, which gives peculiar force to the language of the Apostle. If we fall into the hands of an enemy we may cherish the hope that he may be removed, or that we may make our escape; but no such hope can visit those who fall into the hands of the living God, in whom we live and move and have our being, in whose hand is our breath and whose are all our ways. He executed terrible vengeance on the nations of old. He drowned Pharaoh and his hosts in the Red Sea—He blotted out the name of Amalek from under heaven—He destroyed the seven nations of Canaan. Where are now the Philistines, the Moabites, and Ammonites? Where is the proud Assyrian? Where is Babylon the great? They have all perished. But what is all this when compared with the worm which never dies, the fire which never shall be quenched? There has mercy been mingled with every temporal judgment, however severe; but those who have professed the faith and drawn back into perdition, have thus trodden under foot the Son of God, have rejected His propitiatory sacrifice and blasphemed the Holy Spirit, shall drink abundantly the wine of the wrath of God poured out into the cup of His indignation for ever and ever. To such His mercy is clean gone for ever, and He will be favourable no more. We read that all Israel that were round about them fled at the cry of Korah and his company when the earth opened her mouth and swallowed them up, and all that appertained to them; but what was this in comparison of being cast into the bottomless pit, into that place where hope can never enter ?

V. 32.—But call to remembrance the former days, in which, after ye were illuminated, ye endured a great fight of afflictions.

Knowing the terrors of the Lord, the Apostle persuaded men, yet for love's sake he preferred beseeching them, and hence we find with what wisdom he mingles the most alarming warnings with the most affectionate recollections. We have a very striking example of this in the passage before us. A most awful description had been given of the doom of apostates. There were, perhaps, others approaching the brink of the precipice, and, as a nurse cherisheth her children, the Apostle recalls to their minds the trials they had gone through. He remembered the kindness of their youth, the love of their espousals, when after they were illuminated, when the Sun of Righteousness had arisen upon them with healing in his wings, they had endured a great fight of afflictions ; they had braved persecution, and had not been moved by their afflictions.

V. 33.—Partly, whilst ye were made a gazingstock both by reproaches and afflictions ; and partly, whilst ye became companions of them that were so used.

These consisted, partly, in their being made a gazing-stock by the reproaches cast upon

them, and the various afflictions which they
had passed through in their own persons; and,
partly, while they became companions of them
that were so used, not forsaking their brethren,
but giving them their countenance and sympathy.

*V. 34.—For ye had compassion of me in my bonds, and
took joyfully the spoiling of your goods, knowing in yourselves that ye have in heaven a better and an enduring
substance.*

For ye had compassion.—Paul was in bonds
in Jerusalem for the sake of Christ, Acts xxi.
23, and they had not been ashamed of his
chain, although their compassion for him exposed them to having their goods spoiled.
This, however, did not discourage them;
" they took joyfully the spoiling of their goods,
knowing," &c. They remembered the Lord's
words, how He said, " And every one that
hath forsaken houses, or brethren, or sisters,
or father, or mother, or wife, or children, or
lands, for my name's sake, shall receive an
hundredfold, and shall inherit everlasting life."
Matt. xix. 29. They obeyed His commands,
who said, " Lay not up for yourselves treasures
upon earth, where moth and rust doth corrupt,
and where thieves break through and steal:
but lay up for yourselves treasures in heaven,
where neither moth nor rust doth corrupt, and

where thieves do not break through nor steal."
Matt. vi. 19, 20.

*V. 35.—Cast not away therefore your confidence, which
hath great recompence of reward.*

Cast not away, &c.—In all their trials they
had been supported by the assured hope of the
joy set before them, but he that endureth to
the end shall be saved; therefore, He warns
them not to cast away their confidence, which
would issue in a great reward. Their sufferings were not worthy to be compared with
the glory which should be revealed in them,
Rom. viii. 18. The Apostle appears to glance
at what our Lord said for the support of His
people under their afflictions for His sake,
" Rejoice, and be exceeding glad: for great is
your reward in heaven." Matt. v. 12.

*V. 36.—For ye have need of patience, that, after ye
have done the will of God, ye might receive the promise.*

They had, however, need of patience. In
the world they must have tribulation: they
were appointed thereto. They must suffer
with Christ here, in order that they might
reign with Him hereafter. The Lord would
lead them in the right way, only let them hold
fast the faith, and not be moved away from the
hope of the Gospel. The promise of eternal

glory would make rich amends for their present light afflictions.

V. 37.—For yet a little while, and he that shall come will come, and will not tarry.

For yet a little while.—The prophecy of Habakkuk, from which this quotation is taken, had foretold the destruction of Jerusalem by the Chaldeans, chap. i. 5, 6, and the Apostle applies the words of the prophet to the destruction of the city by the Romans, Acts xiii. 40, 41. This was doubtless the chief event foretold, although it had what may be termed a preliminary fulfilment in the destruction of the city by the King of Babylon; just as the Lord, being brought from Egypt, was the fulfilment of Hosea xi. 1, although it had a previous fulfilment in Israel being brought from the bondage of Egypt. In the passage before us, the Apostle refers to the language of the same prophet, " He that shall come will come, and will not tarry." The great promise of the Old Testament is the coming of Christ in the flesh. This supported the minds of God's people from Adam to Christ. The great promise of the New Testament is the coming of Christ to judgment. All believers are represented as waiting for Him. This is the great and terrible day of the Lord, when He shall judge the world in righteousness, receiving

His people into everlasting mansions, and punishing the wicked with everlasting destruction from the presence of the Lord, and the glory of His power.

While His coming to judgment is the *great day* of His coming, He is represented as coming both in the way of mercy to His people, and of judgment upon His enemies. He promised to come to His disciples, John xiv. 18, and He fulfilled the promise, not by His personal presence, which they only enjoyed forty days, but by coming in the power of His Spirit, the Comforter who abides in the Church for ever, John xiv. 16, and without whom the Church of Christ could not subsist. On one occasion the Lord informed His disciples that some were standing there who should not taste of death till they saw the Son of man coming in His kingdom, Matt. xvi. 28, which was fulfilled in the rapid progress of the Gospel. Again, He describes the coming of the Son of man in the clouds of heaven, with power and great glory, Matt. xxiv. 40, evidently referring to His coming to destroy Jerusalem, for He adds, " Verily I say unto you, This generation shall not pass, till all these things be fulfilled." Matt. xxiv. 34.

The passage under consideration appears especially to refer to the Lord's coming to de-

stroy the city, which was soon to take place,
and would be connected with a partial deliverance from the persecution of the disciples.

*V. 38.—Now the just shall live by faith: but if any
man draw back, my soul shall have no pleasure in him.*

For the just by faith shall live.—This passage
is frequently quoted in the New Testament,
and points out the way of our acceptance with
God, Gal. iii. 11. " The just shall live by
faith" has much the same meaning, although
the former is according to the order of words
in the original. The Hebrews were called to
remember that the coming of the Lord was at
hand. He had warned the disciples of the
awful destruction of Jerusalem, and it was now
at hand, and the vengeance He would then inflict on the inhabitants was an emblem of the
destruction of the wicked. The Lord had also
mentioned the signs that should precede the
desolation of Jerusalem, by the observance of
which His disciples might escape the impending danger. Their safety would depend on
their attention to those signs, and their readi-
ness to abandon all. If they let slip the warnings He delivered, or ceased to observe what
was taking place, they would be involved in the
destruction of the wicked.

Our translators have introduced the words
" any man," but this is unauthorized. Its

object probably was to prevent the passage being employed in opposition to the doctrine of the perseverance of the saints. But this doctrine is explicitly stated in the Word of God, and is not affected by the passage before us: Men go out from the disciples, because they were not of them, 1 John ii. 19. We are here warned that he who endureth to the end shall be saved, which is the uniform doctrine of the Word of God. Let a man profess what he pleases, if he draw back, God's soul shall have no pleasure in him.

The passage quoted by the Apostle is Hab. ii. 4,—"Behold, his soul which is lifted up is not upright in Him: but the just shall live by his faith." Here faith is opposed to high-mindedness, which is directly contrary to faith. The believer has no confidence in the flesh, but rejoices in Christ Jesus. He rests wholly on Christ; he feels he has no strength; he lives out of himself: all which are directly contrary to high-mindedness. God knoweth the proud afar off, and has said his foot shall slip in due time.

V. 39.—But we are not of them who draw back unto perdition; but of them that believe to the saving of the soul.

This sufficiently shows that the supplement, *any man,* in the former verse, is unnecessary.

" The just shall live by faith : but if," says the Apostle, " he draw back, my soul shall have no pleasure in him. But we are not of those that draw back unto perdition; but of them that believe," &c. He was " confident of this very thing, that he which hath begun a good work in you will perform it until the day of Jesus Christ," Phil. i. 6. Faith is the gift of God, and the gifts and calling of God are without repentance : He does not forsake the work of His hands. 1 Sam. xii. 22. The Apostle's words, however, do not imply that none of those whom he addresses should draw back, but he expresses his confidence in them as formerly, chap. vi. 9. He speaks of all believers, " They are not of those who draw back unto perdition : but of them that believe to the saving of the soul ; " literally, " But of faith to the salvation of the soul." There are, no doubt, apostates, who promised fair ; but man only looks on the outward appearance, God searcheth the heart; and when the heart is right with God, and we, under a habitual sense of weakness, have fled to Christ, and are living by faith in Jesus, our path shall be as the shining light, which shineth more and more unto the perfect day.

CHAPTER XI.

V. 1.—Now faith is the substance of things hoped for, the evidence of things not seen.

The substance. It gives things hoped for and not seen a substance, or reality, in the mind. This can hardly be called a definition of faith, for it is a simple idea and can only be defined by synonymous terms. The word here rendered substance is repeatedly rendered confidence, 2 Cor. ix. 4, xi. 17, Heb. iii. 14, and in the margin of this passage, and it would seem preferable to render it confidence ; here faith is the confidence of things hoped for, the evidence, or rather conviction of things not seen, a more accurate description of faith cannot be given.

V. 2.—For by it the elders obtained a good report.

The elders, or ancients, obtained a good report ; they are mentioned with approbation in the Scriptures, and their names handed down to us with honour.

V. 3.—Through faith we understand that the worlds were framed by the word of God, so that things which are seen were not made of things which do appear.

It is by *faith that we understand that the worlds were made by the word of God.* The heathen philosophers did not deny that God was the Creator of the world, but they supposed that creation consisted in reducing to form and order the matter of which all things were made.

The idea of all being made out of nothing appears to have been an idea too vast for their comprehension. But by faith we understand that the things which are seen were not made of matter which had a previous existence. The formation of matter is described in the Scriptures, " In the beginning God made the heavens and the earth," and then we have an account of their being reduced to order. The work of creation is so vast, bearing the impress of its divine author, and is so different from the works of man, that even the heathen are without excuse in not recognising in it God's eternal power and Godhead. " The heavens declare the glory of God, and the firmament showeth his handiwork;" although there is no voice proceeding from the sun and moon, yet their line is gone to all the earth, and their words to the end of the world, and were it not for the determined enmity of fallen man against God, and that a deceived heart has turned them aside, all who behold the glories of creation would be led by the contemplation of them to their great Original; but they feed on ashes; a deceived heart hath turned them aside, and prevents them from seeing that, in supposing the earth to have been eternal, or produced by chance, there is a lie in their right hand.

V. 4.—By faith Abel offered unto God a more excellent sacrifice than Cain, by which he obtained witness that he was righteous, God testifying of his gifts: and by it he being dead yet speaketh.

The next instance of faith adduced by the Apostle is that of Abel. By faith he offered a more excellent sacrifice than Cain. We learn from the history of Cain and Abel, that in connexion with the promise that the seed of the woman should bruise the head of the serpent, bloody sacrifices were instituted; Abel offered the firstlings of his flock, Cain the fruit of the ground. The latter thereby acknowledged his dependence on God, the former acknowledged his guilt as a sinner and his hope of acceptance through the promised Saviour, whose heel was to be bruised in bruising the head of the serpent.

The way of salvation was revealed after the fall; in the emblematical language the seed of the woman bruising the head of the serpent. This may be viewed as the first parable, and its interpretation is given Heb. ii. 14. The bruising of the heel of Christ describes his

death, by which he destroyed the power of
Satan. The sting of death is sin. It could not
injure an innocent person, but Christ took part
in flesh and blood with his people, and by his
death removed the sting of death, transforming
it into a state of transition from pain and sin,
and suffering and vanity, to an exceeding, even
an eternal weight of glory. Through death,
Christ, the head of the family, entered into this
glory, and it behoves all his people to follow
his steps, to have fellowship with him, their
glorious head, in the troubles and trials of life,
and at last to be conformed to his death, that
they may have fellowship with him in his
victory which they all share. In connexion
with the obscure revelation of the plan of
salvation, in the curse pronounced upon the
serpent, bloody sacrifices were appointed, and
thus, as in other ordinances, the truth of the
great atonement was embodied. But Cain disregarded the Divine appointment, confessing
indeed his obligations to the Divine bounty,
but making no account of his sinfulness,
and disregarding the intimation that without
shedding of blood there was no remission
and no satisfaction to justice. The history
of Cain and Abel exactly corresponds with
the parable of the Pharisee and Publican.
The former was exemplary in many re-

spects. He acknowledged his obligations to God, but forgot that he was a sinner and needed mercy. This occupied all the thoughts of the publican, and he looked for it through the propitiation. There is but one name given under heaven whereby a sinner can be saved, and previously to his appearing, sacrifices, which can never take away sin, were offered on God's altar. Abel's offering was by faith in the Saviour, who was described as the seed of the woman, and his faith was manifested by offering the appointed sacrifices.

He thus obtained witness that he was righteous. —God is angry with the wicked every day; but he testified his acceptance of Abel's gifts. We are not told in what manner, not improbably by fire coming down and consuming his offering. Our Lord speaks of righteous Abel. He was, like all God's people, righteous by faith, and, although dead, he yet speaketh, teaching us that there is but one way in which sinful man can come to God, and that the blood of Jesus cleanseth from all sin all who believe in Him as their substitute who has satisfied Divine Justice.

V. 5.—By faith Enoch was translated that he should not see death; and was not found, because God had translated him; for before his translation he had this testimony, that he pleased God.

The Apostle's next example was Enoch. He was the seventh from Adam, and was translated without tasting death. This privilege he shared with Elijah; Enoch was translated before the law, Elijah under the law. This was not only a most honourable testimony to those distinguished servants of God, but an intimation that when Christ shall come to judgment, his people who are alive and remain shall not die but be changed and caught up to meet the Lord in the air. Hence the translation of Enoch and Elijah is termed a mystery, 1 Cor. xv. 51, of which what shall take place on the great day is the explanation, or hidden meaning.

Our translation says, Enoch walked with God. The Apostle, quoting from the Septuagint, has it, he pleased God; the expressions are nearly synonymous. "How can two walk together except they be agreed?" God, in his Word, bears this testimony to Enoch, that he pleased God, which implied his being reconciled to God by Jesus Christ; for, like all other men, he had been shapen in iniquity, and in sin did his mother conceive him, and while in the flesh he could not please God, he was washed and sanctified and justified in the name of the Lord Jesus Christ, and by the Spirit of God.

V. 6.—But without faith it is impossible to please him; for he that cometh to God must believe that he is, and that he is a rewarder of them that diligently seek him.

But without faith it is impossible to please God; for, in order to please God, we *must believe that He is, and that He is the rewarder of those that diligently seek Him.*

It is evident that in coming to God we must necessarily believe his existence, and without the conviction that He is a rewarder of them that diligently seek Him we can have no motive to serve Him.

This illustrates both parts of the definition given. Heb. xi. 1. No man hath seen God at any time, but by faith we have a conviction of His existence. We believe that He is, and that He is a rewarder of them that diligently seek Him, is the confidence of things hoped for. It satisfies us that we shall not seek His face in vain, that He will hear our prayers, and send us an answer in peace.

It is true that men are inexcusable in not perceiving the Creator's eternal power and Godhead by His works; but such is the utter blindness and depravity of fallen man, that not only have they not discovered the true God by the works of creation, but when God had revealed himself in the seed of the woman, the incarnate Saviour, they completely lost the knowledge of God, and changed the image of

the incorruptible God into an image made like
to corruptible man, and to birds and four-
footed beasts and creeping things.

In the passage before us the Apostle not
only speaks of our belief in a God, but in the
living and true God, whom no man knows but
as He is revealed in His Son Jesus Christ.
Hence it follows that the character of the man
who believes that God is, and that He is the
rewarder of them that diligently seek Him, must
be confined to the believer in Christ who knows
that God is a Spirit, and that they who worship
Him must worship Him in spirit and in truth.

*V. 7.—By faith Noah, being warned of God of things
not seen as yet, moved with fear, prepared an ark to the
saving of his house ; by the which he condemned the world,
and became heir of the righteousness which is by faith.*

The next example given by the Apostle is
that of Noah, who was warned of God of
things not seen as yet. He was informed of
the impending flood 120 years before it took
place ; and, although there was as yet no appearance of the catastrophe, by that faith
which is the conviction of things not seen, he
was moved with fear, which led him willingly
to embrace the way of escape made known to
him. He prepared an ark for the preservation
of his house. This could not be done in a
corner, nor, we may be assured, was the object

he had in view concealed. In the obedience yielded by Noah, and in the indifference of those who witnessed the preparation which he was making, we have an illustration of the opposite effects of faith and unbelief. Actuated by a spirit of obedience, Noah was busily employed in preparing the Ark; while, under the influence of indifference, the inhabitants of the world were eating and drinking, marrying and giving in marriage.

Thus he condemned the world; such of them as were in his neighbourhood, or to whom the report extended, treated the notion of a flood with contempt. Such a thing had never before occurred.

It is even doubtful whether there was any rain previously to the flood. We read, Gen. ii. 5, 6, " For the Lord God had not caused it to rain upon the earth . . . but there went up a mist from the earth, and watered the whole face of the ground." It is probable this continued till the flood, and here we find the explanation of Gen. ix. 12—16, " And God said, This is the token of the covenant which I make between me and you and every living creature that is with you, for perpetual generations: I do set my bow in the cloud, and it shall be for a token of a covenant between me and the earth. And it shall come to pass, when I bring a cloud over the earth, that the bow shall be seen in the cloud: and I will remember my covenant, which is between me and you and every living creature of all flesh; and the waters shall no more become a flood to destroy all flesh. And the bow shall be in the cloud; and I will look upon it, that I may remember the everlasting covenant between God and every living creature of all flesh that is upon the earth."

Had there been rain previously the rainbow would have appeared; but, as this was not the case, it seems most reasonable to suppose that the ground had been watered by the mist, and, consequently, that the rainbow was not seen till the rain began to descend. The windows of heaven had been opened and the earth deluged, which would naturally create apprehension when rain began to fall, but then the bow was to appear as a pledge that the earth should no more be overwhelmed.

Thus we see how Noah became heir of the righteousness which is by faith. Noah was a sinner, and therefore exposed to wrath as well as others. He did not escape by his innocence but by his faith. Our Lord frequently said, "Thy faith hath saved thee," and thus did Noah's faith save him; hence he is said to have become heir of the righteousness which is by faith. He is termed a preacher of righteousness, calling his fellow-men to repentance, warning them of what was about to take place which had been communicated to him. But they made light of it, and so perished in their unbelief. God's long-suffering waited an hundred and twenty years, during the whole, or a part, of which Noah was not only engaged in preaching, but in preparing the Ark; thus, at once, addressing by what they saw and heard, and thus are men addressed by the preaching of the Gospel and the appointed ordinances in which this doctrine is embodied.

The Apostle describes Baptism, which now saves believers, as the antitype of Noah's preservation in the Ark; not, indeed, the putting away of the filth of the flesh, which is all that water can do, but the answer of a good conscience toward God by the resurrection of Jesus Christ. Baptism is the profession of our faith that Jesus died for our sins according to the Scriptures, was buried and rose again according to the Scriptures, and in virtue of our unity with Christ our glorious head, His resurrection is our resurrection, and His justification is our justification. As Noah was preserved from the flood by faith, so are believers preserved from the wrath to come through faith in Him who bore their sins in his own body on the tree, thereby cancelling their guilt.

V. 8.—By faith Abraham, when he was called to go out into a place which he should after receive for an inheritance, obeyed ; and he went out, not knowing whither he went.

We have already observed that immediately after the fall God had revealed himself in Christ the seed of the woman ; in other words, the Son of man. To Him, or to God, as revealed in Him, men were taught to look for victory over their adversary the devil; and those who ceased to view God as there revealed very soon lost the knowledge of God altogether, and bowed down to stocks and stones. Noah alone in that generation had retained the knowledge of God. Gen. vii. 1. He viewed God not merely as a subject of contemplation, but as his God and Saviour; and experienced, as all believers do, His power to save.

Before the days of Abraham, God, as we have seen, had revealed Himself in the seed of the woman. Cain, in consequence of the murder of his brother, had been driven out from the presence of the Lord, and another seed had been given to Eve, named Seth. Among his posterity the knowledge of the true God seems to have been maintained; and they appear to have lived in a state of separation from the posterity of Cain, who, it is probable, soon fell into idolatry. At length the separation was broken by the sons or worshippers of God contracting marriages with Cain's posterity, called the daughters of men, which seems to have produced general ungodliness, and was the immediate cause of the Flood. The same controversy has been carried on in every age. God afterwards separated the seed of Abraham, Isaac, and Jacob; but they learned the way of the heathen, and corrupted themselves. After the ascension of Christ, God said to His people, "Come out from among them, and be ye separate, and touch not the unclean thing," &c.; but they disregarded the admonition, and mingled with the nations, satisfied with the name of Christians, while few possessed the spirit of Christ. Thus we see that in every age the great controversy between God and His people has been their proneness to mingle themselves with those who know not God.

Abraham is the father of believers, and his life is their pattern and example. Hence the Apostle dwells more upon his history than he had done upon the preceding examples which he had adduced.

He for a time served other gods. This does not imply that he was an idolater, bowing down

to stocks and stones.   When Jacob and Laban
entered into a friendly league, Laban swore by
the God of Abraham and the God of Nahor,
the God of their father; and Jacob sware by
the fear of his father Isaac.   Both seem to
have sworn by the living and true God; but
Jacob sware by Him who had revealed Himself to his grandfather and his father as their
God, and who had appeared to him at Bethel,
and assured him of his protection, and into
whose hands he had committed himself.

Abraham was called to go out into a place
which he was afterwards to receive for an inheritance, and by faith he obeyed, although he
knew not whither he went.

*V. 9.—By faith he sojourned in the land of promise, as
in a strange country, dwelling in tabernacles with Isaac
and Jacob, the heirs with him of the same promise.*

By faith he sojourned in the land of promise,
as in a strange country, in which he had no
inheritance, but dwelt in tents with Isaac and
Jacob, the heirs with him of the same promise.

*V. 10.—For he looked for a city which hath founda-
tions, whose builder and maker is God.*

This was not grievous to him, for he looked
for a city which hath foundations, whose
builder and maker is God.   Here we are
taught that Abraham's faith looked beyond

this earth.   This is more expressly stated, ver. 16, where Abraham, Isaac, and Jacob are said to desire a better country, even an heavenly, of which they saw only a shadow in the land of promise.   The same language is employed, chap. xii. 22, where we read of the city of the living God, the heavenly Jerusalem, and Jerusalem that is above.   Gal. iv. 26.

V. 11.—Through faith also Sara herself received strength to conceive seed, and was delivered of a child when she was past age, because she judged him faithful who had promised.

Sarah is the next example of faith.   She received strength to conceive seed when past age, and strength was communicated to her through faith.

The Lord had promised to Abraham that Sarah should have a son, and be a mother of nations, Gen. xvii. 15, 16; and the promise was fulfilled to her through faith.   The Lord, with two attendant angels, appeared to Abraham as he sat in his tent.   With the greatest hospitality he prepared food for them, and stood by them under the tree while they did eat.   Gen. xviii. 18.   On the Lord's inquiring for Sarah his wife, Abraham replied she was in the tent.   The Lord then assured him that she should have a son.   Sarah, although unseen, heard the promise, and laughed within herself at the supposition of her being a mother at so advanced an age. The Lord inquired why Sarah had laughed, and asked if anything was too hard for the Lord. She denied having laughed, which was an equivocation; she had not laughed aloud, but she was conscious of having laughed, and the Lord's reproof removed her unbelief. She had heard the question, "Is anything too hard for the Lord?" and that faith through which she received strength to conceive seed sprang up in her mind. The scene here described reminds us of Nathanael. When Jesus said, "Before that Philip called thee, when thou wast under the fig-tree, I saw thee," conviction flashed into his mind, and he said, "Rabbi, thou art the Son of God; thou art the King of Israel." Thus it seems to have been with Sarah. She was in the tent; no human eye was upon her; but her incredulous smile had not escaped the eye of Him who seeth in secret; and thus it appears that faith, by which she judged Him faithful who had promised, was produced in her mind.

V. 12.—Therefore sprang there even of one, and him as good as dead, so many as the stars of the sky in multitude, and as the sand which is by the sea shore innumerable.

And thus there sprang from an individual, and him as good as dead, being naturally incapable of procreating children, so many as the stars of the sky in multitude, and as the sand by the sea shore innumerable.

V. 13.—These all died in faith, not having received the promises, but having seen them afar off, and were persuaded of them, and embraced them, and confessed that they were strangers and pilgrims on the earth.

These all.—The Apostle does not here refer to Abel, Enoch, and Noah; for Enoch did not die; and, not being mindful of that country from which they came out, is not applicable to Abel and Noah, but to Abraham, Sarah, Isaac, and Jacob, who all died in faith, holding fast the beginning of their confidence stedfast to the end. They died in faith, not having received the promises; but they saw them afar off, were fully persuaded that they should be accomplished, embraced them as their portion, the joy and rejoicing of their heart, and confessed themselves strangers and pilgrims on the earth. This illustrates what had been previously said, that Abraham looked for a city which hath foundations, whose builder and maker is God; and that they desire a better country, that is, an heavenly. Had a portion in this world been what they desired, the stronger the desire the more would their souls have cleaved to the dust; but they did not mind earthly things; they looked beyond this vain and perishing world to the better and heavenly country, the

city of which they had become citizens by faith.
Thus were their hearts purified by faith ; they
sought the things that were above; they felt
that here they had no continuing city, that they
were strangers and pilgrims on earth. Faith
brought the glories of the better country to
their view, and this dimmed the lustre of all
earthly splendour, and worldly pursuits and
enjoyments.

The promises include not only that of Christ,
but of the land which He was to inhabit. But
all that was earthly and temporal in the promises derived its value in their eyes from its
connexion with the promise of Him who delivers His people from this present evil world.

V. 14.—*For they that say such things declare plainly
that they seek a country.*

For they that say such things, viz., that they
are strangers and pilgrims on earth, declare
plainly that they seek a country ; they do not
reckon themselves at home. Thus the Psalmist
says, " I am a stranger with thee, and a
sojourner, as all my fathers were." Psalm
xxxix. 13.

V. 15.—*And truly, if they had been mindful of that
country from whence they came out, they might have had
opportunity to have returned.*

The patriarchs are here represented as having
forgotten the country from whence they came

out. Thus the Church, the Lamb's wife, is
exhorted to forget her own people, and her
father's house, Ps. xlv. 10 ; to set her affections
on things above, not on things on the earth.
Had the patriarchs been mindful of the country
whence they came out, they might have had
an opportunity of returning. We repeatedly
read of famines in the land of Canaan in the
days of Abraham, Isaac, and Jacob. Sometimes
they went down to Egypt on such occasions,
but they never thought of returning to the land
of Chaldea. When Abraham commanded his
head servant to go to his kindred, and take a
wife for his son Isaac, the servant inquired
whether, in case the woman was not willing to
leave her country, he should bring Isaac back
to the land of his fathers. Abraham prohibited
his doing so, at the same time expressing his
confidence that God would incline the heart of
the woman to accompany him ; but, having no
particular promise on this subject, he made the
servant swear that he would not on any account
carry Isaac back. The promise of Abraham
being the father of Christ was connected with
the patriarch's dwelling in the land of Canaan,
which was a pledge of the fulfilment of the promise, and was called Immanuel's Land. But,
while they lived in the land, they were not to
mix with the inhabitants.

*V. 16.—But now they desire a better country, that is,
an heavenly: wherefore God is not ashamed to be called
their God: for he hath prepared for them a city.*

It is apparent from their history that they
desired a better country, even an heavenly, and
God had prepared for them a city. Here we are
expressly taught that the attention of the
patriarchs was directed to a better, even a
heavenly country, and that God had provided
for them a city, which is elsewhere described
as having foundations, whose builder and
maker is God. This is illustrated by our Lord
putting to silence the Sadducees, who denied
that there was a resurrection, by quoting
God's declaration to Moses, in which He describes Himself as the God of Abraham, Isaac,
and Jacob. He would have been ashamed of
describing Himself as standing to them in this
relation had He bestowed on them nothing
better than this world can afford. An earthly
king would be ashamed of any of his near relations being placed in a low or subordinate
situation. And the King of kings would have
been ashamed of permitting him whom he acknowledges as His friend, and whom He had
promised to bless, to be put off with the perishing enjoyments of this present life. God is
unchangeable, the same yesterday, to-day, and
for ever; and the relation between Him and

those to whom He described Himself as standing in the relation of a God must be eternal,
not confined to the brief period of our present
life.

*V. 17.—By faith Abraham, when he was tried, offered
up Isaac: and he that had received the promises offered
up his only-begotten son.*

Abraham was not permitted to accomplish
his intention to offer up his son Isaac; but the
trial was the same.   Never was any one subjected to so great a trial.   Isaac was his beloved son, the only child of Sarah his wife,
who, after being long barren, was made a
joyful mother.   For Ishmael had been sent
away from his father's house, and Isaac remained the hope of his aged father.   The promises, for the sake of which Abraham had
passed his life in a foreign land, were expressly
limited to Isaac, and therefore his death appeared to nullify them all; so that paternal
affection, and the hope of being the father of
the Saviour of the world, concurred in leading
Abraham to shrink from obedience to so revolt-
ing a commandment.

*V. 18.—Of whom it was said, That in Isaac shall thy
seed be called.*

*Of whom it was said, In Isaac shall thy seed
be called.*—God had promised that in Abra-

ham's seed all the families of the earth should
be blessed, and He had said as expressly that
this should be fulfilled in the line of Isaac.
Must not, then, the death of Isaac preclude the
fulfilment of the promises? No; Abraham
was persuaded that the promises should all be
fulfilled. He knew that He was faithful who
had promised, and therefore on this subject
there could not be any doubt.

*V. 19.—Accounting that God was able to raise him up,
even from the dead ; from whence also he received him in
a figure.*

We have seen that the commandment to
offer Isaac was express ; he was not only to be
slain, but reduced to ashes ; and there was but
one way in which the express commandment
and the positive promise could be reconciled,
viz., by God raising him from the dead ; but,
considering his almighty power, what was incredible in this ? Acts xxvi. 8. Here we see
Abraham's faith. He had never seen a person
raised from the dead ; he had never seen the
ashes of a body, which had been consumed and
dissipated in smoke, reorganized and reani-
mated ; but, when he reflected on the power of
the Creator, who spoke, and it was done ; who
commanded, and all things stood fast ; who
called into existence and harmony all the
various parts of this fair creation ; all difficulty

was at an end. He knew not how Isaac's bones
had grown in the womb of Sarah. Eccl. xi. 5.
Yet so it had been, and he was convinced that
with God nothing was impossible; and he was
no less fully convinced of the Divine faithfulness. He knew that it was impossible for God
to lie, that He was faithful. We may make
promises, and something may occur which may
prevent our fulfilling them. We may, although
our inclination be the same, have lost the
power of doing what we intended and said; but
with God there is no variableness, neither
shadow of turning. He sees the end from the
beginning. All is under His absolute control;
and, in the faith of this, Abraham hesitated not
to make the required sacrifice.

The commandment to offer Isaac is called a
temptation or a trial. Jas. i. 13. His faith
was triumphant; and he experienced that, in
keeping God's commandment, there was an
exceeding great reward. This was the greatest
trial of the patriarch's faith, and he did not
lose his reward. It had been promised that all
the families of the earth should be blessed in his
seed; and his obedience to the commandment to
offer his son, in whom his seed was to be called,
was the means of making known to him how
the promise was to be fulfilled, namely, by the
death and resurrection of Christ. There is a

remarkable correspondence in the circumstances of Abraham's offering up Isaac, and the death and resurrection of the Lord Jesus. Abraham was required to offer up his son. He obeyed, and proceeded to the land of Moriah. Moriah was the name of the mountain on which the temple was built. It was adjacent to Calvary, and it may be that Calvary was the scene of this transaction. On the third day Abraham saw the place afar off, so that during three days Isaac was under sentence of death, the exact period of our Lord's being free among the dead. Again, Abraham leaving his servants, laid the wood for the burnt-offering upon Isaac, as the cross was laid upon Jesus. Again, Isaac must have submitted without resistance. We know not his age; but Abraham was far advanced, and probably incapable of struggling with a youth who had been able to walk so far, and afterwards to carry the wood for the burnt-offering. These circumstances coincide with what took place at the death of Jesus; and the Apostle appears to put it beyond a doubt that the whole of the transaction was figurative, from our being taught that Abraham received his son from the dead in a parable. Hence it appears that, in Abraham giving up his son, and voluntarily offering him up as a burnt sacrifice, is represented the love of God in not sparing His Son, but giving Him up for all His redeemed. The narrative is indeed, as the Apostle had previously said of the law, not an image, but a shadow of the death of Jesus; but there seems no doubt that, in this parable, Abraham obtained a more distinct view of the manner in which all the families of the earth were to be blessed in his seed; and it has been supposed with great probability that the Lord especially refers to this transaction when He says, "Abraham saw my day afar off, and was glad;" and probably this transaction was the means not only of comforting and instructing Abraham, but also many of his children in their generations.

V. 20.—By faith Isaac blessed Jacob and Esau concerning things to come.

Isaac blessed Jacob concerning things to come. —The Apostle does not speak of the deceit which Jacob practised in order to obtain the blessing. He simply refers to the blessing which each of them received. The blessing of Abraham, viz., of being the father of Christ, was given to Jacob contrary to Isaac's intention; but it was given him according to the Divine purpose, of which Isaac was afterwards fully aware, and said, "I have blessed him, and he shall be blessed." Nothing is said of the impropriety of Jacob's conduct in deceiving

his father. He acted under the direction of his
mother, to whom it had been revealed before
the birth of the children that the elder should
serve the younger, Gen. xxv. 23, by which
the Apostle illustrates the doctrine of election,
Rom. ix. 11, 12. At the same time, Jacob
seems to have suffered much during his lifetime. He says to Pharaoh, " The days of the
years of my pilgrimage are an hundred and
thirty years : few and evil have the days of the
years of my life been, and have not attained
unto the days of the years of the life of my
fathers in the days of their pilgrimage," Gen.
xlvii. 9 ; and he thus describes the twenty
years he served Laban, " This twenty years
have I been with thee ; thy ewes and thy she
goats have not cast their young, and the rams
of thy flock have I not eaten. That which was
torn of beasts I brought not unto thee ; I bare
the loss of it ; of my hand didst thou require
it, whether stolen by day, or stolen by night.
Thus I was ; in the day the drought consumed
me, and the frost by night ; and my sleep departed from mine eyes. Thus have I been
twenty years in thy house ; I served thee four-
teen years for thy two daughters, and six years
for thy cattle ; and thou hast changed my wages
ten times," Gen. xxxi. 38—41. (Psa. xcix. 8.)
Into these things, however, the Apostle does

not enter; he simply states that Isaac blessed Jacob and Esau concerning things to come, and that he did so by faith, and he did so according to the description given of faith, chap. xi. 21.

V. 21.—By faith Jacob, when he was a dying, blessed both the sons of Joseph; and worshipped, leaning upon the top of his staff.

By faith Jacob, when dying, blessed both the sons of Joseph, appointing them to be heads of tribes, thus giving the birthright to Joseph, 1 Chron. v. 1, and proving his faith in the promises of God—*staff*, Gen. xlvii. 31 ; this was connected with the oath he required of Joseph that he should be buried in the land of Canaan, which proved his faith in the promises made to his fathers.

V. 22.—By faith Joseph, when he died, made mention of the departing of the children of Israel: and gave commandment concerning his bones.

Joseph, the next example, when dying, expressed his confidence in the departure of the children of Israel from Egypt that they might obtain the inheritance which God had promised them, and gave commandment concerning his bones, Gen. l. 24, 25, Exod. xiii. 19. Joseph's conduct, in regard to his bones, was not only a proof of his own faith, but was calculated to confirm the faith of his brethren that God would deliver them. This might be disregarded in prosperity, but remembered when oppressed.

V. 23.—By faith Moses, when he was born, was hid three months of his parents, because they saw he was a proper child; and they were not afraid of the king's commandment.

The next example is the faith of the parents of Moses. The king had commanded all the male children of the Israelites to be cast into the river. At this period Moses was born, and, being very remarkable for his beauty, his parents, undismayed by the king's commandment, concealed him three months. Their doing so is ascribed by the Apostle to faith. Whether this faith rested on a Divine communication by a dream to his father, as the Jewish historian, Josephus, relates, or on their confidence in the power of the God of Israel, we are not informed. It is not improbable that the latter was the case; the child was so very remarkable for beauty that his parents concluded that God would preserve him, and they therefore braved Pharaoh's tyrannical edict. Indeed, the Apostle appears to intimate that such was the case, when he says he was hid three months, because they saw he was a proper child.

V. 24.—By faith Moses, when he was come to years, refused to be called the son of Pharaoh's daughter.

The next example of faith is Moses, himself one of the most remarkable personages of whom we read in Scripture. He is placed by our Lord at the head of the prophets, when He speaks of Moses and the prophets, Luke xvi. 29. Moses was the lawgiver of Israel, and a remarkable type of Christ, uniting in his own person the offices of prophet, priest, and king. When Aaron and Miriam alleged that they were prophets as well as Moses, they were sharply rebuked, and reminded of his superiority, Num. xii. 6—8. What the Apostle relates respecting him demonstrates his faith. He had been wonderfully preserved and adopted as her son by Pharaoh's daughter. He was learned in all the wisdom of the Egyptians, and was mighty in words and deeds; but when he was grown up, he renounced all the advantages which he possessed.

V. 25.—Choosing rather to suffer affliction with the people of God, than to enjoy the pleasures of sin for a season.

And chose rather to share the afflictions of God's chosen people than to enjoy for a season the pleasures of sin.

V. 26.—Esteeming the reproach of Christ greater riches than the treasures in Egypt: for he had respect unto the recompence of the reward.

God had promised that Abraham should be the progenitor of the Saviour of the world, and had given him the sign of circumcision as a seal of the righteousness of the faith which Abraham had exercised in the promise, and it was also the token of the covenant. We do not read of Moses having been circumcised, but there can be no doubt that, in obedience to the commandment, he had been circumcised on the eighth day. Hence he bore in his body the marks of the Lord Jesus, the token of the covenant with Abraham. No doubt this was a reproach in the opinion of the Egyptians. In the state in which Israel then was it was a mark of degradation and slavery; but Moses preferred the reproach of Christ to all the treasures of Egypt, which were at his command, but which he was aware must be forfeited by his casting in his lot with Israel. But he had respect to the recompence of the reward of enjoying the blessing of Abraham and sharing with him in the glories of the resurrection, which were included in the promise of being his God. Matt. xxii. 32. Whether Moses had received an intimation that God by his means would deliver Israel, we are not informed. But, either he had received such an intimation, or had formed the design of attempting it, and had confidence in the God of Abraham, Isaac, and Jacob that he would prove successful. Stephen tells us that he supposed his brethren would have understood that God by his hand would deliver them. Acts vii. 25. Had the Lord accomplished his desire, had he with all the advantage of his station succeeded in delivering Israel, his success might have been ascribed to his personal rank and influence; but he was stripped of all his glory, reduced to the situation of a shepherd; and when he received his commission, pleaded his unfitness to engage in the service, and only undertook it by the express commandment of God. We see the same thing in Gideon's victory over the Midianites. He had collected a numerous army, though far inferior to the enemy; but it was diminished to a third of its number by a proclamation, that as many as chose might withdraw. Still it was too numerous. It was further reduced to 300 men, and then obtained a decisive victory over the enemy, when their own strength was gone, Deut. xxxii. 36; and they were strong only in the Lord and in the power of his might.

V. 27.—By faith he forsook Egypt, not fearing the wrath of the king: for he endured, as seeing him who is invisible.

By faith he forsook Egypt, &c.—This refers
to the first deliverance of Israel. Moses, after
slaying the Egyptian, feared the wrath of the
king, and fled out of Egypt; but after he
had, by the direction of God, wrought all the
miracles, he had no apprehension. The king
commanded him to see his face no more.
" And Moses said, Thou hast spoken well, I
will see thy face again no more," Exod. x. 29 ;
previously informing him that " All these thy
servants shall come down unto me, and bow
down themselves unto me, saying, Get thee
out, and all the people that follow thee : and
after that I will go out. And he went out
from Pharaoh in a great anger." This was the
effect of faith,—he disregarded the displeasure
of Pharaoh, having his eyes directed to the
invisible God.

V. 28.—*Through faith he kept the passover, and the
sprinkling of blood, lest he that destroyed the firstborn
should touch them.*

The Lord had intimated his intention to slay
the firstborn of Egypt, and commanded that
the blood of the paschal lamb should be
sprinkled on the doorposts, and that He would
pass over and not inflict the plague on those
whose houses were thus distinguished, and
through faith in the Divine intimation Moses

kept the Passover and the sprinkling of blood ;
at once giving credit to the judgment to be
inflicted on the Egyptians, and to the prescribed means of preservation of the Israelites.

*V. 29.—By faith they passed through the Red sea as
by dry land; which the Egyptians assaying to do were
drowned.*

When Israel came to the Red Sea Moses
was commanded to stretch out his rod over the
sea, which was divided, so that the Israelites
passed over as on dry land, which the Egyptians assaying to do were drowned.   Here the
whole of Israel are represented as believing.
They followed their leader.   The miracles
wrought on the Egyptians must have given
them confidence in God and in Moses, and
under the influence of this confidence they
entered the sea, which was indeed the only
way in which they could escape the pursuit
of the Egyptians.   The Apostle tells us they
were baptized unto Moses in the cloud and
in the sea.   1 Cor. x. 2.   By following him
while the waters stood on their right hand and
their left, the cloud having removed and gone
behind them, they proved their confidence in
him, and consequently in God, under whose
guidance and direction they had come out of
Egypt, just as it is said of believers, that

by Him (Christ) they believe in God.   1 Pet.
i. 21.

*V. 30.—By faith the walls of Jericho fell down, after
they were compassed about seven days.*

Israel received a lesson in Jericho how Canaan was to be conquered, not by their own
sword, but by the power of God.   But their
faith was not abiding.   When they had passed
safely over then believed they God's words,
but soon forgat His works. Ps. cvi. 13.   Thus,
also, our Lord speaks of some who for a while
believe, Luke viii. 13 ; and the Apostle teaches
us that we are partakers of Christ, if we hold
the beginning of our confidence stedfast to
the end, Heb. iii. 14 ; and our Lord tells us,
He that endureth to the end shall be saved,
Matt. xxiv. 13 ; by which we learn that temporary impressions may be made upon the
mind, producing appearances which it may
be impossible to distinguish from saving
faith, except by their continuance or non-
continuance.

*V. 31.—By faith the harlot Rahab perished not with
them that believed not, when she had received the spies
with peace.*

The next example is that of Rahab.   She
told the spies that she knew that the Lord had
given them the land ; she had heard of His

drying up the sea, and declared her faith in the
God of Israel as God in heaven above and in
the earth beneath; and, under this conviction,
she received the spies and concealed them, and
did not perish with the unbelieving Canaanites;
who, although so greatly alarmed by all they
had heard of the Israelites, that they fainted
because of them, Josh. ii. 24, still madly
persisted in resisting them, and brought on
themselves swift destruction.

*V. 32.—And what shall I more say? for the time
would fail me to tell of Gedeon, and of Barak, and of
Samson, and of Jephthae; of David also, and Samuel,
and of the prophets.*

Although the Apostle had adduced a sufficient number of examples, he had not ex-
hausted the subject, but here names several
others whose faith was conspicuous: Gideon,
who by faith triumphed over the Midianites,
Judges vii.; Barak, who overcame the army of
Jabin, Judges iv. 6. Samson, whose faith appears
not only from his mighty actions, but from
acknowledging the Lord as the author of his
success, and calling upon him when ready to
perish with thirst, Judges xv. 18; Jephthæ, whose
faith was manifest by his message to the King
of the Ammonites, stating that God had given
to Israel all the lands to which the Ammonites
laid claim, and at the same time appealing to

God for the justice of his claim. Judges xi. 12—27. It is unnecessary to particularize instances of the faith of David, of Samuel, and of the prophets.

V. 33.—Who through faith subdued kingdoms, wrought righteousness, obtained promises, stopped the mouths of lions.

David through faith subdued all the neighbouring kingdoms. Samuel was a most righteous judge. The prophets enforced men's obligations to act justly; obtained promises, as Phinehas obtained the promise of an everlasting priesthood; whilst Daniel stopped the mouths of lions.

V. 34.—Quenched the violence of fire, escaped the edge of the sword, out of weakness were made strong, waxed valiant in fight, turned to flight the armies of the aliens.

Quenched the violence of fire, like the three who were cast into the midst of the burning fiery furnace ; escaped the edge of the sword ; out of weakness were made strong ; waxed valiant in fight ; turned to flight the armies of the aliens.

V. 35.—Women received their dead raised to life again : and others were tortured, not accepting deliverance; that they might obtain a better resurrection.

Women received ;—as the woman of Zarephath, 1 Kings xvii. 21 ; and the Shunammite, 2 Kings iv. 34 ; others were tortured, not accepting deliverance, that they might obtain a better resurrection—a resurrection to a better and more glorious life.

V. 36.—And others had trial of cruel mockings and scourgings, yea, moreover of bonds and imprisonment.

Others had trial of cruel mockings, as, Jer. xx. 7, bonds and imprisonments.

V. 37.—They were stoned, they were sawn asunder, were tempted, were slain with the sword: they wandered about in sheepskins and goatskins; being destitute, afflicted, tormented.

Stoned, as Zechariah, 2 Chron. xxiv. 20, 21; Matt. xxiii. 37; were sawn asunder (such, it is said, was the fate of Isaiah by Manasseh; tempted; tried in various ways, especially by sufferings; were slain with the sword; they wandered, as Elijah, destitute, &c.

V. 38.—(Of whom the world was not worthy:) they wandered in deserts, and in mountains, and in dens and in caves of the earth.

Thus did David, and Elijah, and others, of whom the world was not worthy.

V. 39.—And these all, having obtained a good report through faith, received not the promise.

Those whom the Apostle had mentioned, and many others, having received a good report through faith, received not the promise. The promise here is the promise of the resurrection and the enjoyment of the better country, v. 16. The hope of the resurrection was general in

Israel, and the Sadducees were remarkable for
denying it. The Apostle describes himself as
having hope,—" And have hope toward God,
which they themselves also allow, that there
shall be a resurrection of the dead, both of
the just and unjust," Acts xxiv. 15; and
again,—" And now I stand and am judged for
the hope of the promise made of God unto our
fathers: unto which promise our twelve tribes,
instantly serving God day and night, hope to
come. For which hope's sake, king Agrippa,
I am accused of the Jews. Why should it be
thought a thing incredible with you, that God
should raise the dead?" xxvi. 6—8. This is
the promise which supported the minds of all
in Israel who truly possessed the fear of God,
and the worthies mentioned by the Apostle
had not received. The Apostle says,—" These
all died in faith." This is not to be understood
of all who had been mentioned; for instance,
all Israel who came out of Egypt, of whom it
is said,—" They are a very froward generation,
children in whom there is no faith." Deut.
xxxii. 20. The fall in the wilderness of the
generation which came out of Egypt is held
out as a warning, 1 Cor. x. 11, 12. But many
to whom the Apostle referred were partakers
of precious faith, and looked for eternal life
beyond the grave.

*V. 40.—God having provided some better thing for us,
that they without us should not be made perfect.*

God having provided some better thing for us,
&c.—With the exception of Enoch and Elijah,
all the family of Adam have returned to the
dust. One generation has passed away, and
another come to occupy the earth. The people
of God have entered into rest, although their
bodies have mouldered in the dust. But,
while the soul remains in a state of separation from the body, they are not made perfect,
they are in a state of transition, they are
present with the Lord; but their body, so
fearfully and wonderfully made, is reduced to
its first elements, and appears to be turned to
destruction. Christ is the first-born from the
dead; the Holy One of God saw no corruption.
He did, indeed, taste of death, and has become
the first-fruits of them that sleep. They came
into the world in successive generations, but
they shall all be made perfect in one. John
xvii. 23. When the Lord shall descend with
a shout, with the voice of an archangel and
the trump of God, the dead in Christ shall
arise. There will be no priority of those who
lived in the early ages of the world. They
are all members of Christ, of His flesh and of
His bones, and His body cannot be mutilated.
Believers are members of Christ's body, of

His flesh and of His bones.   Each individual
believer, therefore, is necessary to the perfection of the whole; so that, while some
remain in the grave the body of Christ is
incomplete.   This passage seems to be a conclusive argument against the notion of first and
second resurrection.   The first resurrection is
figurative, as John the Baptist was figuratively
Elijah.   The body of Christ is compared to
the human body.   Every member, the smallest
and, apparently, the most insignificant, is
essential to the perfection of the natural
body, and not less to the mystical body of
Christ; which, like the other, is one body
composed of many members.   1 Cor. xii. 10.

CHAPTER XII.

V. 1.—Wherefore seeing we also are compassed about with so great a cloud of witnesses, let us lay aside every weight, and the sin which doth so easily beset us, and let us run with patience the race that is set before us.

THE witnesses here spoken of are commonly understood of those to whom reference had been made in the preceding chapter, who, having themselves obtained the victory, are now spectators of those who are engaged in the combat; and, no doubt, reference is made in the New Testament to those games which were so celebrated in Greece. But the testimony borne by the elders, who obtained a good report, as stated in the preceding chapter, rather seems to be their testimony to the efficacy of faith, to which the Apostle had ascribed all the great actions they had performed.

Faith is the spring of all holy affections and of all noble actions, of which a variety of examples had been brought forward in the preceding chapter. Now the witnesses sum-

moned were so numerous, and the testimony
delivered so various, that believers are warned
and encouraged to lay aside every weight, and
the sin which doth so easily beset us, and to
run with patience the race that is set before
us.   The sin which doth so easily beset us, is
evidently unbelief.   The Apostle is treating of
faith, than which there is nothing in which we
are so prone to fail.   We naturally walk by
sight, but the Christian life is a life of faith.
The world, and the things of the world, are
constantly soliciting our attention, and by
means of them the god of this world is ever
attempting to draw our minds away from God,
but we are to resist him stedfast in the faith.

The prophet condemns our natural proneness
to self-confidence in the following striking
passage :—" For thus saith the Lord God, the
Holy One of Israel : In returning and rest
shall ye be saved ; in quietness and in confidence
shall be your strength : and ye would not.   But
ye said, No ; for we will flee upon horses ;
therefore shall ye flee ; and, We will ride upon
the swift ; therefore shall they that pursue you
be swift.   One thousand shall flee at the rebuke
of one ; at the rebuke of five shall ye flee : till
ye be left as a beacon upon the top of a
mountain, and as an ensign on an hill."   Isaiah
xxx. 15—17.   Our Lord, when asked how the

Jews might work the work of God, replies, " This is the work of God, that ye believe in Him whom He hath sent;" but we are ever prone to let slip the truth, and to mind the things which are seen and temporal, rather than those things which are unseen and eternal. Faith is the gift of God implanted by his Spirit, and the same power is requisite for maintaining as for implanting it at first. So that if the believer grieves the Holy Spirit of God he is like Samson shorn of his locks, and becomes weak and as another man. We are constantly apt to start aside from God, like a deceitful bow; so that the Apostle may well term unbelief the sin that doth most easily beset us. Faith is the principal, indeed we may say the material, of which the Christian armour is forged; the shield of faith, and for an helmet the hope of salvation, founded on faith; the feet shod with the preparation of the gospel of peace, which profits only when mixed with faith ; and the sword of the Spirit, which is the Word of God, which profits nothing unless mixed with faith ; praying always, with all prayer and supplication in the Spirit, we must ask in faith, nothing wavering, else we need not expect to obtain anything of the Lord. In short, faith, so to speak, is the staple of every part of the Christian armour.

Let us run, &c.—The Christian life is here compared to a race. It is worthy of notice that it is sometimes described as a rest, a state of repose, and at other times as demanding the greatest exertion: " For thus saith the Lord God, the Holy One of Israel: In returning and rest shall ye be saved; in quietness and in confidence shall be your strength: and ye would not." Jer. xxx. 15. " For we which have believed do enter into rest, as he said, As I have sworn in my wrath, if they shall enter into my rest." Heb. iv. 3. Again, " So run that ye may obtain." 1 Cor. ix. 24. " I therefore so run, not as uncertainly; so fight I, not as one that beateth the air: But I keep under my body, and bring it into subjection; lest that by any means, when I have preached to others, I myself should be a castaway." 1 Cor. ix. 26, 27. " I press toward the mark for the prize of the high calling of God in Christ Jesus." Phil. iii. 14. But these apparently opposite characteristics are perfectly consistent. All the believer's confidence is in the power and grace of Christ, without whom he can do nothing. All his springs are in Christ, Psalm lxxxvii., who works in him to will and to do of his good pleasure; but at the same time he is to be sober, to be vigilant, to fight the good fight of faith, that he may lay hold on eternal life. He is to take to him all the armour of God, of which, while we have seen faith is the chief, we might say the sole material, the greatest diligence and activity are required in using it. Nothing requires more of persevering activity than a race, and here we are called to run with patience the race set before us. The believer requires patience, that after he has done the will of God he may inherit the promises. Chap. vi. 12.

V. 2.—Looking unto Jesus the author and finisher of our faith; who for the joy that was set before him endured the cross, despising the shame, and is set down at the right hand of the throne of God.

Here again faith is introduced under the figure of *looking unto Jesus;* he is here described as our pattern and example. Some suppose that the Apostle here represents Jesus as the judge who determines who shall receive the prize; but he is rather represented as our model, our leader. In the witnesses whom the Apostle had summoned in the preceding chapter we see many great actions performed through faith, but where are the actors? They have, with the rest of mankind, descended to the grave; but in looking to Jesus we see faith perfected and completed. For the joy set before Him of redeeming his people from death, of ransoming them from the power of the grave, and, in the midst of the great congregation, singing praises to his Father. Chap. ii. 12.

He *endured the cross, despising the shame, and is set down at the right hand of God.*— Here we see faith perfected or completed. In all the other instances we see but the beginning of faith, but in our great pattern we see its complete triumph. As the Apostle had already stated that the worthies who lived under the old dispensation had not received the promise; they were dead and buried, they were, so to speak, detained in the grave, that they, and those who trod in their steps, might all be made perfect in one glorious body; but we behold Jesus, after unexampled sufferings, wearing the conqueror's crown, and gone before to prepare mansions in which his followers may for ever dwell.

V. 3.—For consider him that endured such contradiction of sinners against himself, lest ye be wearied and faint in your minds.

Believers are exposed to sorrow and affliction, but there never was sorrow like that with which Jesus was afflicted, Sam. i. 12; and, by considering Him, His original glory, and the depth of His humiliation and sufferings, in connexion with the glory in which He is now enthroned, and into which He is about to introduce all His blood-bought sheep, they ought to be guarded against weariness and fainting.

V. 4.—Ye have not yet resisted unto blood, striving against sin.

They had indeed suffered much, but they had not been called, as many who had gone before them, and as the Captain of their salvation had done, to seal their testimony with their blood.

V. 5.—And ye have forgotten the exhortation which speaketh unto you as unto children, My son, despise not thou the chastening of the Lord, nor faint when thou art rebuked of him.

And they had forgotten the exhortation, in which they are addressed as children, " My son, despise not thou the chastening of the Lord, nor faint when thou art rebuked of him."

V. 6.—For whom the Lord loveth he chasteneth, and scourgeth every son whom he receiveth.

For whom the Lord loveth.—So far from the chastening of the Lord being an evidence of indifference or disregard, it is a proof of love.

V. 7.—If ye endure chastening, God dealeth with you as with sons; for what son is he whom the father chasteneth not ?

This is illustrated by the conduct of a wise and affectionate father. In chastening you,

God dealeth with you as with sons; for what son does not the father chasten ?

V. 8.—But if ye be without chastisement, whereof all are partakers, then are ye bastards, and not sons.

But if ye be without chastisement, whereof all the children of God are partakers, then are ye bastards, and not sons. Men are ashamed of their illegitimate children ; they remind them of their sins, and send them out of the house, and pay little attention to their education.

V. 9.—Furthermore we have had fathers of our flesh which corrected us, and we gave them reverence : shall we not much rather be in subjection unto the Father of spirits, and live ?

Besides, we have had fathers, &c., who corrected us, and, so far from diminishing our respect for them, it led us to give them reverence ; and shall we not much rather be subject to the Father of our spirits, and live ? *

V. 10.—For they verily for a few days chastened us after their own pleasure ; but he for our profit, that we might be partakers of his holiness.

Parents often chastise their children, not so much from principle as from passion; not so much with a desire to do them good, as to

---

* There is probably a reference here to Deut. xxi. 18, in which the rebellious son was commanded to be put to death.

gratify their own irritation: but the Father
of our spirits only chastens His children for
their profit. He makes their own wickedness
correct them, and their backslidings to reprove
them, that they may know and see that it is an
evil thing that they have forsaken the Lord
their God, and that His fear was not in them.
Jer. ii. 19.

*V. 11.—Now no chastening for the present seemeth to
be joyous, but grievous: nevertheless afterward it yieldeth
the peaceable fruit of righteousness unto them which are
exercised thereby.*

It is true that no chastening seemeth for
the present to be joyous, but grievous: but
afterwards, &c. "Ye have heard of the
patience of Job, and know the end of
the Lord; that the Lord is very pitiful, and
of tender mercy." James v. 11. When Joab
refused to come to Absalom, he commanded
his servants to set his field of barley on fire.
Thus, we are prone to forget God, to restrain
prayer, and to sink into formality, but are
reminded by affliction of our entire dependence
upon God. We forsake the fountain of living
water, and hew out for ourselves broken cisterns, cisterns that can hold no water; but are
reminded, by their being dried up, of our folly,
and then are made to turn to the strong hold.
Hosea ii. 6, 7. Moses describes the Lord

chastening Israel as a man chastening his son as a mark of his love.   Deut. viii. 5.

V. 12.—Wherefore lift up the hands which hang down, and the feeble knees.

This may either refer to themselves or others.   If the former, those whose hands hang down, and their knees are feeble through weariness and fatigue, are exhorted to lift them up, to resume their courage.   If it refers to others, it is an exhortation to bear one another's burdens, to take a lively interest in the welfare of their brethren, and to endeavour to animate and encourage them, sympathizing with them in their sorrows, and to comfort and exhort each other by the motives which had been suggested.

V. 13.—And make straight paths for your feet, lest that which is lame be turned out of the way ; but let it rather be healed.

And to beware of casting a stumbling block in the way of others, as far as lies in our power, to facilitate each other's progress by our influence and example, lest the weak be turned out of the way; but we should rather aim at their being strengthened and restored to soundness.

V. 14.—Follow peace with all men, and holiness, without which no man shall see the Lord.

The exhortation implies that there may be

difficulty in maintaining peace, men's tempers and interest frequently clash, and this produces strife and division, James iv. 1. Peace is much enforced both on believers and others in the Word of God. We ought not only to be peaceably disposed ourselves, but to endeavour to promote peace among others. " Blessed," says our Lord, " are the peacemakers, for they shall be called the children of God," Matt. v. 9; and His Apostle says, " If it be possible, as much as lieth in you, live peaceably with all men. Let us therefore follow after the things which make for peace, and things wherewith one may edify another." Rom. xii. 18; xiv. 19. A peaceful disposition is intimately connected with success in diffusing the truth. The Apostle tells us the fruit (or seed) of righteousness is sown in peace of them that make peace, James iii. 18. Connected with peace is holiness, or conformity to God. We shall all receive the deeds done in the body, whether they were good or bad. We are all far deficient. In many things we all offend. If we say we are perfect, it only proves us to be perverse. There is a struggle in the mind of every believer, a law in his members warring against the law of his mind, and bringing him into captivity to the law of sin in his members. But he is, through the

Spirit, communicated to every believer through
Christ to mortify the love of sin, to crucify the
flesh with its affections and lusts.   Faith puri-
fies the heart, and, although this purification is
very partial, yet we are to follow after it, to
remember that faith without works is dead,
being alone; and that it is vain to call Christ
"Lord, Lord," if we do not the things which
He says. We shall all be judged by our works,
and therefore we ought to walk, not as fools,
but as wise.   The nearer we live to God,
the more effectually the truth is working in
us, the more of it we shall perceive; but if we
give place to the devil, if we say, The Lord
delayeth His coming, we are in danger of
stumbling on the dark mountains.   It is true,
our acceptance with God is founded solely on
the righteousness of Christ, but every man who
possesses the hope of the Gospel purifieth
himself, even as He is pure. He that doeth
righteousness is righteous, even as He is
righteous.

*V. 15.—Looking diligently lest any man fail of the
grace of God; lest any root of bitterness springing up
trouble you, and thereby many be defiled.*

Looking, &c.—We ought to maintain a holy
jealousy over ourselves, knowing how prone we
are to sin and to apostacy, and that our adversary, the devil, goeth about like a roaring lion,

seeking whom he may devour; but the Apostle
appears to have in view our watching over each
other in love. The precept is in direct opposition to the question, "Am I my brother's
keeper?" The word is repeatedly rendered
"come short," Rom. iii. 13; Heb. iv. 1. It
is in the margin "fall from;" and, indeed,
while we may be confident that He who hath
begun a good work will carry it on to the day
of Christ, and that the election shall obtain
eternal life, we can only know that we are the
subjects of Divine grace by holding fast the
truth as it is in Jesus, and abiding in the
doctrine of Christ. "For some receive the
word with joy, but have no root, and in time
of temptation fall away;" and although there
is an essential difference between saving and
temporary faith, it may be impossible for a
time to distinguish them. Empty professors
go out from believers, because they were not
of them; had they been so, they would no
doubt have continued with them; but, in the
meantime, their profession and practice may be
such as to make it meet for others to think that
God has begun a good work in them.

But, from the connexion of the passage, it
would appear that the Apostle is treating of
that watchfulness which believers are commanded to exercise over their brethren; not

watching for each other's halting, but, knowing the temptations and dangers to which all are exposed, not only to mind their own things, but the things of others, and to be prepared to caution those who are exposed to peculiar temptations; at least, this is included in the precept; and they were not only to obey this exhortation from regard to their brethren, for they were personally concerned. One sinner destroys much good; and, as a spark may kindle a great flame, so many might be defiled by one root of bitterness springing up to trouble them. The Apostle here refers to Deut. xxix. 18, " Lest there should be among you a root that beareth gall and wormwood," and thereby many be defiled. In general, men do not perish alone in their iniquity; they infect others, and embolden them to transgress.

V. 16.—Lest there be any fornicator, or profane person, as Esau, who for one morsel of meat sold his birthright.

Lest there be.—This is one of those sins which we are expressly taught exclude men from the kingdom of God, 1 Cor. vi. 9, 10. This is one of those fleshy lusts which war against the soul. The word is frequently employed in regard to Israel departing from God, being seduced into the worship of idols;

but whether taken literally or figuratively, it is an act of rebellion against God.

Or profane person; that is, one who disregards spiritual blessings, preferring things which are seen and temporal, to those things which are unseen and eternal. The character is illustrated by the example of Esau, who, for a morsel of bread, sold his birthright. Esau was the firstborn, but this did not entitle him to the blessing of Abraham; for before the children were born it had been said, " The elder shall serve the younger." But he was probably unacquainted with this. His seniority appeared to give him a claim to be the representative of his father and grandfather, and, consequently, to obtain the high privilege of being the progenitor of Christ. But for one morsel of meat he sold his birthright. His conduct affords a striking emblem of those who prefer the gratification of their appetites to the enjoyment of the eternal inheritance. What do they enjoy here ?—A momentary gratification, to which they sacrifice all their future wellbeing.

It appears, from the history of Jacob's family, that, although the blessing of Abraham did not necessarily descend to the firstborn, 1 Chron. v. 1, yet there appears to have been a preference of the elder. Accordingly Jacob, in blessing his sons, passes over the three eldest, Reuben, Simeon, and Levi, on account of their conduct, and sets Judah above all his brethren. Now, the preeminence both of Jacob over Esau, and of Judah over his three elder brethren, was according to the purpose of God, as appears by the names given them at their birth. Jacob means "supplanter," and he did supplant Esau ; Judah means "praise," and, said his father, " Judah, thou art he whom thy brethren shall praise." Thus, the purpose of God was effected through the wickedness of those who appeared to have the best right to the blessing.

V. 17.—For ye know how that afterward, when he would have inherited the blessing, he was rejected : for he found no place of repentance, though he sought it carefully with tears.

Esau was very desirous of inheriting the blessing. He carefully obeyed when commanded by his father to procure him savoury food ; and when, in his absence, Jacob had been blessed, Esau in vain besought his father with tears to bestow it upon him. It could not be ; the blessing was irreversibly bestowed ; he found no place of repentance. Some understand repentance in his father, leading him to revoke the blessing ; but it rather appears to refer to himself. His sorrow was unavailing.

It was not godly sorrow. He was disappointed; his pride was hurt at being overreached. His repentance did him no good; it was of no advantage to him. His history is a warning to all who mind the things which are seen and temporal, rather than those which are unseen and eternal. The same truth is inculcated in the parable of the ten virgins. Five were excluded; they besought that the door might be opened; but it was too late. The door was shut.

V. 18.—For ye are not come unto the mount that might be touched, and that burned with fire, nor unto blackness and darkness, and tempest.

On the third month after leaving Egypt Israel came to mount Sinai, " And Moses brought forth the people out of the camp to meet with God; and they stood at the nether part of the mount." Exod. xix. 17. On that occasion God delivered the ten commandments in the hearing of all Israel, assuring them of His peculiar favour and protection if they obeyed His voice. Ex. xix. 5, 6. Thus they came to a mount that might be touched, a material mountain, which burned with fire, and to blackness and tempest. Hence it is called a fiery law, Deut. xxxiii. 2, and its being given was accompanied with everything calculated to inspire terror and apprehension. The blackness and darkness and tempest intimated the obscurity of the dispensation, under which the Jewish lawgiver wore a vail. 2 Cor. iii. 13.

V. 19.—And the sound of a trumpet, and the voice of words; which voice they that heard intreated that the word should not be spoken to them any more.

This is particularly noticed in the giving of the law. We read that the trumpet sounded long, and waxed louder and louder. Ex. xix. 19. This was the signal for Israel to approach. Ex. xix. 13. Accordingly " when the voice of the trumpet was exceeding loud, so that all the people that were in the camp trembled," Moses " brought forth the people out of the camp to meet with God; and they stood at the nether part of the mount." Exod. xix. 16, 17.

Connected with the sound of the trumpet was the voice of words. We read that the law was given by the disposition of angels, Acts vii. 53, and ordained by angels, Gal. iii. 19. Yet we are expressly told that God spake all these words. Exod. xx. 1. These different statements are harmonized by the word of the Psalmist, " The Lord gave the word: great was the company of those that published it." Ps. lxviii. 11. And again, " The chariots of God are twenty thousand, even thousands of angels: the Lord is among them, as in Sinai, in the holy place." Ps. lxviii. 17. The thunder, the lightning, with the tempest, and the sound of the trumpet waxing louder and louder, were very dreadful, but still more tremendous was the voice of God. It demanded supreme love to God, and to love our neighbour as ourselves, Matt. xxii. 37—40, a demand which no man can answer; by which, therefore, every mouth is stopped, and all the world become guilty before God.

V. 20.—For they could not endure that which was commanded, And if so much as a beast touch the mountain, it shall be stoned, or thrust through with a dart.

They could not bear that which was commanded; the fiery law was too broad for them. It is true that only the moral law, contained in the ten commandments, is here spoken of, but it was necessarily connected with the rest of the Jewish dispensation, the meats and drinks and carnal ordinances, else it would not have been a shadow of good things to come. However insufficient the blood of bulls and goats might be to take away sin, such sacrifices were necessary for the time then present to keep up the expectation of the sacrifice of Christ.

To increase the terror and awfulness of the scene, and to make Israel feel their distance from God, " who is of purer eyes than to behold iniquity, and who cannot look upon sin, but hateth all the workers of iniquity," " if so much as a beast touched the mountain, it was to be stoned, or thrust through with a dart."

V. 21.—And so terrible was the sight, that Moses said, I exceedingly fear and quake.

And so terrible was the sight, that Moses said, I exceedingly fear and quake. This is probably referred to Ex. xix. 19. Moses spake, and God answered him with a voice, probably encouraging him.

V. 22.—But ye are come unto mount Sion, and unto the city of the living God, the heavenly Jerusalem, and to an innumerable company of angels.

In opposition to Israel's coming to mount Sinai, (the material mountain,) the true Israel, to whom the Epistle is addressed, are represented as having come to mount Zion (not a material but a spiritual mountain). In the description of the giving of the law, in the preceding verses, everything is material and earthly. Blackness, darkness, and fire, with lurid smoke, and the sound of the trumpet, are all calculated to affect the senses and inspire terror. Here, on the contrary, everything is spiritual and heavenly. Believers are come to mount Sion. It is remarkable that Jerusalem, which under the old dispensation was chosen for the residence of the God of Israel, where his temple was built, and the sacrifices were offered, was the last place in the promised land of which Israel obtained possession in the reign of David. 2 Sam. v. 7. Hence the God of Israel is said " to have dwelt in His holy hill of Zion," Ps. ii. 6, and " to love the gates of Zion more than all the dwellings of Jacob." Ps. lxxxvii. 2. Hence Zion is called " the joy of the whole land." Ps. xlviii. 2. On this account mount Sion is represented as the dwelling-place of God under the new and better dispensation. This is His rest for ever ; here Christ is laid for a foundation, 1 Pet. ii. 6, and here He is said to stand at the head of His redeemed. Rev. xiv. 1. The city of the living God, the heavenly Jerusalem. This is the city which God hath prepared for His people. Ch. xi. 16. It is called Jerusalem that is above, Gal. iv. 26, and the holy city, new Jerusalem, Rev. xxi. 2.

To an innumerable company of angels.—We have seen that thousands of angels were present at the giving of the law, and myriads of the same glorious beings are represented as all ministering to the heirs of salvation, under the direction of Him who is the head of all principalities and powers.

The whole of Israel were assembled at Sinai, and there formed into a nation, to which allusion is here made.

V. 23.—To the general assembly and church of the first-born, which are written in heaven, and to God the judge of all, and to the spirits of just men made perfect.

The firstborn of Israel were sanctified, Ex. xiii. 2, and the Levites taken in place of them to minister in the sanctuary. The congregation of Israel was an emblem of the general assembly and church of the firstborn, the true Israel, the righteous nation that keepeth the truth. It was a grand sight to behold all Israel assembled before God at Sinai. Israel is called the firstborn. Ex. iv. 22. The genealogies of the different tribes in Israel were carefully kept, as emblems of the Lamb's book of life. Isaiah iv. 3.

God the judge of all—He is revealed as such in his Son. God appeared at Sinai as the God of Israel, Ex. xx. 2, 2 Cor. v. 10, and as such believers have access unto him. At Sinai everything was calculated to alarm, but in Christ God has revealed himself to all his people as love.

Perfect—1 Pet. v. 10.—The people of God are not made perfect till the soul and body are reunited, but life and immortality are brought to light. The resurrection is exhibited in the resurrection of Christ, and therefore we are said to have come to the spirits of just men made perfect; behold them clothed with their spiritual bodies, the house which is from heaven.

V. 24.—And to Jesus the mediator of the new covenant, and to the blood of sprinkling, that speaketh better things than that of Abel.

Moses was the mediator of the old covenant, and stood between God and Israel; but believers are come to a better and more glorious Mediator, *the Mediator of the new covenant,* not written on stone, but in fleshy tables of the heart, 2 Cor. iii. 3, *and to the blood of sprinkling.* Believers are saved by the blood of sprinkling, 1 Pet. i. 2. Christ is their passover, and as Israel escaped by the sprinkling of blood, so do believers. Israel was sprinkled at Sinai with the blood of the covenant, and thus it was ratified. It *speaketh better things than the blood of Abel,* which cried for vengeance, this ensures mercy.

V. 25.—See that ye refuse not him that speaketh. For if they escaped not who refused him that spake on earth, how much more shall not we escape, if we turn away from him that speaketh from heaven.

Him that speaketh—Chap. i. 2.—Him that spake on earth. How vain to expect to escape from mount Sinai. At Sinai the worldly kingdom was established, the rewards and punishments of which were all temporal; now he speaketh from heaven in a far more excellent way,—better promises.

V. 26.—Whose voice then shook the earth: but now he

hath promised, saying, Yet once more I shake not the earth only, but also heaven.

Voice shook mount Sinai, Ex. xix. 18, refers not only to the mountain shaking, but to the great change produced by taking the nation of Israel to be his peculiar people, setting them apart for himself, giving them laws and commandments, while all the other nations were left in darkness and ignorance. But now a much greater shaking was to take place, not only the earth, but the heaven was to be shaken. The first shaking only affected one nation. It took them out of their former order. It gave privileges to one nation which no other enjoyed; but now a far greater shaking was to take place, by which all nations would be affected. The heaven is higher than the earth. By the first shaking God established an earthly kingdom, confined to one nation; by the second, a heavenly kingdom, whose influence should extend to all nations, was to be established.

V. 27.—And this word, Yet once more, signifieth the removing of those things that are shaken, as of things that are made, that those things which cannot be shaken may remain.

Now this word, once more, signifies the removing of things shaken, as of things that are made, that the things that cannot be shaken may remain.— All the law and the prophets hang on the precepts to love God and our neighbour. These things remain, while the meats and drinks and carnal ordinances in which the kingdom of Israel stood are shaken and removed. The shaking of heaven refers to the far greater alteration made by the new covenant, the gathering of the saints into one body under Christ, and bestowing on them the kingdom.

V. 28.—Wherefore we receiving a kingdom which cannot be moved, let us have grace, whereby we may serve God acceptably with reverence and godly fear.

We, believers, receiving a kingdom, are made kings and priests to God. This kingdom cannot be moved; it is not like the Jewish dispensation temporary and introductory, but it is abiding. From this consideration let us have grace to serve God acceptably with reverence and godly fear. Let us consider that the greater our privileges the more our responsibility. To whom much is given of them much shall be required.

Let us then have grace to serve God acceptably with reverence and godly fear.—This is altogether different from slavish fear; it is that godly fear which arises from right views of the glorious character of God; his purity, holiness, kindness, and compassion, blended with abhorrence of sin, on which he cannot look.

V. 29.—For our God is a consuming fire.

The Apostle refers to Deut. iv. 24,—" For the Lord thy God is a consuming fire, even a jealous God;" and while the Gospel exhibits the boundless riches of the love of God, it gives a more awful display of His justice, and abhorrence of sin, than if all mankind had been destroyed. He pardons sins of the deepest dye, but it is only through the death of His only begotten Son. Here we see that He is of purer eyes than to behold iniquity, and that He cannot look upon sin. When Jesus stood in the place of sinners, the sword was called to awake against the man who was the fellow of the Almighty, and He drank to the very dregs the cup of wrath; so that while the believer joys in God through Jesus Christ, whose mercy endureth for ever, the more clear his apprehension of the way in which this mercy flows to him, the more is he impressed with the evil of sin, which is that bitter thing which God cannot look upon.

CHAPTER XIII.

V. 1.—Let brotherly love continue.

Brotherly love is Christ's new commandment. It is at once a new and an old commandment. It is old, as it was from the beginning. It is new, as it was enjoined by Jesus on his disciples. The love of believers to each other, which is implanted in them by Divine teaching, 1 Thess. iv. 9; was shadowed forth by the preference which the children of Israel were commanded to cherish towards each other. Believers of every nation are to be the objects of our love. It is to continue. It is the perfect bond by which the subjects of the kingdom of God are knit together. They are heirs of God, and joint-heirs with Christ. Their inheritance is ample. However great the enjoyment of one, it does not impoverish others, so that there is no room for jealousy.

V. 2.—Be not forgetful to entertain strangers: for thereby some have entertained angels unawares.

Hospitality to strangers is inculcated from the consideration that some have, without knowing it, entertained angels, as was the case with Abraham and Lot.

V. 3.—Remember them that are in bonds, as bound with them; and them which suffer adversity, as being yourselves also in the body.

This a reference to those who are in bonds for the cause of Christ. They were to sympathize with them and to pray for them. Such persons had peculiar claims upon them as their brethren, and being placed as it were in the front of the battle. Indeed, it became them to sympathize with all who were in adversity, from the consideration that they were also in the body and liable to like afflictions.

V. 4.—Marriage is honourable in all, and the bed undefiled: but whoremongers and adulterers God will judge.

Marriage is honourable in all.—The Roman Catholics extol celibacy as more honourable, and do not permit their clergy to marry; but God has declared it to be honourable in all. But God will judge whoremongers and adulterers; they may escape the judgment of men, but they cannot escape Divine vengeance.

V. 5.—Let your conversation be without covetousness; and be content with such things as ye have: for he hath said, I will never leave thee, nor forsake thee.

Here, and in many other passages of Scripture, we are cautioned against covetousness, and urged to be content with the situation and circumstances in which we are placed in the course of God's providence, and the motive to contentment is the promise of God, that He will never leave us nor forsake us. This passage is remarkable for the number of negatives which it contains. I will never, never leave thee; no, I will never, never forsake thee. This was originally said to Joshua, after the death of Moses. Josh. i. 5. David repeated the promise to Solomon, 1 Chron. xxviii. 20; and it is repeated in substance to Israel. Isa. xli. 10, 14. The Apostle teaches us that " whatsoever things were written aforetime were written for our learning, that " we through patience and comfort of the Scriptures might have hope," Rom. xv. 4; and as " all the promises of God in him are yea, and in him Amen, unto the glory of God by us," 2 Cor. i. 20, all believers are encouraged to appropriate this precious promise in all their straits and difficulties.

V. 6.—So that we may boldly say, The Lord is my helper, and I will not fear what man shall do unto me.

We may therefore boldly say,—" The Lord is my helper," &c. " The Lord is on my side;

I will not fear: what can man do unto me ? "
Ps. cxviii. 6.

V. 7.—Remember them which have the rule over you, who have spoken unto you the word of God : whose faith follow, considering the end of their conversation.

The Apostle seems to refer to their leaders or elders, who had spoken to them the word of the Lord, and had departed this life ; for he refers to the end of their conversation. They had finished their course, they had kept the faith, and entered into the joy of their Lord.

V. 8, 9.—Jesus Christ the same yesterday, and to-day, and for ever. Be not carried about with divers and strange doctrines. For it is a good thing that the heart be established with grace ; not with meats, which have not profited them that have been occupied therein.

This is often understood as being connected with the preceding verse; but it is evidently to be connected with what follows. From the consideration that Jesus is the same yesterday, to-day, and for ever, the believers are cautioned against being carried away with those winds of doctrine which arise from time to time—they are termed diverse and strange doctrines. There appears, from what follows, to be a reference here to the Judaizing teachers who " taught the brethren, and said, Except ye be circumcised after the manner of Moses, ye cannot be saved," Acts xv. 1 ; for the Apostle goes on,—" It is a good thing that the heart be established with grace, not with meats," &c. It appears from the epistle that many had either apostatized, or were in danger of apostacy and of returning to the weak and beggarly elements. This error is exposed in almost all the epistles, especially in that to the Galatians ; and those who inculcated such doctrine are characterized as false teachers. The Apostle would have the hearts of believers established with grace, with enlarged views of the boundless riches of Divine grace, through the one sacrifice of Christ.

V. 10.—We have an altar, whereof they have no right to eat which serve the tabernacle.

The Jewish sacrifices were offered upon the altar. Now we have an altar, by which is evidently meant Christ. He is at once the altar, the sacrifice, and the Priest. The whole of the Jewish dispensation pointed to Him on whom alone believers depend. The priests in Israel who waited at the altar were partakers with the altar, 1 Cor. ix. 13 ; part of the sacrifice was burnt on the altar and part eaten by the priest ; but those who serve the tabernacle have no right to eat the sacrifices of the Christian altar.

V. 11, 12, 13.—For the bodies of those beasts, whose

blood is brought into the sanctuary by the high priest for sin, are burned without the camp. Wherefore Jesus also, that he might sanctify the people with his own blood, suffered without the gate. Let us go forth therefore unto him without the camp, bearing his reproach.

For the bodies of those beasts, whose blood is brought into the sanctuary by the high priest for sin, are not to be eaten, but burnt without the camp, according to Lev. xvi. 17 :—" And there shall be no man in the tabernacle of the congregation when he goeth in to make an atonement in the holy place, until he come out, and have made an atonement for himself, and for his household, and for all the congregation of Israel." All the sacrifices prefigured Christ, and more especially the sacrifice on the great day of atonement. Now, as the priest was not permitted to eat of the flesh of the sacrifice offered on that day, but it was burnt without the camp, it is evident that the worshippers in the tabernacle have no right to eat of our altar; for, in exact correspondence with the Levitical law, Jesus, that He might sanctify the people with His own blood, suffered without the gate. Let us then go forth to Him without the camp, bearing His reproach, turning our back on the legal sacrifices, and on the altar where they were offered.

V. 14, 15.—For here have we no continuing city, but

we seek one to come. By him therefore let us offer the
sacrifice of praise to God continually, that is, the fruit of
our lips giving thanks to his name.

And let us be encouraged so to act by the
consideration that here we have no continuing
city, but we look for one to come, that city
which hath foundations, whose builder and
maker is God. This verse is a parenthesis.
The 15th verse is connected with the 13th. In
it we are encouraged to go forth without the
camp, bearing His reproach; and, in verse 15,
are exhorted by him to offer the sacrifice of
praise to God continually, namely, the fruit of
our lips, Hos. xiv. 2; Ps. lxix. 30, 31; giving
thanks to His name. As Israel approached
God through their high priest, we are to approach through the great High Priest of our
profession, for no man comes to the Father but
by Him.

V. 16.—But to do good and to communicate forget not:
for with such sacrifices God is well pleased.

But while we are to offer the sacrifice of
praise to God continually, we are not to forget
to do good to others, and to communicate of
our substance to the poor. Phil. iv. 18. Probably the Apostle particularly refers to the
fellowship or contribution for the poor, which
is so frequently enjoined in Scripture. These
are the sacrifices which the Lord now requires

of His people, and with these sacrifices He is
well pleased.

*V. 17.— Obey them that have the rule over you, and
submit yourselves : for they watch for your souls, as they
that must give account, that they may do it with joy, and
not with grief: for that is unprofitable for you.*

In verse 7th and 9th the Apostle had exhorted the Hebrews to remember their departed leaders, who had spoken to them the
word of the Lord, and cautioned them against
being carried away with diverse and strange
doctrines, from the consideration that Jesus is
the same yesterday and for ever.   Here he
admonishes them to obey their leaders, and to
submit to them.   The authority given by the
Lord to the bishops or elders of the churches
of Christ is altogether different from the authority with which civil rulers are invested.   The
authority of the spiritual ruler is to be maintained by instruction and persuasion, and is not
to be enforced by civil pains and penalties, like
the authority of the civil ruler.   We have an
illustration of this in the history of our Lord.
In consequence of the doctrine in one of His
discourses proving very offensive, many of His
disciples went away.   He neither prevented nor
threatened them, but said to the twelve, " Will
ye also go away ?"   But they were restrained
by the conviction that He was the Christ,

the Son of God. John vi. 67, 69. So the overseers are to commend themselves to every man's conscience, and to rule by the Word of God. The duty of submission is enforced, first, because they watch for the souls of those over whom they are placed, and must give account of the manner in which they have fulfilled their trust.

V. 18.—Pray for us: for we trust we have a good conscience, in all things willing to live honestly.

The Apostle then requests their prayers, and he does this the more confidently because he trusted he had a good conscience. He was indeed maligned by many; but, whatever his calumniators might allege, he had the testimony of his conscience. " For our rejoicing is this, the testimony of our conscience, that in simplicity and godly sincerity, not with fleshly wisdom, but by the grace of God, we have had our conversation in the world, and more abundantly to you-ward." 2 Cor. i. 12. It may appear strange that the Apostle does not speak with more confidence. He trusts he had a good conscience, in all things willing to live honestly. Here he seems to glance at the deceitfulness of the heart. We may compare this with 1 Cor. iv. 3, 4 :—" But with me it is a very small thing that I should be judged of you, or of man's judgment: yea, I judge not mine own self. For I know nothing by myself; yet am I not hereby justified: but he that judgeth me is the Lord." He was not conscious of acting unfaithfully, but this did not justify him. His heart was deceitful and desperately wicked. He might form a false estimate of himself, but the judgment was the Lord's; and here he does not affirm that he has a good conscience, but he trusts he has a good conscience, in all things willing to live honestly.

V. 19.—But I beseech you the rather to do this, that I may be restored to you the sooner.

He had requested in general to have their prayers, and he desires them for a specific purpose, that he might be the sooner restored to them. He was exposed to many dangers. He was exposed to deaths oft, 2 Cor. xi. 23 ; and in many perils, ver. 26; and he desires the prayers of his brethren that he may be the sooner restored to them. Amidst all his varied and extensive labours he always felt peculiar interest in his countrymen, and appears glad of an opportunity of seeing and conversing with them.

V. 20.—Now the God of peace, that brought again from the dead our Lord Jesus, that great Shepherd of the sheep, through the blood of the everlasting covenant.

Here, in drawing to a close, he offers an affectionate prayer for his brethren; and it is expressed in a manner calculated for their instruction and edification.

He describes God as the God of peace.* He preaches peace to them that are far off, and to them that are nigh. He is the author of peace in all the Churches of the saints, 1 Cor. xiv. 33. The same Apostle prays that the Lord of peace may give the brethren peace always, by all means, 2 Thess. iii. 16. By the blood of His Cross Christ hath not only reconciled His people to God, but made peace between Jews and Gentiles, making of two one new man, so making peace by abolishing the enmity arising from their separation by the peculiar dispensation under which the Jews were placed.

The prayer, then, is addressed to the God of peace, who is characterized as having brought from the dead the great Shepherd of the sheep. He feeds His flock as a shepherd, Isa. xl. 11, and describes Himself as sustaining this character, John x. 11, and speaks of His sheep consisting both of Jews and Gentiles, verse 16, as given to Him, verse 29. He received a commandment to lay down His life for them, verse 18. Pastors are exhorted to feed the flock, but He is the great Shepherd of the sheep.

Through the blood of the everlasting covenant.

* It is an argument for Paul being the author of this Epistle that this title is only to be found in his writings.

—Some understand this to signify that Christ is the great Shepherd of the sheep through the blood of the everlasting covenant, having purchased the Church with His own blood. But it is rather to be connected with His being brought from the dead through the blood of the everlasting covenant. His being brought from the dead, or His resurrection, was the fruit of the perfection of His sacrifice, by which the sins of His people were cast into the deeps of the sea. He proclaimed with His dying breath that the work of redemption was completed, and the Father set His seal to the declaration when He raised Him from the dead. He is, therefore, said to be brought from the dead through the blood of the everlasting covenant. He had been made sin for His people, but their guilt was fully expiated by His blood. He had received the wages of sin, but, having made an end of sin, death could not retain him under its dominion; hence He was brought from the dead through the blood of the everlasting covenant, by which the covenant was ratified; and through the same blood all His blood-bought sheep shall be brought.

The everlasting covenant is opposed to the temporary covenant with Israel, which they broke, and the removal of which made room for the better covenant, which can never wax old, having been in the mind of God from eternity, and shall abide for ever.

V. 21.—Make you perfect in every good work to do his will, working in you that which is well pleasing in his sight, through Jesus Christ; to whom be glory for ever and ever. Amen.

Make you perfect in every good work.—Thus He prays for their progress, for their growth in grace, and increasing conformity to their great pattern and example.

Working in you, &c.—Believers are God's workmanship, created in Christ Jesus unto good works. They were at first created in Adam; but they are born of the Spirit, and possess a new and divine nature, derived from their glorious Head; and, as they were at first changed into the image of Christ by the contemplation of His glory, the transformation proceeds till they see Him as He is, and are completely conformed to Him.

V. 22.—And I beseech you, brethren, suffer the word of exhortation: for I have written a letter unto you in few words.

He entreats them to listen to the instructions He had delivered, for He had written to them very concisely.

V. 23.—Know ye that our brother Timothy is set at liberty: with whom, if he come shortly, I will see you.

He informs them that Timothy was set at liberty, and expresses His intention to visit them along with him.

V. 24.—Salute all them that have the rule over you, and all the saints. They of Italy salute you.

All the Epistles were addressed to the Churches, and thus we are guarded against the error of considering the clergy, as they have been improperly called, as in themselves constituting the Church. The brethren are directed to salute their pastors, overseers, or rulers. Respect to them is intimately connected with the peace of the Church, 1 Thess. v. 13.

The Apostle adds, " and all the saints." He also sends the salutation of the brethren in Italy, which shows the Epistle was written from thence.

V. 25.—Grace be with you all. Amen.

Grace, the Lord's free and undeserved favour : He prays it may rest on them all.

The Epistle is said to be written from Italy, which is evident from verse 24; but it could not be sent by Timothy, for Paul only expected his arrival, and the notes appended to the Apostolic Epistles are of no authority.

Note on Hebrews ii. 9. *P.* 65.

ON THE EXTENT OF THE ATONEMENT.

A GREAT deal of disputation on this subject arises from a doubtful interpretation of the meaning of the word Atonement. In the Bible the sacrifice of Christ is always represented as a price paid to Divine Justice. Rev. v. 9. But the adversaries of the Vicarious Sacrifice calumniously represent orthodox Divines as placing the Father and the Son in an adverse relation. Scripture and all orthodox creeds represent the Godhead as acting in unison from the Councils of Eternity. The Father, in his boundless love for the world, sends the Son to shed his blood and offer a sacrifice, as an atonement for all who believe; the Son, comes in the fulness of time, to offer himself as a good Shepherd, giving his life for the sheep; and the Holy Spirit applies the benefits of Christ's sacrifice and intercession for all whose names are written in the Lamb's Book of Life. It is from confounding the infinite value of the sacrifice with its limited application as an atonement that many have been beguiled into those errors which explain away the vicarious sacrifice, making Christ an example only and not a victim, and introducing the fatal but delusive notions of Universal Pardon or Universal Restoration.

It is, however, supposed by many, generally sound Divines, in our days, that if they hold that Christ died only for his people the invitations of the Gospel must be restricted. On this subject the following extract is taken from Robert Haldane's Exposition of Romans v. 11 :—

" Many suppose that in preaching the Gospel it is necessary to tell every man that Christ died for him, and that if Christ did not actually atone for the sins of every individual, the Gospel cannot be preached at all. But this is very erroneous. The Gospel declares that Christ died for the guilty, and that the most guilty who believe it shall be saved. ' It is a faithful saying, and worthy of all acceptation, that Christ Jesus came into the world to save sinners,' even the chief of sinners. The Gospel does not tell every individual to whom it is addressed, that Christ died for him, but that if he believes he shall be saved. This is a warrant to preach the Gospel unto all men ; and it is only as he is a believer that it is known to any man that Christ died for him individually. To preach the Gospel then to every man, and call on every one to believe and be saved, is quite consistent, as it is a truth that whoever believes shall be saved. If the most guilty of the human race believe in Jesus, there is the most perfect certainty that he shall be saved. If any man is straitened in preaching the Gospel, and find a difficulty in calling on all men to believe, except he can at the same time tell them that Christ died for every individual of the human race, he does not clearly understand what the Gospel is. It is the good news that Christ died for the most guilty that believe, not that He died for every individual, whether he believe or not. To the truth that every man shall be saved who believes, there is no exception.

" The difficulty of those who feel themselves restrained in exhorting sinners to believe the Gospel, on the ground that the atonement of Christ was not made for all, is the same as that which is experienced by some who, believing the doctrine of election, suppose it inconsistent to exhort all indis-criminately to believe the Gospel, since it is certain that they who are not chosen to eternal life will never be saved. In this they err. The Gospel, according to the commandment of the everlasting God, is to be made known to all nations for the obedience of faith. It is certain, however, that they for whom Christ did not die, and who do not belong to the election of grace, will not believe. These are secret things which belong to God, to be revealed in their proper time. We are not, then, to inquire first, either for ourselves or others, for whom Christ died, and who are chosen to eternal life, before we determine to whom the Gospel is to be preached ; but to preach it to all, with the assurance that whoever believes it shall receive the remission of sins. In believing it, we ascertain for ourselves that Christ bare our sins in His own body on the tree, and that God from the beginning hath chosen us to salvation, through sanctification of the Spirit and belief of the truth." (Vol. I., p. 386. Eighth Edition.)

Macintosh, Printer, Great New-street, London.

THE DOCTRINE AND THE DUTY OF SELF-EXAMINATION

James Haldane

"Examine yourselves, whether ye be in the faith; prove your own selves. Know ye not your own selves, how that Jesus Christ is in you, except ye be reprobates?"

2 Corinthians 13:5

The apostle Paul, in writing to the church at Corinth, exhorts the Gentile converts, *Examine yourselves, whether ye be in the faith; prove your own selves: know ye not your own selves, how that Jesus Christ is in you, except ye be reprobates?* Although he had confidence in the Corinthians, that they were in general sincere in their belief, and members of the true church of Christ, yet he felt that it was possible that they might be destitute of the faith of the gospel—that they might have been imposing upon themselves, and were the objects of divine displeasure instead of their *life being hid with Christ in God.*

It is a serious thing for the professor of Christianity to reflect on this possibility, but it is on this account the duty of self-examination is urged on him by the highest sanctions.

In endeavoring to explain and enforce this duty, I shall

I. Make some general observations on the subject.

II. Consider the end which we ought to have in view in self-examination.

III. Suggest some topics to which our inquiries should be directed in attending to this divine precept.

1st. Consider, the commandment to examine ourselves does not imply that we may not be immediately sensible that we believe the gospel, and consequently have joy and peace in believing. The mind perceives, and is acquainted with all its own thoughts, judgments, and emotions. When we believe any thing to be true, we feel that we do so; and we may know when we believe the gospel of God, as well as when we believe any report upon the authority of a fellow creature. But let it be remembered, that even in the things of this life, we are apt to impose upon ourselves. The deceitfulness of the heart is especially manifest in regard to things unseen and eternal; and hence so many cry peace, peace, to themselves when there is no peace. One fruitful cause of self-deception in every country called Christian, is that most men have been accustomed from their earliest years to hear what is called the gospel, and to acknowledge its truth, without understanding its meaning, attending to its evidence, or feeling its importance. We may be conscious that we believe what we deem to be the gospel, and yet be in the gall of bitterness and the bond of iniquity. It is necessary, therefore, for all to examine, not only whether they believe something to which they attach the name of gospel, but whether it be indeed the gospel which they believe.

2nd. From the very nature of the gospel, as well as from the express declarations of God, we are certain that the faith of Christ must produce sentiments, experience, and practice peculiar to itself. The connection between faith and practice is uniformly declared to be so inseparable that the latter must always exactly correspond with the former.

3rd. Great pains have in consequence been taken to distinguish with accuracy between common and saving faith. And persons have been directed to judge favorably or unfavorably of their state, according as they have exerted the saving and not merely the natural acts of faith. The certain consequence of this must be to lead men to endeavor to perform such saving acts, and to trust in these, when they suppose that they have performed them. The mind is thus diverted from Jesus Christ, from the glory of His atonement, and the mercy of God revealed in Him, which is the only foundation of hope, to a delusive search after something else which may quiet the conscience. Thus a system of self-righteousness is established, under the name of salvation by faith.

Besides, nothing can lay us more open to self-deception. When instead of being engaged in contemplating the truth, our minds are occupied in considering the manner of our believing, we are laid under very strong temptations to persuade ourselves that our faith possesses all the qualities of saving faith, and hence to draw our consolation. The Scriptures show us a more excellent way. They address the common sense of mankind, teach us what we are to believe, and describe the effects which the belief of the truth must necessarily produce. Thus, our minds are constantly directed towards the testimony of God, and a far more unequivocal test is given us by which we may prove whether we believe the gospel.

4th. We ought ever to bear in mind that we are extremely prone to take refuge in the opinion of others, especially of those who rank high in our esteem for judgment and piety. The opinions of others may indeed be very useful to the Christian. It is, however, often more important for us to regard the sentiments of those who are prejudiced against us than those of our friends.

Caution is the more necessary, as there is a strong tendency in those who are weak in the faith—and especially in persons under recent impressions—to be very solicitous about the opinions of those around them. And it is to be feared that many, by imagining that others entertain a favorable opinion of them, are buoyed up by delusive hopes, and hardened to their own destruction.

5th. The doctrine of Jesus is addressed to the heart, and never fails to affect it when understood and believed. It does not merely produce outward reformation, while the mind remains under the dominion of sin. *It is mighty through God to the pulling down of strongholds, casting down imaginations, and every high thing that exalteth itself against the knowledge of God, and bringing into captivity every thought and affection to the obedience of Christ.*

In self-examination, therefore, we ought to attend to our inward feelings, as well as to the general tenor of our conduct. In this respect many have erred. While some have considered true religion as consisting almost exclusively in certain emotions of mind, without paying due attention to the conduct; others, observing how little the practice of some professors corresponds with what they profess to feel, discard the consideration of inward emotions entirely, and look only to the outward behavior. Both are in error. By attending to the workings of our minds, as well as to our practice, we are in less danger of being deceived. The one is a check upon the other. Our conduct may in many respects appear good, while it proceeds from a corrupt principle. And in judging of our feelings, without bringing them to the test of practice, we are ever apt to impose upon ourselves, and to cherish, those feelings which give us pleasure, without considering whence they spring. It is only when our feelings and practice correspond that we can have well-grounded satisfaction.

6th. We ought to beware of forming a judgment of ourselves by partial and detached views of our conduct. To this we are extremely prone. Ever ready to depart from universal regard to the ways of God, we are disposed to rest on some one action, or series of actions, as an evidence that all is well with us, and thus to flatter ourselves that we are in truth the servants of Christ.

7th. The evidence of our being in the faith is always capable of increase. We are not then to be satisfied with the presumption that upon the whole the balance is in our favor, but to seek after the most decisive evidence. We are not to lull ourselves asleep by saying we are right in the main, although imperfect in very many respects, and certainly weak in the faith. According to the evidence of this imperfection, or of our weakness in the faith, we are in danger of making shipwreck of faith altogether.

In short, the greater progress we make, we shall be the less disposed to admire or depend upon our attainments, for our standard of holiness will always be proportionately raised.

8th. The revelation of God—that His love is unchangeable, that believers shall finally and certainly persevere, and that the gifts and calling of God are without repentance—is often abused to the neglecting or setting aside the necessity of self-examination. When lukewarm in our love, and backsliding from God, we are prone to quiet our consciences with such considerations. The saints shall indeed persevere, but we can have no evidence that we are of the number unless we are abiding in the truth.

The Scriptures uniformly distinguish the saving operations of God on the soul by their permanence. The children of God are not of those who draw back unto perdition, but of them that believe to the saving of the soul; while those who receive the Word with joy, but have no root, are manifested by their stumbling and falling away, being unable to endure temptation. Hence it follows, that whatever we have done or suffered for the gospel, unless we abide in the faith, we cannot be saved. We can only be saved by the gospel if we keep in memory the truth. None, therefore, can lawfully take comfort from the promises of God—that believers shall persevere—unless they are actually persevering, and under the influence of these promises, working out their own salvation with fear and trembling. Hence, in self-examination, the question is not, whether we did actually believe at any former period, but whether we are now in the faith of Christ.

II. Let us next consider what purposes and ends we ought to present to our mind in self-examination.

1st. Self-examination, then, is not calculated to quiet the conscience, to banish slavish fear, or to remove doubts and apprehensions of our being unbelievers.

When the mind is apprehensive of divine displeasure and its consequences, we have for our relief, the testimony of God, that the blood of Christ cleanseth from all sin. We are invited to draw near to the throne of grace for mercy, and are assured that Christ will in no wise cast out the most vile who come to Him. If this does not relieve us, God has provided no other ground of comfort and we ought to beware of seeking such, either for ourselves or others. If this does not give us peace, it must be because we believe not the record of God, because we are not willing to be indebted to free and sovereign mercy alone. And in such a state of mind we need to be excited to fear and jealousy of ourselves, and to be called to repentance, not to be quieted in our unbelief and rebellion.

2nd. The object of self-examination, according to the Scriptures, is to prove the genuineness of the peace and comfort which we enjoy.

Peace and comfort are the necessary effects of the

gospel, when its meaning is properly understood and its certainty deemed by us unquestionable. But there is a false peace which may be mistaken for true. True peace arises from the knowledge of the atonement of Christ, and is always connected with deep and lively views of eternal things. False peace arises from indifference about eternal things; and of this we see enough in the world lying in the wicked one.

Thus we see that while self-examination is not calculated to restore peace to the troubled mind, it is highly important in order to ascertain whether the hope we enjoy be scriptural. Without much self-examination, we shall not long continue in the possession of solid peace.

3rd. The object of self-examination, according to the Scriptures, is to detect *the hidden evils of the heart.*

Many fleshly lusts war against our souls. We are surrounded with snares, and are ever apt to be led aside; not only to fall into open sin, but to impose upon ourselves, and while outwardly walking religiously, not to be living to God—going on in cold formality, not mortifying our members, but in some secret, and perhaps unperceived manner, serving the flesh. By frequently bringing our hearts to the test of Scripture, and comparing our spirit and conduct with the precepts of the Word of God, we shall more easily avoid the snares of Satan and maintain more habitually a suitable and becoming conversation.

4th. One great object for which self-examination is enjoined in Scripture, is to increase our joy in the Lord.

Joy is a fruit of the Spirit, *But the fruit of the Spirit is love, joy, peace, longsuffering, gentleness, goodness, faith* (Gal. 5:22), and of the very greatest importance and much insisted on in the Word of God. *The joy of the LORD is your strength* (Neh. 8:10). It animates us in duty and supports us under trials. It prevents the innocent enjoyments of this life from engrossing an immoderate share of our affections. It renders insipid the pleasures in which the men of the world chiefly delight, and encourages us to devote our all to the Lord, in whose service we enjoy the greatest happiness. Many do not seem to be aware of this, nor of the vast importance of having the soul filled with joy in God. They even look upon it with a suspicious eye, as if it proceeded from presumption, and were inconsistent with that humility which ought to distinguish the disciple of the lowly Jesus. Nothing can be more false and unfounded. The idea can only arise from inexperience of the joy which flows from the gospel.

That there is a presumptuous confidence among some professors, who speak great swelling words of vanity about their joy, is alas! too manifest. But we are not on this account to contradict the whole revelation of God, which represents joy as an eminent characteristic of believers. Paul tells us that the kingdom of God is righteousness, and peace, and joy in the Holy Ghost, and exhorts his brethren to rejoice always in the Lord (Phil 3:1; 4:4).

Nothing recommends the gospel of Christ to the world more than His followers being filled with joy and peace. Ungodly men are ever prone to mistake and misrepresent religion as productive of gloom and melancholy, and they have had too much reason for this from the conduct of many professors. We have every reason to believe that the uncomfortable views of religion which so many entertain arise from their not discerning the glory and fullness of the gospel, together with the carnality of their minds, which leads them to endeavor to keep their consciences at ease, while not living near to God. Hence they flatter themselves, that their want of comfort is the fruit of their humility, and that the joys of others are the offspring of pride, if not a mere pretense. It is no uncommon thing for Satan to be transformed into an angel of light, and to represent the genuine fruits of the Holy Spirit as proceeding from the heart not being right with God.

Upon the whole, it appears that, while our peace and joy must, in the first instance, arise entirely from believing the testimony of God, and can only be preserved by abiding in His doctrine, it is most highly important and necessary—as we would guard against self-deception, as we would correct what is amiss in us, as we would increase our joy, and consequently our activity in the Lord's service—that we closely and constantly examine ourselves whether we be in the faith.

III. Let us now suggest some topics, to which our inquiries should be directed, while engaged in the duty of self-examination.

1st. Let us inquire how the gospel has affected us. Does it give us hope, while we regard ourselves as justly deserving of the wrath of God on account of sin? Do we see in it a reply to the accusations of conscience? Are these answered by the considerations of its truth? This is the first and necessary effect of the gospel, if we know what it means, and have received it not in word only but by the Holy Spirit, and in much assurance. It is an effect, without which no other can exist, and upon the existence and degree of which every fruit of the Spirit depends. But though this is first in order, it is never solitary. What other effects then has the gospel produced in our minds? I do not mean that we should inquire whether these have been suddenly produced by it; but whether it has, either more gradually or immediately, wrought effectually in us, changing the objects of our pursuit, and the tempers and dispositions of our hearts. Many things, and these highly interesting, may be believed, which leave the heart as they found it. Not so the gospel of Christ; this opens a new scene to the eyes of all who receive it; it brings them, as it were, into a new creation. The things which formerly engrossed their minds now appear mean and contemptible, compared with those revealed in the gospel; and those things which were once considered as unworthy of their regard, now appear to be all-important. Being risen with Christ, by the faith of the operation of God who raised Him from the dead, the Christian seeks *those things which are above, where Christ sitteth at the right hand of God* (Col 3:1). Begotten again to the lively hope of an inheritance incorruptible, undefiled, and unfading, he accounts himself a stranger and pilgrim on earth, and plainly declares that he seeks a heavenly country. Is this the case with us? Have the vast and momentous concerns of eternity made all that is in the world appear vain in our eyes? *This is the victory that overcometh the world, even our faith* (1 John 5:4). If therefore the world is not crucified to us and we unto the world by the doctrine of the cross, we have never beheld the glory of that doctrine, and are consequently rejecting the testimony of Jesus.

2nd. We should examine the general principles on which we act.

Faith works by love to God. Believers are con-

strained *for the love of Christ constraineth us;
because we thus judge, that if one died for all, then
were all dead* (2 Cor 5:14); i.e., all endured death in
Him, the substituted sacrifice, for their sins. *And
that He died for all, that they which live should not
henceforth live unto themselves, but unto Him
which died for them, and rose again* (2 Cor 5:15).
They consider themselves not to be debtors to the
flesh to live after the flesh; they account themselves not their own, but bought with a price. They
are the willing servants of their Redeemer, desiring to glorify Him with their bodies and spirits,
which are His. Does this description correspond
with our character? What views have we of the
character of God? Do we tremble like slaves in His
presence, esteeming Him a hard and austere master, or are we destitute of reverence and holy awe
of His majesty? The faith of the gospel produces
the most profound awe and veneration of God. The
believer views Him as a consuming fire, while, at
the same time, he has boldness in His presence,
and is taught to cry, *Abba Father*! The comforts of
the Holy Spirit are ever found united with the fear
of God.

What views do we entertain of sin? Does it appear
to us a light matter, or does the sense of it drive us
to despondency or despair? In either case, we may
be assured, on the authority of God, that we are
not believing the gospel. The gospel produces self-
abhorrence on account of sin, and that in the

greatest degree. It gives a view of sin, so dreadful, as may well confirm every fear which the loudest alarms of conscience can excite. But it also stills these alarms, and produces peace, and joy, and lively hope in believers, without diminishing in any degree their sense of the malignity and awful consequences of sin. We remember and are confounded, and never open our mouths any more, because of our shame, when we know that God is pacified towards us for all that we have done (Eze 16:63).

Again, we should inquire what things chiefly occupy our thoughts, whether the things of the flesh or of the Spirit. *They that are after the flesh do mind the things of the flesh; but they that are after the Spirit the things of the Spirit* (Rom 8:5). In which channel do our minds run? Thus, ought we not only to keep, but to examine our hearts with all diligence. But, as we are apt to impose on ourselves, when we judge merely by our feelings, and to imagine our minds to be spiritual, while our conversation is carnal, we ought to inquire:

3rdly. How far we actually sacrifice everything to the will of God? Does our practice decidedly prove that we are seeking first the kingdom of God and His righteousness? Does our conduct plainly show that we sit loose with regard to the world? Do our lives make it manifest that neither the wealth, the honors, nor the pleasures of the world are the chief object of our regard; that we are not conformed to this world, but transformed by the renewing of our minds? This is the certain consequence of holding fast the truth.

4thly. How do we employ the talents God has committed to us? Do we seriously consider what talents we possess? Do we act as those who must give account—not endeavoring, on the one hand, ostentatiously to display them, and thus to acquire honor for ourselves; nor, on the other, from sloth or false humility, neglecting to occupy them because they are small and inconsiderable, or because they are of such a nature as not to excite the admiration of men? Do we conscientiously employ them with an eye to the glory of God? This opens a wide field for self-examination.

5thly. How do we bear the trials which God appoints for us? Are we like the bullock unaccustomed to the yoke? Do we faint in the day of adversity or fret under our afflictions? Or do we despise the chastening of the Lord; with a sullen and stoical firmness braving distress, and steeling our minds to disappointment? It is the characteristic of the believer to *glory in tribulations* (Rom 5:3), to account them light and temporary, not worthy to be compared with the far more exceeding and eternal weight of glory for which these afflictions are preparing him (2 Cor 4:17-18). The language of faith, therefore, will always be, *The cup which my Father giveth me to drink, shall I not drink it?* The believer, knowing that all things shall work together for good to those who love God, in every thing gives thanks. He has learned, in whatever state he is, therewith to be content. His soul is as a weaned child. While he may keenly feel the rod of his heavenly Father; while he is, it may be, in heaviness through manifold temptations, yet he greatly rejoices, adding fortitude and patience to faith.

6thly. How do we act towards our brethren? *If a man say, I love God, and hateth his brother, he is a liar; for he that loveth not his brother whom he hath seen, how can he love God whom he hath not seen?* (1 John 4:20). Do we consider Christ as our great pattern, whom we are bound to imitate in doing good to all men as we have opportunity, and especially to those of the household of faith? Do we really love the disciples of Jesus: do we esteem them the excellent of the earth; do we associate with them, and testify our love to them by every act of kindness in our power? Nothing ascertains character more than the company with whom we delight to associate. We must needs go out of the world, were we altogether to avoid the ungodly. But their society is not to a Christian a matter of choice and satisfaction. He is aware of the danger to which it exposes him, and is ever fearful and watchful of its effects.

If self-examination be properly conducted, the result will always be a deep sense of our sinfulness and a growing conviction of our constant need of pardoning mercy. This must be the case with the most zealous, circumspect, and conscientious. The more we are convinced of the reasonableness, and struck with the wisdom and excellence of the commandments of Christ, and the more we know of the happiness of those who obey them, the more severely shall we condemn ourselves, and lament that we have not hitherto regarded them as we ought.

If, on self-examination, we have reason to conclude, or if we suspect, that we are not in the faith, it is our present duty to believe in Jesus who died for the ungodly, and confidently to trust in Him for salvation. Nothing we can do or suffer can prepare us better for receiving the testimony of God. Salvation is proclaimed to men as sinners. The gospel is addressed to all, in the circumstances in which it finds them. We cannot indeed enjoy the blessings it conveys without faith, yet we need no other qualification for divine mercy but guilt and wretchedness; and if we dream that we do, or that we shall ever possess any other, we deceive ourselves. It is only pride and the love of sin, with the blindness and error inseparable from them, which prevent all men from gladly receiving the gospel. They desire to have something whereof to glory; they wish to feel something which shall warrant them to believe. But in so doing they err, not knowing their own character, nor the grace of God.

Do some object, *We cannot believe; faith is the gift*

of God; no man can come to Christ except the Father draw him? This is true and, properly understood, what every Christian must feel and believe. But many, it is to be feared, misapprehend and wrest these Scriptures to their own destruction. They lament their own inability as if it were their misfortune, and not their crime, and then they quiet their consciences, considering the uneasiness they feel, as an evidence that there is some good thing in them towards God, and that in due time all will be well.

But in what does this inability consist? We can receive the testimony of men; we conduct ourselves every hour by faith in human veracity; and why can we not receive the testimony of God? Is it less weighty or more questionable? Are we laid under an invincible necessity to account the God of truth a liar? No; but His gospel pours contempt on all to which we are attached. It shocks the pride of the human heart. It describes our righteousness as filthy rags, and proclaims salvation to the most sober and decent, on the same terms as to the murderer and the sensualist; it acknowledges no difference among men as a recommendation to divine mercy. Thus it levels all human glory, and cuts off all occasion of boasting. Hence Christ is a stumbling block and rock of offense, and Satan, in the form of an angel of light, suggests to those who are blinded by him, that as this doctrine confounds all moral distinctions and depreciates human virtue, it cannot be of God.

Add to this, the gospel makes no provision for the lusts of the flesh or of the mind. It spares not a right eye nor a right hand, but proclaims complete deliverance from all sin. This salvation is not future, but present. Now, to suppose an ungodly man truly desirous of being made holy, is to suppose that he loves holiness, which the Scriptures uniformly deny. If then a sinner's inability to believe consists in pride and the love of iniquity, it is plain that so far from being an alleviation, it is the greatest aggravation of unbelief. *The carnal mind is enmity against God: for it is not subject to the law of God* (Rom 8:7). Yet this God, to whom men are enemies, pitying their ruined condition, has given His Son to die for sinners, and beseeches them to turn to Him and live. But they cannot think of it; they cannot find in their hearts to be reconciled to God; and they quiet their consciences by alleging, *I am tempted of God; He but tantalizes me; I am unable to believe.*

When men object that they cannot believe and that faith is the gift of God, their ideas are altogether different from what is meant in the Scriptures by these declarations. We naturally consider faith as something which is to recommend us to the favor of God. However blinded the human mind may be, few are able to persuade themselves that they can fully keep His holy law. They think they can do something, but not quite enough, and they go about to establish their own righteousness under the name of faith, which, though imperfect, they consider to be an acceptable obedience. If their consciences, however, still continue uneasy, they take shelter in the delusion that they must wait till God gives them faith. Such have yet to learn that they are utterly lost and ruined; and till they see this to be the case, the preaching of the cross must appear to them foolishness. In the meantime, they dream of doing what they can that they may obtain faith, and thus attempt to purchase the blessings of salvation. But unbelievers are never required in the Scriptures to use means to believe. This would in fact be a contradiction to the whole gospel. It would be a commandment to men to go about to establish their own righteousness to endeavor to reconcile God to them; as if He were their enemy, while they were desirous of His friendship.

We are taught in the gospel that we can do nothing, more or less, to procure the favor of God; that we are destitute of every good disposition; that our hearts are filled with enmity against Him; and that the only bar to our being reconciled is our aversion to reconciliation. He commands every creature to place confidence in the finished work of Christ, which He has declared to be all-sufficient for the remission of sins of the deepest dye. And so long as men disobey this commandment, they plainly show, whatever their profession may be, that they love the darkness more than the light, that they hate both Christ and His Father. Eternal life is preached to all, as a free gift through Jesus Christ; and those who reject it, plainly show that they prefer the gratification of their pride and evil passions to the enjoyment of the blessings of the salvation of Christ.

Through the deceitfulness of the human heart, many who do not believe, imagine that they desire to be delivered from sin. But if the power of sin in the heart be such as the Scriptures uniformly assert; if men are completely under its dominion—ungodly, and without strength, till Christ sets them free; and if he only that believeth is thus delivered by Christ, then it is absurd to suppose that any unbeliever truly desires salvation. He may wish to be freed from some particular sin which exposes him to inconvenience, but the dominion of iniquity is so firmly established in his heart that he cannot possibly desire to be delivered from his bondage, which consists entirely in his depraved inclinations.

Some suppose that to call in question their own state is a rejection of the testimony of God, and thus set aside all self-examination. To doubt their eternal salvation, is according to them, to make God a liar. But God has not testified to any individual that he shall be saved. His testimony is true, whether men believe it or not, that he who believeth in Jesus Christ shall never perish, but shall have eternal life. Hence the necessity of inquiring, Am I in the faith?

Others, who do not go so far, too easily admit that any suspicions concerning their state are temptations, of which they endeavor to get rid of as soon as possible. But let such remember that their apprehensions may be perfectly well-founded. As far as their conduct and conversation do not correspond with what the Scriptures declare to be inseparable from the belief of the truth, they have reason to doubt, to search and try their ways. All doubts of our personal interest in Christ, it is true, have their origin in unbelief. If we were fully persuaded of the truth of the gospel, if our eyes were always fixed upon it, if we always clearly perceived the glorious fullness and freeness of the salvation of Christ, we should constantly rejoice with joy unspeakable and full of glory; and we should also be proportionately sanctified by the truth, be fruitful in every good work, and thus possess the full assurance of the hope which God hath published in the gospel. It is owing to our not discerning the glory of this doctrine, that we at any time stand in doubt of our obtaining eternal blessedness. But we shall not improve our situation by imposing on ourselves, and concluding, without reason and evidence, that notwithstanding our uneasiness, all is well with us. We should consider these doubts as the symptoms of some internal disorder; and that we have at all times an almighty Physician to whom we may with confidence apply, whose skill is equal to the most desperate case; believing in whom, no sinner of the human race shall ever perish, but shall undoubtedly obtain eternal life. Amen

To Set Them In Order

*Some Influences of the Philadelphia
Baptist Association Upon Baptists in
America to 1814*

by Dr. James L. Clark

The Philadelphia Baptist Association, organized Saturday, September 27, 1707 was for 44 years the only such association in America. In many aspects of both doctrine and polity the Philadelphia Association set the standards of Baptist faith and practice in America. In this book, Dr. Clark examines some of these more enduring influences of this association on Baptist development in America, from the time of its formation in 1707 until the formation of the General Missionary (or Triennial) Convention in 1814. As he states in the introduction, the aim of the work is "to treat these influences as they had a bearing upon the education, doctrine, organization, and discipline of the Baptists of this country to 1814."

This work is the second release in our *Philadelphia Association Series*, and contains in facsimile form, a copy of the Philadelphia Baptist Confession of Faith of 1742, from the oldest extant sixth edition of 1743, printed in Philadelphia by Benjamin Franklin. In addition there is included a facsimile copy of the *Baptist Catechism* of 1782, which was also published under the auspices of the association, and the histories of two of the older churches of the association (Pennepek and Great Valley) by Pennsylvania historian Horatio Gates Jones, Jr.

"The Influence of the Philadelphia Association has been greater in shaping Baptist modes of thinking and working, than any other body in existence."

> The Baptist Encyclopedia,
> edited by William Cathcart (1881), p. 917.

Navy grade B buckram binding, smyth sewn, with gold stamping on the spine and front cover. Acid-free paper. 466 p. Illustrated, with a full index. $32.00 plus shipping

Other Publications

THE LIFE AND MINISTRY OF JOHN GANO
Vol I
by Terry Wolever

This is a new work that Mr. Wolever has prepared for those who have an interest in early American Baptist History, early American History, and those who want to know more of this great man.

Volume I Contains the complete *Biographical Memoirs of John Gano* which has been out of print since 1806. These *Memoirs* are about 100 pages of a 450 page book full of important, well documented history.

Gano pastored the First Baptist Church of New York, which disbanded when the British Army occupied the city. Gano served the Continental Army as a chaplain and is reported to have administered believer's baptism to General George Washington. This full account will be in the forthcoming Volume II.

Volume I contains:
Biographical Memoirs of John Gano
Account of Gano by Richard Furman
Gano's sermon outline on Eph. 1:6
Sermon preached at Gano's ordination
Pastorate at Morristown, New Jersey
Ministry at the Jersey Settlement in North
Carolina
App. A - The Particular Baptists in North
Carolina - an Appraisal Appraised.
App. B - Biographical Sketches of the
Children of John and Sarah Gano

This book is hard bound in grade B buckram and is printed on acid free paper. It is gold stamped on the front and spine. $32 plus shipping.

Particular Baptist Press
2766 W. Farm Road 178
Springfield, MO 65810

An Anthology of Early Baptists in New Hampshire

Compiled and edited by Terry Wolever

"This book inaugurates our 'Anthology Series,' focusing on the Regular Baptist heritage of the Early Republic period in the United States. It was during that time that the Particular, later designated Regular, Baptists represented the mainstream current of Baptist life in America. It was a time of tremendous growth and associational expansion, marked by leaders of conspicuous ability.

It is the desire of the publishers that these anthologies will reacquaint contemporary Baptists more fully with their history. In so doing we not only find an important part of our identity in the past, but bring with us an inspiring legacy to the present."

- *From the Foreword*

Cloth, grade B buckram. Smyth sewn. Acid free paper. 604 pages, illustrated. Complete Index of Persons, Index of Churches, General Index and Scripture index. $36.00 plus shipping

Contents:

Other Publications

The Annual Register of Indian Affairs
1835 - 1838
by Isaac McCoy

Hard bound, grade B buckram, acid-free paper - 341 pages with index. $55 plus shipping.

Early Indian Missions
by Dr. Edward Roustio

Hard bound, grade B buckram, acid-free paper - 462 pages with index. $38.50 plus shipping.

Minutes of the Philadelphia Baptist
Association 1707 - 1807. Tricentennial Edition
by A. D. Gillette

Hard bound, grade B buckram, acid -free paper - 546 pages with *new and expanded indices. Illustrated* 7 X 10 trim size with marble end sheets. $38 plus shipping.

A Commentary on the Epistle to the Romans
by John Gill

Hard bound, grade B buckram, acid-free paper with dust jacket 637 pages New completely retypeset edition - $28 plus shipping.

The British Particular Baptists

This will be a three volume set when completed. Each volume contains informative biographical sketches of the British Particular Baptists from 1638 - 1910. This set is edited by Dr. Michael Haykin of the Heritage Baptist College and Seminary in Ontario, Canada.

Volume I

British Particular Baptist Biography - Michael Haykin
John Spilsbury (1593-c1662-1668) - James M. Renihan
Hanserd Knollys (c1598-1691) - Barry H. Howson
William Kiffin (1616-1701) - Paul Wilson
John Bunyan (1628-1688) - Allen E. Smith
Benjamin Keach (1640-1704) - Tom J. Nettles
The Stennetts - B. A. Ramsbottom
John Gill - (1697-1771) - Robert W. Oliver
Benjamin Beddome (1717-1795) - Michael Haykin
John Collett Ryland (1723-1792) - Peter Naylor
Robert Hall Sr. (1728-1791) Michael Haykin
Caleb Evans (1737-1791) - Kirk Wellum
Samuel Medley (1738-1799) - B. A. Ramsbottom

This volume is hard bound on grade B buckram with gold leaf stamping and is printed on acid free paper. $22.50 plus shipping

Volume II

Introduction by Michael A. G. Haykin
Benjamin Francis (1734-1799) by Michael Haykin
Abraham Booth (1734-1806) by Robert W. Oliver
John Rippon (1751-1825) by Sharon James
John Ryland Jr. (1753-1825) by Grant Gordon
Andrew Fuller (1754-1815) by Tom J. Nettles
William Carey (1761-1834) by Timothy George
William Steadman (1764-1837) by Sharon James
Samuel Pearce (1766-1799) by Tom Wells
Christmas Evans (1766-1838) by Geoffrey Thomas
Robert (1764-1842) & James (1768-1851) Haldane
by George McGuinness
Joshua (1768-1837) & Hannah (1767-1847) Marshman
by A. Christopher Smith
William Ward (1769-1823) by A. Christopher Smith

This is a matching volume to Volume I and is $23.50 plus shipping

Particular Baptist Press

The Three Mrs. Judsons
by Arabella Stuart

This book was printed in 1875 and Particular Baptist Press has completely retypeset this excellent inspiring missionary story. We have added 24 pictures and documents, plus two important historical appendices. Appendix A is the sermon that was preached at the ordination of Adorniram Judson, Luther Rice and the other missionaries in February 1812. Appendix B is the sermon on Baptism by Adoniram. Judson, after he had become a Baptist. 375 pages, 6 X 9 in grade B buckram hard bound on acid free paper. $24 plus shipping.

The Life & Works of Joseph Kinghorn
Volume I
Edited by Mr. Terry Wolever

This excellent work is a reprint of the mid nineteenth century edition of Martin Wilkin's biography of Kinghorn. Kinghorn was an early supporter of William Carey and the modern missions movement, as well as a notable scholar. His ability in the Word was much in demand by his peers and much respected by those with whom he differed. He was considered second only to John Gill in his rabbinical learning and was one of the godliest of pastors.

When complete this will be a four volume set. Volumes 3 and 4 will contain the complete debate between Kinghorn and his good friend Robert Hall over the communion issue. Mr. Kinghorn took issue with Hall's *open communion* position and a congenial, thorough debate followed. Both sides will be presented, so that any interested person will get the best arguments of each position from these two scholars.

Vol I is a hard bound, grade B buckram work on acid free paper. 530 pages. $24.50 plus shipping.